MUSLIMS

AND THE

WEST

A MUSLIM PERSPECTIVE

Khan Hussan Zia

authorHOUSE™

1663 LIBERTY DRIVE, SUITE 200
BLOOMINGTON, INDIANA 47403
(800) 839-8640
WWW.AUTHORHOUSE.COM

First published by AuthorHouse 11/10/05

ISBN: 1-4208-6770-9 (sc)

Printed in the United States of America
Bloomington, Indiana

This book is printed on acid-free paper.

In fond memory of my parents and their love of truth, knowledge and justice.

CONTENTS

INTRODUCTION ix

DEMONIZING ISLAM..1

THE CRUSADES...11

SPAIN 26

EAST EUROPE 37

CHECHNIYA..47

EUROPEAN COLONIZATION.......................................56

PALESTINE...75

IRAQ...94

KASHMIR 119

THE BALKANS...130

AFGHANISTAN 149

ESSENTIAL WEST..195

PAX AMERICANA..222

IN DEFENCE OF ISLAM...233

EPILOGUE...259

POSTSCRIPT 272

ANNEX..310

INTRODUCTION

It was shortly after the Gulf War in 1991. A white man was working his way towards the immigration desk in a queue at Jeddah airport. When the Pakistani ahead of him in the line presented his passport the Saudi official at the desk pushed it aside and invited the white man to come forward. He took his American passport, kissed and touched it to his eyes before stamping it and letting the man through. It was an expression of gratitude and appreciation on the part of an Arab, convinced that USA had gone to war to save his country from falling into the hands of the ogre Saddam Hussein.

A little over ten years after this incident, CNN interviewed the then Secretary of State Lawrence Eagleburger and President George Bush Senior to reminisce about the Gulf War on television. Among other things, Eagleburger related how he had managed to keep the Israelis from joining the conflict by raising the question, *'When we are fighting this war for you, why do you want to make things complicated for us by insisting on sending in your own troops?'*

Bush Senior recalled that initially he was afraid to sanction the war on Iraq for fear of a backlash among the other Muslim states. This was until Henry Kissinger assured him that his fears were unfounded. Not only was there no adverse reaction from the Muslim countries but many of them contributed their forces to defeat Iraq and, later, more than generously compensated the United States for the expenses incurred in the war.

Today, as another war against Iraq looms over the horizon, things are a little different but not significantly as far the ruling elites in the Muslim countries are concerned. They have again pledged their support and agreed to provide military bases for operations to the United States. This is despite the overwhelmingly popular sentiment in these countries being against a repeat of the earlier conflict and the tragedy that resulted from it.

The feelings among the Muslims generally, even if not reflected in the actions of their governments, are being echoed by men of conscience in the West, especially in Europe. Despite the inherent political and economic risks involved in displeasing the United States, countries like France, Germany and Belgium have taken a principled stand on the issue. Admirable as these are, in the end, what will matter most is what the Muslims do to save themselves.

The actions of the United States, contrary to popular belief among the Muslim masses, are not directed against Islam or the Muslims per se. These are primarily aimed at securing her own political and economic objectives. It was not so long ago, in the days of the cold war, that the West had formed partnerships with Muslim religious parties all over the world to contain communism. It is just that the situation has changed and Muslims now happen to be at the wrong end of the equation.

If Islam and the Muslims are being maligned in the West today it is a deliberate act, not motivated by religious hatred, but intended to influence and manipulate public opinion within their own countries. The process dates back to the 1973 Arab-Israeli war and the embargo by the oil-producing countries that threatened economic prosperity in the West. Within five years the two main architects of the embargo ---- King Faisal of Saudi Arabia and the Shah of Iran ---- were gone.

After the revolution in Iran the ayatollahs balked at the idea of submitting to western dictates. It was not long before Saddam Hussein, with active backing from the West as well as other Arab states, invaded Iran to provoke a war that lasted eight years. Shortly afterwards it was time to clip Saddam's wings for venturing into Kuwait and we had the Gulf War.

There is a need to explain the necessity and justification for such actions to the people in order to win their continued support. In this case, they are told that Muslims are hostile to the West, not for what it does to them, but because they belong to a fanatic creed that is intolerant of western ideals and civilization and the freedoms vested in them.

People like Bernard Lewis and Samuel Huntington have hypothesized about the issue at length, curiously, only after the loss of the Soviet Union as the enemy. Their theories are basically centred on the premise that Islam, because of inherent differences, is an enemy of the West. Despite glaring and obvious flaws, such assertions have received consistent and widespread circulation. The attacks of 11th September 2001, regardless of whoever was responsible for the dastardly acts, are claimed as proof of Islam's villainy.

It would be a grievous mistake to band together the entire West in this conspiracy which appears to be primarily the work of a few governments and vested corporate interests. Neither all westerners nor all Christians and Jews fall under this category. In fact, the thinking majority of them are opposed to the current policies.

The old saying that history is written by the victors is still true. People in the West are generally restricted to what is available in the western media for their sources of information. Even most of the Muslims who write depend upon these sources. They also tend to be apologetic for how the Muslims feel and act for some reason. In the end, what is produced is regurgitation and re-processing of much the same basic data. The process has inadvertently created a vicious circle of misinformation about Islam and the Muslims.

Inevitably, there is some bias involved in whatever gets written about such subjects as religion, politics and history. In order to reduce it to as little as possible, western writers have been quoted verbatim in the book, wherever possible, even on Islamic religious issues. It is hoped that it will help to dispel some of the myths, misgivings and misconceptions that have become prevalent in the West about Islam.

The basic purpose, however, is to inform the Muslims of the background, present state of inter-action between their world and the West and its implications for the future, as observed by one of their own. Hopefully, the review would prove useful in drawing appropriate conclusions and lessons for the difficult times that lie ahead. If, in places the tone appears blunt or emotive, it is only reflective of the feelings experienced by the vast majority of the Muslims in the present traumatic and anxiety filled conditions.

K. Hussan Zia
147 Ahmed Block
New Garden Town, Lahore.
14th February 2003.

DEMONIZING ISLAM

'At worst, bloody and dangerous; at best, false'. This is how Bishop J. Delano Ellis, advisor to the US Congressional panel on faith related matters, described Islam in August 2001. Evangelist Jerry Falwell, a prominent 'Moral Majority' and 'Christian Right' leader, said on CBS' programme *'60 Minutes'*, *'In my opinion ------ Jesus set an example of love, so did Moses, and Mohammed set an opposite example'*. He has also described the Prophet of Islam variously as a 'terrorist', a 'violent man', a 'man of war' and worse. Reverend Franklin Graham, whose father Billy Graham is also an evangelical preacher and has enjoyed full access to the White House since the 1950s, said last year that Islam *'is a very evil and wicked religion'*. Graham was the minister who delivered George W. Bush's inaugural prayer last year.

Pat Robertson, the founder of Christian Coalition and highly sought after fund raiser for the Republican Party, told his TV audience recently, *'Islam is not a peaceful religion that wants to co-exist. ----- Muslims want to co-exist until they can control, dominate and then, if need be, destroy'* (*'The Uncivil War Against Islam'* in *'The Chicago Tribune'* of 27th October 2002, by Law Professor M. Cherif Bassiouni, DePaul University). He also went on ABC's TV programme *'This Week'* and told George Stephanopoulos, *'Hitler was bad but what the Muslims want to do to the Jews is worse'* (*'Imams of Inanity'* by Richard Cohen in *'The Washington Post'*, 3rd December 2002). These and other Christian ministers have also told radio and TV audiences that Mohammed was 'an inherently violent man'. Apart from Jerry Falwell's Moral Majority and Pat Robertson's

Christian Coalition there are other more virulent Christian organizations like 'Reconstructionism' and 'Christian Identity' with even more extremist agenda against Islam in the United States.

These are not the ravings and rantings of some foolish and bigoted clergymen that could be ignored as such. All of the men of cloth mentioned above are highly influential in the United States. Christian Right ideology has increasingly influenced its mainstream politics especially in the past thirty years. Today, no less than 130 members of the House of Representatives are 'born-again' Christians. Pat Robertson and other prominent evangelists speak of a new political religion that would direct its efforts at taking control of all major American institutions, including mainstream denominations and the government, so as to transform the United States into a global Christian empire.

The disparate sects belonging to the Christian revivalism in America have joined hands in a movement for gaining political power known as 'Dominionism'. They claim that Jesus has called them to build Christian dominion over the nation and, eventually, throughout the world. America will become an agent of God, and all political and intellectual opponents of America's Christian leaders the agents of Satan.

The Ten Commandments form the basis of its legal system, Creationism and 'Christian values' will be the basis of the educational system. Aside from its proselytizing mandate, the federal government will be reduced to the protection of property rights and 'homeland' security. A number of influential Dominionists advocate the death penalty for a host of 'moral crimes,' including apostasy, blasphemy, sodomy, and witchcraft. The only legitimate voices in this state will be Christian. All others will be silenced.

Chris Hedges, one time foreign correspondent for the *New York Time* and the author of '*War Is a Force That Gives Us Meaning*' and '*Losing Moses on the Freeway*,' attended the annual convention of the National Religious Broadcasters, along with some 1,600 Christian radio and television personalities who claim to reach up to 141 million listeners and viewers, recently in Anaheim, California. He has described its proceedings in the *Harper's Magazine*. Some parts are reproduced below to show what a strange mixture religion and politics make:

'----------- *the convention is meant to serve as a rallying cry for a new and particularly militant movement in Christian politics, one that is sometimes mistaken for another outbreak of mere revivalism. In fact, this movement is a curious hybrid of fundamentalists, Pentecostals, Southern Baptists, conservative Catholics, Charismatics, and other evangelicals, all of whom are at war doctrinally but who nonetheless share a belief that America is destined to become a Christian nation, led by Christian men who are in turn directed by God.---------------*

'*Early Sunday morning, in a ballroom on the second floor of the Hilton Hotel, the Israeli Ministry of Tourism is hosting a breakfast. Several hundred people, all dressed in the appropriate skirts and business suits of American churchgoing people, are seated at round tables with baskets of bread, fruit plates, and silver pitchers of coffee. Waiters serve plates of scrambled eggs and creamed spinach. I count no more than half a dozen people who are not white. On the platform is a huge picture of the Dome of the Rock, the spot in Jerusalem where the third Temple will be rebuilt to herald, at least according to the Christians in the room, the second coming of Christ. Some 400,000 Christian tourists visit Israel each year, and, what with the precipitous decline* in Israel's tourism industry in recent years, these people have become a valued source of revenue.

'The strange alliance in this case is premised upon the Dominionist belief that Israel must rule the biblical land in order for Christ to return, though when he does, all Jews who do not convert to Christianity supposedly will be incinerated as the believers are lifted into heaven; all this is courteously left unmentioned at the breakfast. The featured speakers include Avraham Hirschsohn, who is the new Israeli minister of tourism, and Michael Medved, a cultural conservative and a nationally syndicated radio talk-show host. Medved is also one of the most prominent Jewish defenders of Mel Gibson's biopic The Passion of the Christ.

'Hirschsohn praises the audience for standing "with us for the last four years when nobody else would. Thank you." He then announces, to grateful applause, that the tourism ministry plans to build a "Pilgrim Center" near Galilee.

"A more Christian America is good for the Jews," Medved says. "This is obvious. Take a look at this support for Israel. A more Christian America is good for America, something Jewish people need to be more cognizant about and acknowledge. A more Jewish community is good for the Christians, not just because of the existence of allies but because a more Jewish community is less seduced by secularism."

'The cast of characters that takes the stage next is illuminating. Glenn Plummer, a black minister from Detroit who is active in the Republican Party, assures us that he knows all about Muslims because "I come from Detroit, where the biggest mosque in America is."

"It didn't take 9/11 to show me there is a global battle going on for the souls of men," he says. "When Islam comes into a place, it is intent on taking over everything, not only government but the business, the neighborhoods, everything. ----------------'

In the absence of any debate that would afford an opportunity to present a more true picture of Islam people in the West have little choice but to believe these men. When the same message is repeated over and over again by different individuals it becomes like gospel truth in the minds of unsuspecting listeners. Had the type of language quoted above been used against Moses and Judaism every human rights organization, the press, radio and television in the western world would be up in arms and the gentlemen in question indicted for inciting religious hatred and locked up behind bars.

Muslims and Islam, on the other hand, are fair game these days. In their case every thing goes but that is a separate issue. George W. Bush, his Attorney General John Ashcroft and the vast majority of their colleagues and supporters in the Republican Party share Pat Robertson's 'Christian Right' philosophy. None of them objected to, let aside condemned the utterances by these ministers. This attitude was reflected earlier in a UN resolution in the Human Rights Committee condemning the linking of Islam with terrorism when USA joined India, Israel and twelve other states to vote against the resolution, in effect, insisting that the two were linked.

Such feelings are by no means exclusive to the US politicians and clergy. The men and women of the media are even more strident and virulent in expressing feelings of bias and hate. In a recent editorial the right wing magazine the '*National Review*' suggested that the United States should consider a nuclear attack on Makka. *'Lots of sentiment for nuking Mecca,' 'The Review'* editor Rich Lowry said in an online forum called *'The Corner'*. He also suggested the likeliest sites for first U.S. nuclear strikes would be two countries with overwhelmingly Muslim populations: Iraq and Iran. *'If we have clean enough bombs to assure a pinpoint damage area, Gaza City and Ramallah* (in the Israeli-occupied territories) *would also be on the list'*, he added. Last September, Anne Coulter, writing in the *'National Review'* suggested, *'We should invade their* (Muslim) *countries, kill their leaders and convert them to Christianity'*.

For years, Hollywood has been stereo-typing Muslims, the Arabs in particular, in an unsavoury mould. In films ranging from *'Aladdin'* to *'The Mummy'* to *'Rules of Engagement'*, Muslims are usually portrayed as simplistic, illiterate, one- dimensional, angry, hateful, untrustworthy and, of course, dirty. Mostly, they are presented as gross stereotypes like the wealthy sheikh, the oppressed women and, not forgetting, the Muslim terrorist.

USA is not by any means alone in its anti-Muslim hysteria. Prime Minister Silvio Berlusconi of Italy on three occasions during a visit to Berlin enthusiastically boasted of the 'supremacy' and 'superiority' of western civilization over Islam and called on Europe to recognize its 'common Christian roots' (*'The Guardian'*, 27th September 2001). Hardly any one questioned him about the basis his presumption. Cardinal Giacomo Biffi, the archbishop of Bologna and leading contender to succeed Pope John Paul II, recorded in a pastoral letter that was read out to 300 priests in Bologna in September 2000, *'Christian Europe was in danger of being overwhelmed by a Muslim invasion. There should be no more entry visas for Muslims to Italy. -- --- There was a struggle for the soul of Europe which would either rediscover its Christian roots or convert to Islam'*.

When asked if he was conducting a new Crusade, he replied, *'I have never had anything against the word Crusade'* (*'The Times'*, London, a piece by Richard Owen).

The rest of Europe is no different. More than seven hundred German intellectuals, including the well-known writer of modern Germany and Nobel Prize winner, Guenter Grass, and philosopher Juergen Habermas signed petitions protesting the award of German Book Trade Association's 1996 Peace Prize to the venerable (late) Professor Annemarie Schimmel, for her scholarly works on Islam, describing these as 'a call to murder' simply because she portrayed Islam in factual and not falsely perceived and misleading light (*Associated Press,* 16th October 1995).

A well-known French author of a number of books, Michel Houllebecq, said in an interview recently that Islam is *'the most stupid religion'* and that the *'badly written'* Koran made him *'fall to the ground'*. Most of the French literary community has risen to defend his right to 'freedom of speech' in the court case filed against him (Paul Webster in *'The Guardian'* of 18th September 2002). At the same time, when Germany bans history books and Israel disallows the works of Shakespeare within its borders (*'Baghdad Without a Map'*, by Tony Horwitz, Penguin Books, New York, 1991, p. 136), somehow, there are no such protests and freedom of expression remains unaffected and intact.

Former Bosnian Serb leader Radovan Karadzic told Ed Bradley of CBS's TV programme *'60 Minutes'* that the people of East Europe regarded him as their hero for having murdered three hundred thousand innocent and unarmed Muslim men, women and children in the genocide perpetrated in Bosnia-Herzgovina from 1992 to 1995. Their only apparent crime had been that they were Muslims and not even very strict ones at that. Russian President Boris

Yeltsin's defence minister described the ongoing merciless butchery of poor Chechens by the Russian Army as '*Soldiers of the Lord carrying out the Lord's good work*' (meaning murdering Muslims). The Eastern Orthodox Church in Jerusalem went so far as to confer sainthood on the drunken Yeltsen, who delighted in pinching the bottoms of female employees during a visit to the Clinton White House, for doing the 'Lord's good work' in Chechniya. Its priests routinely blessed Serbian paramilitary executioners as they proceeded to machinegun battered and starving Bosnian Muslim inmates of Serb concentration camps (BBC).

The reasons for the existence of such views and attitudes do not necessarily lie in ignorance. There are a whole host of other factors involved. These vary with each individual and organization and it would be difficult and pointless to argue in this context. It is virtually impossible to try and guess at the motivation behind each individual's expressions of opinion. What can be said with confidence is that in all of history there has never been more information available about Islam and it has never before been better studied, at least in the academic institutions in the West, as it is today.

So why the display of such rabid bias and apparent ignorance? The best guess is that what the academicians find does not fit the pattern nor help in furthering the desired political, economic and religious objectives of certain powerful interests. The information that is made available through the media to the American people, in particular, has been tightly controlled since the World Trade Centre incident. They are told very little of what went on inside Afghanistan, for instance, and it is the same with the impending invasion of Iraq. There is a deliberate effort afoot to distort the image of Islam and the Muslims in general in the eyes of the world to make it easier to pursue thinly veiled political and other objectives.

It is very important that the designated enemy must be presented to the people in a demonized and bestial form in order to generate the required level of hatred and animosity to win support for war. Also, if pictures of the dead and dismembered civilians are kept away from the TV screens, if their race and religion are implied as 'inferior' and if what is happening is for the 'future good' of the primitive and uncivilized natives, the situation becomes easier to live with and explain to the unsuspecting.

One reason why it is Taliban, Saddam and Khomeini who are demonized and not their countries is because they are easier to present as more credible threats to the West as individuals than their weak and impoverished nations. It becomes difficult, if not impossible, to achieve the desired effect if scholars with knowledge, credibility and integrity are seen to hold a different picture of Islam and the Muslims. Hence, the necessity to exclude them from public discussions as far as possible.

The on-going deliberate vilification of Islam for short-term political gains has created a dangerous divide that is filled with extremely worrying portents in the long-term. Regardless of where the abuse and slander originates it has to be countered before any further damage is done and truth gets consigned to oblivion. Left unanswered, it encourages further outrage and allows the less informed to be misled into believing the propaganda to be the truth. Because of the serious nature of the issue, it is time for the policy makers and governments in the Islamic countries to join hands in making a concerted effort to deal with the menacing new developments. It is not something that should be left in the questionable hands of the media alone.

When dealing with this type of onslaught one could get mired in attempting a comparative evaluation of the concerned faiths to counter the falsehoods that are being spread. It would be so easy as well as revealing to take quotations from the present and past Christian and Judaic versions of the Old and New Testaments and compare these with the relevant injunctions in Islam. Strictly speaking, this is an option that is not open to a Muslim for the Koran specifically forbids indulging in ridicule and slander of the other faiths ('*The Koran*' 6:108).

Pointing out the widespread and shameful abuse of children and paedophilia in the Roman Catholic Church, for instance, will not enhance the image of Islam in any way. One could also attempt to explain and answer each piece of criticism that is levelled against Islam but that will hardly have an effect on people who have a specific agenda and whose minds are not open to reason or knowledge. For these considerations it is preferable and also much more interesting, at least from an academic point of view, to examine some relevant issues and situations in a historical perspective and see how the two civilizations in question acquitted themselves in the past as well as the present. Facts should speak better than words especially since, as in this case, they have been sourced mostly from non-Muslims themselves.

THE CRUSADES

The first historically significant encounter between Muslims and the West took place in 638 AD when an Arab army captured Syria and Palestine from the Byzantine Empire in the time of the second caliph, Omer. Contrary to the established practice of the conquering armies in those times, there was no molestation of either the population or any of the churches, temples or synagogues. The Jews, who had been banished from Palestine since 135 AD by the Romans, were allowed to return for the first time after five hundred years of Roman and Christian rule and permitted freedom of worship as they pleased. This is how H. G. Wells described the event in his well known '*The Outline of History*' (vol. 1 pp. 616, 617):

'*Jerusalem fell early, making a treaty without standing siege, and so the True Cross, which had been carried off by the Persians a dozen years before, and elaborately restored by Heraclius, passed once more out of the rule of Christians. But it was still in Christian hands; the Christians were to be tolerated, paying only a poll tax; and all the churches and all the relics were left in their possession. Jerusalem made a peculiar condition for its surrender. The city would give itself only to the Caliph Omer in person. Hitherto he had been in Madina organizing armies and controlling the general campaign. ---------------- He came the six-hundred-mile journey with only one attendant; he was mounted on a camel* (that he had taken turns riding with the slave) *and a bag of barley, another of dates, a water-skin and a wooden platter were his possessions for the journey. ------------ He met the patriarch of Jerusalem, who had apparently taken over the city from its Byzantine rulers, alone. With the*

Patriarch he got on very well. They went round the holy places together.'

When it was time for prayer the Patriarch invited the caliph inside the church of the Holy Sepulchre but the latter declined fearing that it might set the wrong precedence and become an excuse for his followers to appropriate the places of worship of other peoples. Since that day the Church of Holy Sepulchre has remained a Christian place of worship. The only interference by the Muslims has been to ensure that every sect of Christians had access to it and that it was not monopolized by one sect to the exclusion of others. The same is true of the Church of the Nativity of Bethlehem and of other buildings sacred to Christianity. It was not uncommon for Muslims and Christians to share the places of worship in the early days of Muslim rule. Many buildings in Syria were conjointly used ---- at Lud (Lydda), in the Plain of Sharon, a church of St. George and a mosque still exist under the same roof with only a common wall separating them.

If Islam had been inherently violent and anti-Christian, as people like Bernard Lewis wish to convey, what was there to stop its armies from indulging in murder, mayhem and forced conversions as was done to the Muslims and Jews when the Moors were evicted from Spain in 1492? The Charter granted to the Christian monks of Sinai by the Muslims in mid-seventh century AD is still extant. If you read it you will see that it exudes not only goodwill but actual love. In the Koran, Christians and Jews are mentioned as *'people of the Scripture'*. The only war it sanctions is in self-defence. Aggression is forbidden. All life is sacred, *'If you killed one man it is as if you killed all mankind -------'*.

Christians and Muslims have always co-existed peacefully in the East. The difficulties have been almost exclusively with the European brands of Christianity and, as we shall see, these may have more to do with questions of race than religion. It is also true that Christianity before and after Emperor Constantine made it the state religion of Rome are two different things. Apart from a few relics, all vestiges of earlier Christianity were ruthlessly wiped out. Even the fabled ancient library in Alexandria was burnt to the ground in the Christian purge in 4th century AD.

It was not simply that the Romans became Christians but the reverse is more accurate ----- Christianity itself became profoundly Romanized. Many of the festivals, rituals and customs practised by the Christians today, in fact, have Roman origins. Any one interested in the lineage of present-day western Christianity and its pagan roots may like to see '*The Jesus Mysteries; Was Jesus a Pagan God?*' an intriguing study by Timothy Freke and Peter Gandy (Harper Collins, UK). They have put forward an interesting hypothesis that the concepts of Trinity and Resurrection were not original or exclusive to Christianity. A Christ-like figure had also appeared earlier in the mythologies of Egypt (Orisis), Greece (Dionysus), Persia (Mithra), Asia Minor (Attis), Syria (Adonis) and Italy (Bacchus).

Although they are inter-related, culture and religion are two different issues. Islam may be au fait with Christianity and Judaism in terms of religion per se but that does not mean that the reverse is also true. Far from it. As we saw above, the other two regard Islam in a very different light ----- as a heresy and perversion.

We also need to bear in mind that whereas Christianity in Asia and Islam have common cultural roots, the present-day western culture has evolved primarily from the Roman and some Greek traditions with vastly different values and attitudes. Monogamy, for instance, is a Roman tradition that is not supported by the Old Testament but has been imposed on Christianity. Similarly, there is nothing in Christianity that prevents Muslim schoolgirls in the West from wearing the hijab. The ban imposed on it in many western countries is the manifest reaction of a culture feeling threatened and rendered historically insecure ever since the fiasco of Crusades. This may also be true when Messers Berlusconi and Bush feel the need to proclaim the superiority of their civilization in public.

What we are experiencing today in the West, and it has been mostly true in history as well, is more a cultural than a religious problem. Religion is brought in primarily as a convenient tool for arousing passions among the people that would be more difficult to achieve with simply the nebulous, diffused and non-specific notions of culture.

A little over four and a half centuries after the conquest of Palestine by the Muslims it was the turn of the European Christians to take over Jerusalem. This is how Pope Urban II exhorted the faithful in 1095 AD to join the holy war, *'O race of Franks! Race beloved and chosen by God! ---------- - From the confines of Jerusalem and from Constantinople a grievous report has gone forth that an accursed race, wholly alienated from God, has violently invaded the lands of these Christians, and has depopulated them by pillage and fire. They have led away a part of the captives into their own country, and a part they have killed by cruel tortures. They destroy the altars, after having defiled them with their uncleanliness. The kingdom of the Greeks is now dismembered by them, and has been deprived of territory so vast in extent that it could not be traversed in two month's time.*

'------- For this land that you now inhabit, shut in on all sides by the sea and mountain peaks, is too narrow for your

large population; it scarcely furnishes good enough for its cultivators. Hence it is that you murder and devour one another, that you wage wars, and that many among you perish in civil strife.

'Let hatred, therefore, depart from among you; let your quarrels end. Enter upon the road to the Holy Sepulture; wrest that land from a wicked race ------- and be assured of the reward of imperishable glory in the Kingdom of Heaven'. ('The Story of Civilization IV. The Age of Faith' by Will Durant, Simon and Schuster, New York. 1950. P. 587).

A force of 12,000 Crusaders captured Jerusalem from its 1,000 Arab defenders in 1099 AD and proceeded to brutally massacre its Muslim and Jewish population. Karen Armstrong, historian and religious scholar of some repute, writes *'In a massacre that makes September 11 look puny in comparison, some 40,000 people were slaughtered in two days. A thriving, populous city had been transformed into a stinking charnel house. Yet in Europe scholar monks hailed this crime against humanity as the greatest event in world history since the crucifixion of Christ'.*

Bishop Raymond of Agiles, an eyewitness to the event, reported, '------- *wonderful things were to be seen. Numbers of Saracens were beheaded. ------- others were shot with arrows, or forced to jump from the towers; others were tortured for several days and then burned in flames. In the streets were piles of heads and hands and feet. One rode about everywhere amid copses of men and horses'.* ('Medieval Mind, vol I', by Taylor, p. 551).

All the surviving Jews were driven into a synagogue and burnt to death ----- this despite the fact that the first crusade had been substantially financed by the Jews in Europe ('*History of the Jews, III*,' by H. Graetz, p.308, as quoted by Will Durant in *'The Story of Civilization --- The Age of Faith'*, p.366). Henceforth no Jew or Muslim was allowed to enter Jerusalem. All synagogues and mosques were either destroyed or converted into churches, including al-Aqsa mosque that was taken over and turned into the headquarters of the Knights of Templar.

The attitude of the Christian Church towards the Jews at the time of the crusades and much of the rest of history is summed up in the letter that Peter the Venerable, the saintly Abbot of Cluny, wrote to Louis VII, King of France, just before the Second Crusade in 1147. It read in part, *'I do not require you to put to death these accursed beings --- - God does not wish to annihilate them; but, like Cain the fratricide, they must be made to suffer fearful torments, and be preserved for greater ignominy, for an existence more bitter than death'* (*'Israel in Egypt'* by G.F Abbott p.88 and *'History of the Jews, III'* by H. Graetz, p. 350).

The crusades did not end with the capture of Jerusalem. A second Crusade, led by the Holy Roman Emperor Conrad and King Louis of France, was inconsequential but the third, led by the English King Richard, the French King Philip Augustus and the Holy Roman Emperor Frederick Barbarossa (1189-1192) managed to lose Jerusalem and most of Palestine to the Muslims. The fourth Crusade, instead of fighting the infidel, in 1204, ransacked Christian Constantinople and the crusader knights seized domains within the Byzantine Empire for themselves. The last three crusades were rather pointless and unsuccessful raids against Egypt.

There were other crusades as well, not all of them directed against the Muslims. One was authorized against pagan tribes living east of River Elbe, another to put down heretics in the south of France that wiped out entire Cathar communities, and more against King John of England and Emperor Fredrick II, a crusader himself. One of these, composed of English and Flemish contingents, wrested Lisbon from the Moors and laid the foundation of Portugal.

In 1172 Salahuddin became the ruler of Egypt and succeeded in annexing Syria and Northern Iraq to his domain. Alarmed at the looting and hostage-taking of pilgrims and traders by the crusaders, he engaged and defeated the combined armies of all the Christian knights gathered under Jerusalem's King Guy at the Hittin Plateau in September 1187. The distraught Pope dispatched a new army under King Richard of England, a particularly cruel and treacherous individual whose favourite pastime was to watch the execution of Muslim prisoners, mostly women and children. He showed up in the port of Acre in 1191 along with King Philip of France and the Holy Roman Emperor, only to surrender after some desultory warfare, and return home the next year.

Contrary to many legends prevalent in the West, Salahuddin never deigned to meet with Richard. The truce was negotiated by his younger brother al-Adil. At one stage Richard made the bizarre proposal that Al-Adil should marry Richard's sister, Joanna, and the couple should rule the Holy Land together (*'Arab Historians of the Crusades'*, by Francesco Gabrieli, London, 1978, p.226-27). It horrified Joanna and the churchmen. Salahuddin dismissed it as irrelevant and frivolous.

It would be reasonable to expect Salahuddin to exact some revenge from the Christians for all the savagery and butchery that they had perpetrated on the Muslim population during the occupation. There were no reprisals and no looting, burning, torture or any other cruelty inflicted upon the non-Muslims. Salahuddin simply restored the old order, giving

Christian priests their churches and the freedom to worship in them despite the fact that some of them had encouraged the Crusaders to acts of barbarity like eating the flesh of Muslim dead bodies (*'Discovering Islam: Making Sense of Muslim History and Society'* by Akbar S. Ahmed, Rutledge & Keegan Paul Ltd., London, 1988, p. 51).

This kind of acceptance and tolerance was not reserved specifically for the Christians. Other religious minorities were also accorded similar accommodation and privileges under the Muslim rule, extensive misrepresentation and re-writing of history by various individuals and groups in recent times notwithstanding. In the twelfth century, a Jewish Rabbi named Benjamin of Tudela had spent a dozen years traveling across the Muslim world from Spain to India. While his recorded memoirs speak bitterly of intolerance towards the Jews in Christian lands, he is conspicuously warm towards the Muslims describing the caliph of Baghdad as *'an excellent man, trustworthy, kind-hearted towards everyone'* and *'extremely friendly towards the Jews'.*

The Rabbi's principal aim had been to compile a register of the Jewish communities in as many cities of Asia as he could reach. The results were gratifying to him because he found them to be numerous and prospering everywhere in Muslim lands (*'Empires of the Monsoon'*, by Richard Hall, Harper Collins, London, 1996, p.40). Traditionally, the financial affairs of Muslim states, in particular the Ottoman Empire, were handled by Jewish or Christian functionaries as a matter of custom and tradition.

The religious fervour aroused by the Crusades not only had a profound influence on the politics of Western Europe that reverberate to this day but also deeply affected the lives of its ordinary citizens for many centuries to come. Spurred on by over-zealous priesthood, Crusades became an obsession that consumed the continent. More often than not, such blind religious zeal breeds tragedy and the Crusades were no exception. Of all the tragedies none were more poignant than the 'Children's Crusades' initiated in the belief that the innocents would, somehow, succeed where Christian armies had failed.

In 1212 a German youth, Nicholas, announced that God had commissioned him to lead a Crusade of children to the Holy Land. Some thirty thousand teen-agers followed him across the Alps to board ships in Genoa. Very few made it even that far. Many perished in the snow and ice of the Alps. Thieves stole their possessions and stragglers were devoured by wolves. Similarly, a French boy named Stephen had a vision of Christ ordering him to lead a children's Crusade. He led twenty thousand youths to Marseilles, where the ocean was expected to divide and open a dry passage to Palestine. It didn't. The young Crusaders were herded into seven ships. Two of these floundered near Sardinia and the ship owners sold the rest of the boys in the slave markets of Tunisia and Egypt.

Tragedy aside, Crusades served a very useful, if less than celestial, purpose for the church itself. People could hardly refuse to donate money for such a worthy cause as war against the infidels. The Popes exploited this weakness quite unashamedly. At the turn of the sixteenth century, Pope Leo X consecrated Albert of Brandenburg the archbishop of Magdeburg, Germany for a consideration of 24,000 ducats and gave him an eight year indulgence for St. Peter. Albert borrowed the sum from the banking house of Fuggers. To make it possible for him to pay back the loan, the Pope proposed and a new holy war against the Turks to raise the needed cash. Half of the proceeds thus collected went to Fuggers and the rest to Rome. Any pious

Christian who was unable to join a crusade for any reason could obtain an indulgence and remission of sin from the Pope in exchange for a suitable cash donation (*'The Bad Popes'*, by E. R. Chamberlin, The New American Library, Inc. New York, 1971, p. 238).

In the cold light of history, the sum total of achievement in these Christian Crusades can only be described as many centuries of misery for Europe and an even greater tragedy for the Holy Land itself, while most of the Islamic world remained unconcerned and unaffected. They may not have achieved anything positive and may not have been of any great significance when viewed in the context of Islamic history but they remain very relevant to the understanding of Christian attitudes and feelings towards Islam. The failure gave rise to bitterness, frustration and resentment that has been burned deep into the western psyche and keeps manifesting itself at every opportunity till this day.

Regardless of their effect or lack of it on Islam, the Crusades were a defining moment in European history. In his *'The Legacy of Islam'* (reprinted in 2001 by Rightway Publications, Delhi under the title, *'Influence & Impression of Islam'*) Sir Thomas Arnold writes, *'With the Crusades a new era opened. The half-fabulous magnificence traditionally ascribed to the Saracens became a reality to Christendom. A host drawn from every part of Europe came suddenly into close contact with a social order that in every respect outranged the narrow limits of their experience. In every activity of life the reactions of this impact with alien progress soon became apparent -------'* (p. 148).

It was the first time that the Europeans were called upon to look outwards beyond their own borders and the concept of a 'just war' was born whose moral basis was later defined by Saint Thomas Aquinas, the thirteenth century theologian and philosopher in his *Summa Theologica* (*'Applied Ethics'* by David S. Oderberg, Berkeley Calif: University Press Books, 2000). This has been used through the ages and even today by people like Presidents Bush, Pope John Paul II and Archbishop Dr. Robert Runcie of Canterbury, as an excuse to justify western attacks on Muslim states like Iraq and Afghanistan.

This was also when a common enemy was presented to the Europeans as the basis for unification. The moving spirit behind it was religion, hence, the choice of Muslims as the enemy. It divided the world between 'them' and 'us'. There was little choice. You had to be with 'us' or face expulsion from the ranks. That is how the Crusading psyche visualizes the world and this is what was most probably at the back of President Bush's mind when he declared his so called 'war on terrorism' and told the rest of the world to join him. Just as the Pope had brought King Philip of France in line by threatening ex-communication when he showed reluctance to proceed on yet another Crusade in 1189 so too Bush declared, 'You are either with us or against us'.

This Manichaean mindset has no tolerance for divergence or a difference of views. The process becomes self-consuming once you start looking for enemies. It does not take long before they start to appear within. That is when minorities and dissidents become ready-made targets for suspicions and persecution.

This is something the Muslims did not fully comprehend at the time and seem to be having difficulty with it even now. They never regarded the Crusaders as a threat to Islam, as such, even after Nuruddin Zengi the Turkish ruler of Syria foiled a Crusader plot to desecrate the grave of the Prophet in Madina in 1162, reportedly, having been warned of it in a dream. It was only after this incident that the entry of non-Muslims into Makka and Madina was banned. For the most part, the crusaders were accepted as integral to the landscape.

Islam has always tolerated and accepted the existence of other societies and religious groups within its boundaries with more or less equal rights. The only stipulation has been that in return for the exemption from the obligation to fight for the defence of the land they were called upon to pay a poll tax known as '*jazia*'. This is not a discriminatory imposition, as often erroneously portrayed. Muslims too are required to pay '*zakat*', a tax that is exclusively obligatory for them and not applicable to the non-Muslims.

The view from Europe was very different. The Crusades touched the very basis and validity of the faith. The eventual defeat raised many questions, including if God had indeed abandoned the true believers. With these doubts came explanations and reasons as to why this might be so. It has left a sense of uncertainty and insecurity in Christianity that is palpable even to this day. After the six-day Israeli victory and conquest of Jerusalem in 1967, Billy Graham's father-in-law, L. Nelson Bell, wrote '*It gave the students of the Bible a thrill and a renewed faith in the accuracy and validity of the Bible*' (Jim Lobe in '*The Asia Times*', 27th April 2002). Why should it take a war by a Jewish State to validate the Holy Book for Christians? One wonders if he and the rest of America's Christian Right ever stopped to think what the poor Palestinians, who were at the receiving end of this validation, must think of this interpretation of the Bible and what Jesus Christ himself must be feeling when he sees the usurpation of rights and unending suffering of the people among whom he was born and brought up and who believed in him, as all Muslims do?

This is another issue; suffice it to say that the failure of the Crusades has never been far from the European consciousness and keeps surfacing whenever there is an occasion. When Kaiser Wilhelm of Germany paid a visit in 1898 to Jerusalem, then under Turkish rule, he did so dressed as a medieval crusader. British General Allenby, after taking over Jerusalem from the Turks in the closing stages of World War I, made the declaration on 11th December 1917, '*Crusades have now been completed*'. Probably not, because we now hear George W. Bush calling for them again. In reality the Crusades have never ceased in the European mind, as any discerning reader of history would realise. They were merely put on hold for the duration of the cold war with the Soviet Union and have now been revived again by the new knights in shining armour ---- Bush, Blair, Berlusconi & Co.

In a recent article, Karen Armstrong has described the legacy of the Crusades in these terms, '*The crusades destabilised the Near East, but made little impression on the Islamic world as a whole. In the west, however, they were crucial and formative. This was the period when western Christendom was beginning to recover from the long period of barbarism known as the Dark Ages, and the crusades were the first cooperative act of the new Europe as she struggled back on to the international scene. We continue to talk about "crusades" for justice and peace, and praise a "crusading journalist" who is bravely uncovering some salutary truth, showing that at some unexamined level, crusading is still acceptable to the western soul. One of its most enduring legacies is a profound hatred of Islam.*

'*Before the crusades, Europeans knew very little about Muslims. But after the conquest of Jerusalem, scholars began to cultivate a highly distorted portrait of Islam, and this Islamophobia, entwined with a chronic anti-Semitism,* would become one of the received ideas of Europe. Christians must have been aware that their crusades violated the spirit of the gospels: Jesus had told his followers to love their enemies, not to exterminate them. This may be the reason why Christian scholars projected their anxiety on to the very people they had damaged.

'Thus it was, at a time when Christians were fighting brutal holy wars against Muslims in the Near East, that Islam became known in Europe as an inherently violent and intolerant faith, a religion of the sword. At a time when the popes were trying to impose celibacy on the reluctant clergy, western biographies of the prophet Mohammed, written by priests and monks, depict him, with ill-concealed envy, as a sexual pervert and lecher, who encouraged Muslims to indulge their basest instincts.

'At a time when feudal Europe was riddled with hierarchy, Islam was presented as an anarchic religion that gave too much respect and freedom to menials, such as slaves and women. Christians could not see Islam as separate from themselves; it had become, as it were, their shadow-self, the opposite of everything that they thought they were or hoped they were not.

'In fact, the reality was very different. Islam, for example, is not the intolerant or violent religion of western fantasy. Mohammed was forced to fight against the city of Mecca, which had vowed to exterminate the new Muslim community, but the Koran, the inspired scripture that he brought to the Arabs, condemns aggressive warfare and permits only a war of self-defence. After five years of warfare, Mohammed turned to more peaceful methods and finally conquered Mecca by an ingenious campaign of non-violence. After the prophet's death, the Muslims established a vast empire that stretched from the Pyrenees to the Himalayas, but *these wars of conquest were secular, and were only given a religious interpretation after the event.*

'In the Islamic empire, Jews, Christians and Zoroastrians enjoyed religious freedom. This reflected the teaching of the Koran, which is a pluralistic scripture, affirmative of other traditions. Muslims are commanded by God to respect the "people of the book", and reminded that they share the same beliefs and the same God. Mohammed had not intended to found a new religion; he was simply bringing the old religion of the Jews and the Christians to the Arabs, who had never had a prophet before. Constantly the Koran explains that Mohammed has not come to cancel out the revelations brought by Adam, Abraham, Moses or Jesus. Today, Muslim scholars have argued that had Mohammed known about the Buddhists and Hindus, the native Americans or the Australian Aborigines, the Koran would have endorsed their sages and shamans too, because all rightly guided religion comes from God.

But so entrenched are the old medieval ideas that western people find it difficult to believe this. We continue to view Islam through the filter of our own needs and confusions. The question of women is a case in point. None of the major world faiths has been good to women but, like Christianity, Islam began with a fairly positive message, and it was only later that the religion was hijacked by old patriarchal attitudes. The Koran gives women legal rights of inheritance and divorce, which western women would not receive until the 19th century. The Koran does permit men to take four wives, but this was not intended to pander to male lust, it was a matter of social welfare: it enabled widows and orphans to find a protector, without whom it was impossible for them to survive in the harsh conditions of 7th-century Arabia.'

SPAIN

In April 711 AD a small Arab army of seven thousand, reinforced by another five thousand Muslims from North Africa, crossed the straits of Gibraltar into Spain under the leadership of Tarik Bin Ziyad. He met the Spanish Visigoth King Rodrigo's army of seventy thousand in battle at Rio Guadalete. The Spaniards were routed and Muslims ruled over much of Spain for the next almost eight centuries. In all this time they did not engage in any forced conversions, pogroms, pillage or rape in the occupied territories. This is how Dutch professor Reinhart Dozy described their rule in *'Histoire des Musalman d' Espangne, livre II, chap. II'* (as reproduced in *'The Moors in Spain'* by Sir Stanley Lane-pool, pp. 30-34) *'It must not be supposed that the Moors, like barbarian hordes who preceded them, brought devastation and tyranny in their wake. On the contrary, never was Andalusia so mildly, justly and wisely governed as by her Arab conquerors. Where they got their talent for administration is hard to say, for they came directly from their Arabian deserts, and the rapid tide of victories had left them little leisure to acquire the art of managing foreign nations. Some of their counselors were Greeks and Spaniards, but this does not explain the problem; for these same counselors were unable to produce similar results elsewhere and all the administrative talent of Spain had not sufficed to make the Gothic domination tolerable to its subjects -----------*

'The result was that the Christians were satisfied with the new regime and openly admitted that they preferred the rule of the Moors to that of the Franks or the Goths. Even their priests, who had lost most of all, were at first but little

*incensed with the change, as the old chronicle ascribed
to Isidore of Beja, written in 754, shows. The good monk
is not even scandalized at so unholy an alliance as the
marriage between Rodrigo's widow and the son of Moosa*
(a Muslim general). *But the best proof of the satisfaction of
the Christians with their new rulers is the fact that there
was not a single religious revolt during the eighth century.*

'*Above all, the slaves, who had been cruelly ill-used by the
Goths and Romans, had cause to congratulate themselves
upon the change. Slavery is a very mild and humane
institution in the hands of a good Mohammadan* (as indeed
we witnessed in the case of Caliph Omer when he arrived
in Jerusalem). ----------

'*As far as the vanquished were concerned, we have seen
that the conquest of Andalusia by the Arabs was on the
whole a benefit. It did away with the overgrown estates
of the great nobles and churchmen, and converted them
into small proprietorships; it removed the heavy burdens
of the middle classes, and restricted the taxation to the
test-tax per poll levied on the unbelievers, and the land-
tax levied equally on Moslem and Christian; and included
a widespread emancipation of the slaves, and a radical
improvement in the condition of the emancipated, who now
became almost independent farmers in the service of their
non-agricultural Mohammadan masters*'.

Paul Alvaro, an eighth century Spanish layman, writing
in '*Indiculus Luminosus*' (as quoted by R.W Southern in
'*Western Views of Islam in the Middle Ages*', London 1962,
p. 21) describes the state of affairs at the time as '*The
Christians love to read the poems and romances of the
Arabs; they study the Arab theologians and philosophers,
not to refute them but to form a correct and elegant Arabic.
Where is the layman who now reads the Latin commentaries*

on the Holy Scriptures, or who studies the Gospels, prophets or apostles? Alas! all talented young Christians read with enthusiasm the Arab books'.

There was a world of difference in the treatment of slaves by the Muslims and the European Christians. Under Islam a slave, although beholden to his owner, enjoyed the same basic rights in law as any free individual. Many of them rose to high office in the land and even ruled as kings, among them, Salahuddin of the crusading fame.

It was a different story altogether in Christendom. An English lady, Mrs. Jemima Kindersley, on her way to Calcutta in 1765 witnessed the torture and lynching of slaves by the Dutch in Cape Town that she wrote were carried out in public in a manner 'too shocking to repeat'. Any slave accused of a serious infraction, such as an attempt to escape, was stretched live on a torture wheel after smashing his arms and legs with an iron club. Others were impaled on stakes in the ground where they took two or three days to die. The Europeans viewed the slaves not as human beings but as property. There are recorded cases of slaves being beheaded to save expenses, after they had outlived their utility to the owners (*'Empires of the Monsoon',* p. 362).

Interestingly, most of the slave trade in Europe and later in North America was handled by the Jews as evident from this extract from the *'History of the Islamic Peoples'* by Carl Brockelmann, Capricon Books, New York, 1960, '---------- *At this time* (fourteenth century AD onwards) *a very lively slave trade, predominantly in Jewish hands, was flourishing in western Europe. Its victims were principally captives from the wars along the Slavic eastern marches of Germany who were sold into Spain by way of France; Verdun was a principal centre for the preparation of eunuchs* ---------- (p.187). Also see *'The Secret Relationship Between Blacks and Jews*', by Professor Tony Martin, Wellesley College, Boston, 1991 for details of the slave trade in the Americas.

The city of Cordoba, under the Muslim rule, was the unrivaled metropolis of Western Europe. It had a population of six hundred thousand in 950 AD. There were 92,700 shops, 600 mosques, 300 public baths, 50 hospitals, 70 public libraries, 80 schools and a university that catered for 20,000 students. One library alone housed some 400,000 volumes at a time when the largest library in Christendom at the time probably held no more than 400. The institutions of learning were open to students from all over Europe regardless of their race or religion. One of the Christian students in Muslim Spain happened to be Gerbert of Aurillac, the future Pope Sylvester II.

Other cities like Murcia, Seville, Cartagena, Granada, Valencia and Almeria enjoyed similar prosperity. Muslims gave Spain its distinctive architecture still visible in the Giralda of Seville ----- the bell-tower of the cathedral of Seville --- originally, the minaret of its Great Mosque that was demolished and replaced by the cathedral. The Alcazar in Seville and the Alhambra overlooking Grenada are two more examples of what has survived. Under the Islamic law, Spanish women had the right to own property and business, partake in politics, the freedom to divorce and protection from physical abuse by their husbands that was denied to them in the Christian West until much later.

The Muslims brought advanced knowledge of agriculture and introduced oranges, apricots, figs, silk and paper to Europe. In the field of science, their contributions included Algebra, Arabic numerals (originally from India), the concept of zero in mathematics, Khwarzimi's astronomical tables that revolutionized the study of geography, astronomy and navigation at sea and new developments in medicine, chemistry (*al-chemia*), metallurgy and weapons technology. Even the Spanish guitar is a gift from the Persian musician, Ziryab. Morris dancing, popular in the British Isles until recent times, was a reflection of the widespread influence of Muslim Spain. (In popular usage, 'Moorish' became 'Morris' after a period of time).

More importantly, the works of philosophers like Ibne Rushd (Averroes), Razi (Razes), Ahmed Ghazali and Mohiyuddin Ibne Arabi, scientists like Abu Ali Sena (Avicenna), and analysts like Ibne Khaldoon and Al-Beiruni began to influence the minds and paved the way for Renaissance. The intellectual activity that characterized Muslim civilization had a profound effect on the rest of Europe. The writings of ancient Greeks, eclipsed for hundreds of years that had already been translated into Arabic, were now made available in Latin. These included the original versions of the works of Aristotle and Plato, the geometry of Euclid, the medical treatises of Pedanius, Dioscorides and Galen and scores of other classics.

Muslim rule came to an end in Spain in 1492 AD, the year Columbus came to America. The terms of the treaty under which Granada had surrendered to King Ferdinand and Queen Isabella allowed freedom of religious practice to the Moors. These commitments were soon forgotten. Queen Isabella promulgated a decree by which the Moors were told to choose between baptisms or being deported after making a substantial payment to the Crown. All Jewish and Muslim children under the age of fourteen were to be forcibly baptized; many were dragged screaming into the churches for the ceremony. Faced with the prospect of never seeing their children again if they escaped to some other country, scores of thousands of adult Jews and Muslims chose to be baptized themselves and became second class Christians in their own country.

The businesses and properties of all non-Christians were expropriated by the Order of Christ, a particularly intolerant organisation. These were then sold to provide funds for the overseas expeditions. Those who converted to Christianity came to be known as *'Moriscos'*. They continued to be discriminated against as suspect second class citizens with few rights and were not allowed to leave the country. Even a move from one province to another was a crime for them punishable with death. The mosques were closed, thousands of priceless manuscripts burnt and Muslims were threatened and beaten into the Gospel of Peace and Goodwill after the manner already approved by their Catholic Majesties in respect of the no less miserable Jews.

Sir Stanley Lane-Pool records, *'The infidels were ordered to abandon their native and picturesque costume, and to assume the hats and breeches of the Christians; to give up bathing and adopt the dirt of their conquerors* (taking a bath was deemed un-Christian and taboo among the Europeans until fairly recent times); *to renounce their language, their customs and ceremonies, even their very names, and to speak Spanish, behave Spanishly, and rename themselves Spaniards'* (*'The Moors in Spain'*, p. 179).

The harshness and cruelty with which these measures were enforced, gave rise to numerous rebellions that smouldered for the better part of a hundred years. These were put down through wholesale butchery and devastation. Entire communities, including women and children, were wiped out. There is no count of how many were killed, enslaved or converted. No less than three million Moors were banished from Spain, forever, after the fall of Granada. Most of them ended up begging for a living on the streets of North African cities. To this day, many families retain the keys to the houses they had abandoned in Spain. It was the same with the Jews who also fled to safety in Muslim lands under the Ottomans in the Balkans and in North Africa.

The actions of the Spaniards had less to do with any political resentment against eight hundred years of Muslim rule than with religious and racial intolerance and bigotry. This is clearly evident from the Papal Bull promulgated by Pope Benedict XIII in May 1415. Among other things, it forbade all Jews from reading, listening to or teaching the Talmud, which it called a *'depraved doctrine'*. All books that contradicted the dogmas and rites of Christianity were banned. No Jew was permitted to pronounce the names of Jesus, Mary or any of the saints. No new synagogue could be built or old ones refurbished. No person of Jewish faith could become a judge, physician, midwife, trader, watchmaker or moneylender. They were forbidden from renting property, employing Christian servants and living in Christian neighbourhoods. All contracts with Jews were declared null and void.

Each of them was obliged to wear a distinguishing red or yellow badge and attend at least three sermons a year that stressed the coming of Christ, the Messiah, and the errors of the Talmud (*'Historia de los Judios'* by J. Amador de los Rios). They were accused of worshipping Anti-Christ, practicing witchcraft and ritually murdering Christian babies. Jews were the Devil incarnate, an assertion often made in the Christian circles quoting the Gospel of John in the Bible.

This hatred was not confined to the Catholics. Martin Luther, the father of Reformation, was particularly virulent in his attitude towards the Jews *'Thus they call Him* (Jesus) *the child of a whore and His mother, Mary, a whore ------ Reluctantly I must speak so course in opposing the Devil --- - 'Yea, I maintain that in three fables of Aesop there is more*

*wisdom to be found than in all the books of the Talmudists
and Rabbis and more than could come in the hearts of the
Jews* --- (*'The Jews and Their Lies, Luther's Works vol.
47'*, edited by Franklin Sherman and Helmut T. Lehman,
Fortress Press, Philadelphia, 1971, ISBN 0-8006-0347-48).

This was a far cry, indeed, from the position of virtual
equality and privilege enjoyed by them under the Muslim
rule, which they were later to term as their 'golden age'. It
was not only the Jews; the same acceptance and tolerance
was shown to the Christians, many of whom occupied
high office in the Muslim state, among them a bishop
who was Muslim Spain's ambassador to Germany. (For
an understanding of the comparative treatment of Jews
under the Muslim and Christian rules in Spain please see
'The End of Days' ---*A Story of Tolerance, Tyranny and
the Expulsion of Jews from Spain'*. By Erna Paris, Lester
Publishing, Toronto, 1995).

Martin Luther and Pope Benedict XIII were by no means
alone in harbouring such extreme prejudice. Earlier, Lateran
Counsels of 1179 and 1215, as well as Pope Gregory IX, had
passed similar edicts against the Muslims and Jews. Pope
Clement V (1305 - 1314) had declared that Islamic presence
on Christian soil was 'an insult to God' (*'Mohammad --- A
Western Attempt to Understand Islam'* by Karen Armstrong,
Victor Gollancz, London, 1991, p. 28). These were not
the irresponsible utterings of an ignorant bigot or like the
'fatwa' of some foolish mulla who has no authority based
in Islam. In the Roman Catholic faith, Pope is the 'Vicar of
Christ' which is believed to confer divine authority upon
him. His voice is considered to be the 'Voice of God' by the
church and his decrees are regarded as the 'Laws of God'
for the government of mankind. The Pope is also believed
to be 'infallible', as proclaimed by Pope Pious IX as late as
in 1870.

The office of Inquisition, first established by Pope Gregory IX in 1213 to deal with heresy, was revived with a vengeance in Spain. It involved a fearsome bureaucracy of priests, notaries, police, commissioners, spies and informers. The diabolically cruel institution was not officially abolished until 1834, by which time, millions of innocent and helpless victims had met with the most inhuman and excruciatingly painful end at its hands in the name of Christian religion. In the city of Seville alone, in one year, the Holy Office of Inquisition ordered more than two thousand men, women and children to be burnt alive at the stake, with two thousand more burnt in effigy, and awarded varying degrees of other punishments, accompanied by diabolical torture, to seventeen thousand more. The properties of the victims were confiscated and divided up between the Holy Office, the Royal Treasury and the Church. (*'Histoire Critique de l'Inquisition d' Espagne,* by J. de Mariana, p. 239).

Their crimes ---- practicing non-Christian religion, having Arabic names, showing disrespect for Christian sacraments, refusing to eat pork and drink wine and practicing circumcision, to name a few (for more details about the *Inquisition,* please see *'The Spanish Inquisition'* by Henry Kamen, New American Library, New York). Curiously, the Inquisition also prohibited the import and publication of novels in Latin America on the presumption that these were inclined to produce a rebellious spirit among the local population. It is significant that the extreme cruelties associated with Inquisition were not the result of some temporary aberration restricted in terms of time and place. The diabolical institution was ordained and established by the highest religious authority in Christendom, regarded as the 'Voice of God', and it was operated by church functionaries for hundreds of years in all the continents of the world except, perhaps, Australia.

The final act of 'religious cleansing' of Spain came in 1614. Everyone who had any Arab or Moorish blood, even after having converted to Christianity, was ordered to leave *'so that all the kingdoms of Spain will remain pure and clean from these people'*, as the Duke of Lerma phrased it (*'Islam'* by Chegne, p.13). An estimated 300,000 Moriscos, nearly all their remaining population, were forcibly driven out of the country. Many of them ended up in Latin America where remnants of their culture can still be traced.

Racism has been an inherent, ugly and recurrent theme in European culture throughout known history and lurks only just below the surface among the white race wherever it is to be found. In fifteenth century Spain it manifested itself in the cult of *Limpieza de Sangre* (Purity of Blood). Any one with Arab or Jewish mixture or ancestry, even though belonging to the Christian faith, was denied access to universities, colleges and military schools, prevented from holding public or bureaucratic office and even forbidden from living in certain towns and areas. It was a farce and a hoax for, according to Fray Augustin Salucio in *'Discurso'* (1599 AD) by this time there was hardly a family in Spain that did not have at least some trace of the 'impure' blood (*'The Spanish Inquisition'*, p.134).

Sir StanleyLane-Poole, rare among western historians for his unbiased objectivity and willingness to record the truth when it came to Islam, wrote this epitaph to the Muslim rule in Spain: *'The misguided Spaniards knew not what they were doing. -------------- They did not understand that they had killed their golden goose. For centuries Spain had been the center of civilization, the seat of arts and sciences, of learning, and every form of refined enlightenment. No other country in Europe had so far approached the cultivated dominion of the Moors. ---------The Moors were banished; for a while Christian Spain shone, like the moon, with borrowed light; then came the eclipse, and in that darkness Spain has groveled ever since. The true memorial of the Moors is seen in desolate tracts of utter barrenness, where once the Moslem grew luxuriant vines and olives and yellow ears of corn; in a stupid ignorant population where once learning flourished; in the general stagnation of a people which has hopelessly fallen in the scale of nations, and has deserved its humiliation* ('The Moors in Spain', p. 185). This state of affairs lasted until well into the twentieth century.

It is significant that during the liberation of Spain almost all the Christian powers in Europe aided and supported the liberators in one way or another. However, the Moors were left to fend for themselves by the rest of the Muslims. None of the powerful sultanates in Turkey and North Africa took much notice of their plight and suffering and chose not to make common cause with them. Unlike Christendom, the issue was not a religious one for the Muslims, just as it had not been during the Crusades. This has been the case throughout most of history and contrary to the assertions made by writers like Lewis, Huntington, et al. in recent times, Muslims have historically never formed or acted as a religious monolith in confronting non-Muslim powers.

EAST EUROPE

Muslim Turks occupied Constantinople in 1453 putting an end to the Byzantine Empire. Later they expanded their rule to include most of eastern Europe and all of the coastal regions around the Black Sea. Contrary to popular belief in Christian circles they never engaged in forced conversions or expulsions of Christian subjects from their domains, as was done to the Muslim population after the Christian take over in Spain and the Russian expansion southwards.

When the Turkish rule in eastern Europe ended after nearly five centuries it gave rise to more than two dozen different nations with their religions, languages and cultures not only in tact but also profoundly enriched. In fact, the popular cry among the Balkan peasants at the time was, *'Better the turban of the Turk than the tiara of the Pope'* (*'A Concise History of the Middle East'* by Arthur Goldschmidt, Westview Press, Boulder, Colorado, 1988, p.132). It was the same in the other parts that were under Muslim rule. A general belief at the time held, '------- *the God of vengeance delivered us out of the hands of the Romans by means of the Arabs ------- It profited us not a little to be saved from the cruelty of the Romans and their bitter hatred towards us'* (*'The Arabs in History'* by Bernard Lewis, London, 1958, p. 58).

As evidence of the extent of Turkish religious, social and racial tolerance, all the eight grand wazirs of Sultan Suleyman the Magnificent had been humble-born Christians. (During the peak years of the Ottoman Empire, between 1453 and 1623, only five out of the forty-eight persons to hold the office of grand wazir were of Turkish blood. Of the rest, eleven were from Albania, six from Greece, eleven Slavs, one each from Circassia, Italy, Armenia, and Georgia. The origins of the rest are unknown.) The brother of perhaps the greatest of them (Ibrahim) happened to be the Christian Archbishop of Bosnia.

The French political philosopher, Jean Bodin, had said at the time, '*The king of the Turks, who rules over a great part of Europe, safeguards the rites of religion as well as any prince in this world. Yet, he constrains no one, but on the contrary permits everyone to live as his conscience dictates. What is more, even in his seraglio at Pera he permits the practice of four diverse religions, that of the Jews, the Christian according to the Roman rite, and according to the Greek rite, and that of Islam ('The Ottoman Impact on Europe'* by Paul Coles, Harcourt, Brace and World, New York, 1968, p. 151). The entrenched beliefs many westerners today profess about Islam often reveal more about the West than they do about Islam or Muslims. The Ottomans were history's longest-lasting major dynasty; their durability must have had some relation to their ability to rule a multi-faith empire at a time when Europe was busily hanging, drawing and quartering different varieties of Christian believers.

Some things change little with time. One of these is the need for an external enemy to reduce internal strife and ensure willing compliance by the people. There is no tool more useful than religion to stir up emotions. The threat posed by the Turks to Europe could only be countered by a united Christendom and despite what Bodin and others like him may have said, wheels were set in motion to demonize Islam and the Turks in particular. In a way it is true that European identity as such was defined primarily in its opposition to Islam as the enemy. It remains to be seen if history will repeat itself as the efforts to unify and expand the European Union intensify. The portents are not altogether sanguine or reassuring for the Muslims, considering the vituperation against them and their religion emanating from many influential quarters. The fact that Muslim Turkey has been denied entry into the Union, on one pretext after another, for so long may be just one harbinger of things to come.

Christians in all the lands were called upon to unite against the infidel Turks who were characterized, without providing any tangible proof, as the 'scourge of Christendom' and 'ferocious and inhuman barbarians'. Shakespeare described the Turks as '*malignant*' and Carlyle as '*unspeakable*'. Martin Luther saw Islam as a '*movement of violence in the service of the Anti-Christ; it cannot be converted because it is closed to reason; it can only be resisted by the sword, and even then with difficulty*' ('*Europe and the Middle East*' by Hourani, p. 10). Voltaire portrayed the prophet of Islam as a '*theocratic tyrant*' in his essay, '*Fanaticism, or Mohammad the Prophet*'. Dante also expressed equally vitriolic views but that did not stop him from plagiarizing Muslim philosophers like Mohiyuddin Ibne Arabi, an act described as 'piracy' by Professor Asin in his book '*The Sufis*' (p. 140).

As is becoming only too apparent, not much has changed since then. Recently, when Prophet Mohammed was put at the top of the list of persons who had the most profound influence in human history ('*The 100: A Ranking of the Most Influential Persons in History*', by M. Hart) it met with distastefully base criticism in influential western literary and theological circles. The cries that we now hear about the western civilization being threatened by the old bogeyman of Europe and the strident calls for unified action against the resurrected demon from its past all sound disturbingly familiar to those who take an interest in history.

A stream of literature has been churned out by the presses in the West with themes associating Islam and the Muslims in thinly veiled references to the villains in the Biblical prophecies about Armageddon, Antichrist and the rest. In the United States alone novels in the 'Left Behind Book Series' (Tyndale House) have sold millions of copies. This is just one publishing house. It is the same story in every other Christian country. The plot is invariably about religious struggle between the forces of 'good' and 'evil' and it is always centred on the Middle East ------ Palestine, Jordan and, in particular, Jerusalem.

In the spring of 1821, Greeks of Peloponnes started killing local Muslims in an orgy of horrendous proportions. This was the start of the Greek Revolution to get rid of the Turkish occupation. Within a few months more than twenty thousand Muslim men, women and children had been slaughtered. *'The conquerors, mad with vindictive rage, spared neither age nor sex ---- the streets and houses were inundated with blood, and obstructed with heaps of dead bodies. Some Mohammedans fought bravely and sold their lives dearly, but the majority was slaughtered without resistance'* (*'History of the Greek Revolution, vol. I'*, by Thomas Gordon, William Blackwood, Edinburgh, 1832, pp. 254 – 5).

Gordon is indeed rare among the western historians and politicians of the time, most of whom seldom mentioned this start but concentrated instead on highly colourful accounts of the atrocities committed by the Turks in quelling the rebellion. As with George W. Bush today, the revolution was quickly dubbed as a new crusade. One eminent historian rather loftily wrote, '----- *the common earth had received a defilement which needed some rite of lustration to wipe off from the consciences of all mankind'*. The 'indescribable Turk' was generally regarded as the agent of this defilement but the Anglican church attributed it to the 'most nauseous of all abominations, Mohammedism'.

With the passage of time corruption and tyranny took hold and the Turkish Empire slowly shriveled to become the 'Sick Man of Europe' in the nineteenth century, surrounded by squabbling vulture on all sides. The Turks were slow to react to changes that had taken place in Europe and failed to adapt in time. Conservatism took a stranglehold to exclude modern scientific, technological, administrative and political advances and ideas. Trade and industry stagnated, causing economic instability and deprivation.

The empire was gradually rolled back by the combined forces of Christian Europe. As each place was liberated, its Muslim population was given the choice of either converting to Christianity or being expelled from the land. Even after conversion, as in Spain, they were treated as second class citizens and forced by law to change even their Turkish names. The Russians were particularly cruel, ordering forced conversions and indulging in wanton murders of civilians, raping, looting and enslaving Muslim populations.

Ivan IV 'the Terrible' started the process by declaring 'holy war on the infidel' and attacking the khanate of Kazan. He succeeded only after some initial failures and much bloodshed. Orthodox Christian priests, who had accompanied him, immediately embarked upon a programme of forced conversions. Thousands of young widows and unmarried maidens were pronounced Christian, against their will, and presented to Russian soldiers as concubines. The city's mosques and madrasas were destroyed and clerics and teachers put to the sword. Ivan 'purified' the site of the main mosque and laid the foundation stone of what became the Cathedral of Visitation. He also started construction of Saint Basil's Cathedral in Kremlin Square in Moscow, with its onion shaped golden dome that became a symbol for Russia in subsequent years. Its entire cost was extracted from the hapless victims of Kazan.

It took the Russians more than a century to subdue the tiny Muslim states in the Caucuses. Christians from neighbouring Georgia and Armenia, even as far afield as Germany, came to aid the Russians in fighting the Muslims. Some European and American travelers who happened to visit the Caucuses during this period came back with ghastly reports of torture, massacres and destruction of entire towns and villages. There were mass expulsions of populations and numerous accounts of Muslim men killing their wives and children to save them from falling into Russian hands (*'Turco-Tatar Past, Soviet Present, vol. VI'* by P.B Henze, p. 257). By the time Russia had finished with these tiny Muslim states, more than a million Caucasians, a majority of their population had been either killed or deported to the Ottoman Empire. The Russian attitude was exemplified by Prince Kochubey who, while campaigning in Circassia in the eighteenth century, explained to a visiting American, *'The Circassians are like your American Indians ---- untamable and uncivilised ---- and owing to their natural energy and character, extermination only would keep them quiet'*. They did their best to achieve it.

The Russians first ventured into Khiva in Central Asia at the beginning of the eighteenth century. All of the initial half a dozen or so expeditions met with unmitigated disaster. Very few of the Cossack soldiers survived to tell the tale. They were no match for the Khivan horsemen and their tactics. Over the course of the next century and a half, the Russian Army was modernized and equipped with long-range artillery and machine guns to which the Turkmen had no answer. With the balance so heavily tilted in Russian favour, they subjugated Tashkand in 1865 and Samarkand three years later.

Led by the ferocious General Kaufmann, they attacked Khiva simultaneously from four different directions in 1873. After a series of running battles and hard campaigning, Kaufmann forced the Khan, Mohammed Abdul Rahim Bogadur, to surrender and imposed a fine of forty one thousand pounds sterling to be paid within two weeks. There was no way that the Khivans could find the money and Kaufmann ordered their villages to bet set on fire and all grain, fodder, cattle and property confiscated. The Turkmen (locally known as 'Yamud') escaped into the surrounding desert with their women, children and anything else that they could collect. Kaufmann ordered his Cossacks to pursue them. What followed has been recorded by the American journalist, MacGahan, who was accompanying the expedition as representative of The New York Herald. His description is typical of the events that followed the Russian conquests in Central Asia:

'Our lines are broken by the abandoned carts and our progress impeded by the cattle and sheep that are running wildly about the plain. It is a scene of the wildest confusion. Here is a Turkman lying in the sand, with a bullet through his head, then two women, with three or four children sitting down in the sand, crying and sobbing piteously and begging for their lives. A little further on, more carts, carpets and bed coverlets, scattered about with sacks full of grain, and huge bags and bundles, cooking utensils, and all kinds of household goods. Then more women toiling wearily forward, carrying infants and weeping bitterly -- -------. Then camels, sheep, goats, cattle, donkeys, cows, calves and dogs; each, after its fashion, contributing to the wild scene of terror -------. A few yards further on there are four Cossacks around a Turkman. He has already

been beaten to his knees and weapon he has none. To the four sabres that are hacking at him he can offer only the resistance of his arms, but he utters no word of entreaty. Blow after blow they shower on his head without avail. At last, after what seems an age to me, he falls prone in the water, and the Cossacks gallop on. Next morning we continued our march, burning and ravaging every thing as we proceeded. We left behind us a strip of country about three miles wide, in which there was nothing left but heaps of smouldering ashes. --------. Here they had lived in quiet peaceful contentment, for whatever they had to do with war was far away in the Persian and Russian frontiers, in their little oasis surrounded by the great desert, as isolated from the rest of the world as an undiscovered island in the South Pacific. But the torch was applied and they learned all too dearly something of this great outside world.'

The chase continued for a week at the end of which the fleeing Turkmen, in desperation, decided to turn around and confront the Cossacks. MacGahan recalls, *'We rode over the field to count the wounded and the dead. The bodies of the Turkmen were strewn about in great numbers. Here was one lying on his side, both hands still clutching a long stick, to which he had tied a short crooked scythe. He was bare foot, bare headed and was clad only in light linen shirt and trousers; and there was still the stamp of the fierce savage spirit that had led him with such unequal weapons to face the breach loaders of the Russians.*

'But worse still to see were the women cowering under the carts, like poor dumb animals, watching us with fear stricken faces and beseeching eyes, but never uttering a word, with the dead bodies of their husbands and brothers lying around them. I observed one, however, who paid no attention to what was passing around her. She was holding in her lap the head of a man who was dying from

a terrible sabre cut in the head. She sat gazing at his face as motionless as a statue, not even raising her eyes at our approach; and we might have taken her attitude for one of stolid indifference, but for the tears that stole silently down from her long dark lashes, and dropped on the face of the dying man.'

This kind of savagery against innocent and defenceless human beings is not possible unless they have been thoroughly and completely demonized and de-humanized in the eyes of the soldiers first. It is easier for them to accept the enemy has no humanity. These poor people had been subsisting peacefully, eking out a meager living in the desert plains and minding their own business for centuries. They posed no threat and had done no harm to the Russians. What they did not know was that in some far away places the medicine men of the West had declared them to be bloody and dangerous savages who did not wish to co-exist peacefully because of the false and horrible faith that they professed. They were being exterminated because they were violent savages, in the eyes of the Russian Christians, who could not be converted peacefully.

No doubt the same thoughts went through the minds of the western pilots who bombed desperately poor innocent people, sleeping in towns and villages, at the dead of night in already devastated and destitute Afghanistan and exterminated bound and blindfolded Taliban prisoners in jails like Kila Jangi (see chapter 'Afghanistan'). Indeed, Huntington is right in his '*The Clash of Civilizations*'; Islam does have bloody borders ----- the only difference is the blood is that of the Muslims.

After the break-up of the Soviet Union, most of the peripheral small states that had been forcibly annexed, gained independence. This was not the case with a number of Muslim states. Chechniya and Daghestan, for instance, that are overwhelmingly Muslim were retained as parts of Russia against the wishes of their people. Their cries for the same rights as were granted to others in the Baltic, Black Sea and the Caucuses regions fall on deaf ears. Worse still, their struggles for freedom are now classified as 'terrorism' in the western lexicon.

Soon after gaining independence after the demise of the Soviet Union, Christian Armenia attacked neighbouring Muslim Azerbaijan and occupied nearly a quarter of its territory, which it retains to this day, killing thousands of men, women and children in the process. More than one million Muslims were pushed out of their homes and have been living under atrocious conditions on the outskirts of Baku ever since. It has not bothered the conscience of the United Nations or that of the western leaders or their media one bit. It stands in stark contrast to the drumbeat that followed Iraq's invasion of Kuwait at about the same time in 1991. Both of these were clear cases of unprovoked aggression; in one the aggressor happened to be Christian and in the other Muslim. Why was the reaction in the UN and among the western powers so very different in the two cases? Would they have acted in the same manner as they did if the aggressor in the former case had been Muslim Azerbaijan? Hardly likely.

CHECHNIYA

The Caucuses formed part of the Iranian and Turkish Empires until the beginning of the nineteenth century when Russia started to flex her muscles and expand southward. The process was gradual and lasted well over a century. It was brutal and savage with indiscriminate murder, rape and forced conversions to Christianity.

Iran was attacked in 1809 and again in 1827 when the Shi'ite mullas of Baku, Qum and Najaf declared that '*jehad*' against Russia had become obligatory due to her maltreatment of the Muslims. It was not the first time in Islamic history, nor will it be the last, when the ignorant mullas' opinion prevailed over sound political judgement. The results were predictably catastrophic for Iran. She was made to sign humiliating treaties first at Gulistan and later at Turcoman-Chai, mediated by the British, that gave away all the lands around the Caspian Sea, north of Aras River to Russia.

Under the terms of the latter treaty, Iran also agreed to pay heavy war reparations and handed over tens of thousands of priceless manuscripts from the Royal Library of Ardebil to the Russians. During all these proceedings, it is not clear, if there was any realisation in Istanbul that elimination or diminution of Iranian power in the region would, inevitably, mean increased threat to Turkey herself. The traditional dislike between the two Muslim powers was too great to permit contemplation of joint action in the face of the common threat.

A year after the treaty of Turcoman-Chai, the Russians attacked the Ottoman territories in the Caucuses and annexed Circassia on the Black Sea's eastern shore. The familiar killings and forced mass conversions of its Muslim population followed the occupation. These Russian excesses, in the name of Christianity, gave rise to rebellions that kept flaring up for more than fifty years. Starting in Circassia, they spread to Daghestan, Chechniya, Ingushtia, Karabagh and Azerbaijan.

Shaikh Mansur, a Dominican monk who had converted to Islam, managed to unite the tribes of these mountainous regions and put up a fierce resistance. The example set by him was again followed by Imam Shamayl in mid-nineteenth century. Their inspiration mostly came from the Nakshbandi and Kadri orders of Sufism. The deeds of their leaders like Ghazi Muhammad Yukar Yarak, Haji Barzak Dukmah Aka, Mansur Ushurmah, Imam Shamayl and Kunta Haji Kishiev have become legends and their examples continue to inspire and guide the oppressed, ignored and forgotten people of this unfortunate region to this day.

Under the Soviet rule the Caucasus region was divided into several apparently ethnically based autonomous states. However, their borders were carefully drawn to make certain that each of the states had a mixture of different nationalities and tribes. The main purpose was to ensure that mutual jealousies and suspicions within each population would exclude any possibility of the local people uniting on a common platform. It has resulted in creating diabolical complications in the politics of the area to which there is no solution or end in sight.

The Chechens have been resisting their incorporation into the Russian empire for more than 150 years; their fierce determination for independence was chronicled in fiction by leading nineteenth-century Russian writers such as Alexei Tolstoy (*'Haji Murad'*) and Mikhail Lermontov (*'A Hero of Our Time'*).

During the civil war that followed the Russian Revolution of 1917, an attempt to set up an autonomous Muslim state floundered in the face of Bolshevik pressure. In hidden genocide during the 1940s, Stalin had thousands of Chechens shot and 500,000 (half the population) sent in cattle cars to frigid Central Asian concentration camps, where a quarter of the deportees perished. Survivors of Stalin's gulag filtered back to Chechniya in the 1960s.

The western attitudes towards the Muslims never seem to change. After the Soviet Union broke up, its successor state, Russia, allowed the tiny Baltic republics of Lithuania, Estonia and Latvia, along with Belarus, Moldova, Ukraine etc. to regain their independence but not the Muslim states of Chechniya, Daghestan and Ingushtia in the Caucuses. For the past ten years the Russian Army has been using aircraft, tanks, heavy artillery and missiles to suppress the Chechen struggle for independence without any visible signs of success, despite Russian claims to the contrary. The entire land has been laid waste, cities, towns and villages destroyed and hundreds of thousands of innocent people have been either killed or driven from their homes simply because they happen to be Muslims who want to live independently in the same way as their Christian counterparts in the Baltic and Black Sea regions.

As in Bosnia, the gross atrocities and human rights violations committed by the Russians are known to all the powers, including the United Nations, but no one is prepared to lift a finger to protect the poor Chechens. On the contrary, the United States has gone so far as to legitimize the brutal suppression of the hapless people on highly spurious grounds and declared them as 'terrorists' to make common cause with Russia. In 1956 when the Hungarians rose in revolt against the Soviet occupation of their land they were hailed as freedom fighters by the West and their struggle is commemorated as such to this day. Now that the Chechen Muslims are struggling for the same rights they have been labelled 'terrorists'. The western criterion on such moral and political issues, when it comes to the Muslims, has always been unjustifiably flexible and Machiavellian, to say the least.

Eric Margolis gives an over-view of the recent Chechen struggle for independence in the Toronto Sun, 3rd November 2002, '*When the Soviet Union collapsed in 1991, Chechniya, led by Gen. Jhokar Dudayev, declared independence. While Moscow allowed other republics independence, Chechen were denied freedom because of important oil pipelines that ran through their territory and Kremlin fears other Muslim peoples of the Caucasus would seek independence.*

In 1994, Boris Yeltsin ordered an invasion of breakaway Chechnya. Much of the cost of the war was financed by the United States, which sought to support Yeltsin against his domestic political enemies. President Bill Clinton even called Yeltsin "Russia's Abraham Lincoln." In a near military miracle, lightly-armed Chechen fighters defeated and drove out the Russian army, but at appalling cost. Russia razed the Chechen capital, Grozny, and killed an estimated 100,000 civilians. President Dudayev was assassinated by the Russians, thanks to secret electronic equipment supplied to the KGB by the U.S.

In 1996, Russia granted Chechnya de facto recognition and promised a referendum within five years to decide its future. Chechnya seemed free. But in 1999, in an eerie harbinger of the 9/11 attacks on the U.S., a series of mysterious explosions destroyed apartment buildings in Russia, killing 300 people. Then-prime minister Vladimir Putin, a former KGB officer, blamed "Islamic terrorist" Chechens "linked to bin Laden." Russia was swept by nationalist fury and anti-Chechen hatred.

When a FSB (formerly KGB) team was caught planting bombs in another building, and a KGB officer blamed the bombings on the war party in Moscow, the news was hushed up. Putin became president, almost by acclamation, and promptly ordered another invasion of Chechnya.

In spite of massive firepower, including devastating fuel air explosives and carpet bombing, Russian forces have failed to crush small bands of fierce Chechen mujahedin. In mass roundups called zachistki, Russians seize all male Chechens over 16, routinely torture and, often, execute them. International rights groups accuse Moscow of wide scale murder, torture, rape, and looting.

War in Chechnya has degenerated into a savage battle of attrition, with atrocities and banditry committed by both sides. Moscow conducts its brutal operations under a blanket of secrecy. Foreign and Russian journalists who try to report the ugly truth about this conflict are killed or silenced. Russia has lost an estimated 10,000 soldiers, two-third of their total losses in Afghanistan.

The George Bush administration has shamefully adopted Moscow's propaganda line by branding the Chechen independence fighters "Islamic terrorists," the price of Kremlin support for its anti-Islamic campaign. The Kremlin now claims the hostage-taking was "Russia's 9/11."

Not so. "Terrorism" is the only weapon the weak have against the mighty. Russia could end "terrorism" by finally giving Chechens the independence they have long sought and richly deserve - and be well rid of this pointless bloodbath. If America truly cared about human rights, it would be encouraging Moscow to set the Chechen free instead of turning a blind eye to what the rights group, the International Helsinki Federation, calls a second attempted genocide against this tortured, forgotten people'.

Russian journalist Anna Politkovskaya, reporting for the Moscow newspaper *'Novaya Gazeta'*, visited Chechniya twenty eight times since the start of the second conflict three years ago. In her epoch-making book *'A Dirty War'*, she rejects Moscow's claim that the 'terrorists' are being weeded out and order is being restored. Instead, she reveals a region fraught with massive human rights abuses and widespread destruction. What has happened in Afghanistan has also happened in Chechniya: bombing the whole territory without any thought to the people who live there. It was Anna Politkovskaya who brought to the public notice excavation of mass civilian graves with tortured and mutilated bodies. She has seen in Chechniya bodies with their heads cut off and pregnant women with their bellies slit open. People are harassed, tortured and detained by the Russian troops in the villages and along the roads.

Polish writer Krystyna Kurczab-Redlich visited Chechniya recently and wrote a report for the Polish edition of the *'Newsweek.'* It was also published in the *'Sunday Observer'* of 27th October 2002 under the title *'Torture and Rape Stalk the Streets of Chechniya'*. Excerpts from this article are reproduced below:

'At 5am on 14 April 2002, an armoured vehicle moved slowly down Soviet Street. A young brown-haired man, covered in blood, his hands and feet bound, stood onboard. The vehicle stopped and the man was pushed off and brought over to a nearby chain-link fence. The car took off and there

was a loud bang. The force of the explosion, caused either by a grenade or dynamite, sent the man's head flying into the neighbouring street, called Lenin's Commandments. 'It was difficult to photograph the moment, though I have grown somewhat accustomed to this,' says a petite greying Chechen woman, who has spent years documenting what Russia calls its 'anti-terrorism campaign'.

'Blowing people up, dead or alive, she reports, is the latest tactic introduced by the federal army into the conflict. It was utilised perhaps most effectively on 3 July in the village of Meskyer Yurt, where 21 men, women and children were bound together and blown up, their remains thrown into a ditch.

'From the perspective of the perpetrators, this method of killing is highly practical; it prevents the number of bodies from being counted, or possibly from ever being found. It has not always succeeded in this respect, however. Since the spring, dogs have been digging up body parts in various corners of Chechnya, sometimes almost daily.

'Meanwhile, the more traditional methods endure. On 9 September the bodies of six men from Krasnostepnovskoye were found, naked, with plastic bags wrapped around their heads. In June, a ditch containing 50 mutilated bodies was discovered near the Russian army post in Chankala. The corpses were missing eyes, ears, limbs and genitals. Since February, mass graves have been found near Grozny, Chechen Yurt, Alkhan-Kala and Argun.

'-----------The Society for Russian-Chechen Relations, in collaboration with Human Rights Watch, reports that in the span of a month between 15 July and 15 August this year, 59 civilians were shot dead, 64 were abducted, 168 were seriously wounded and 298 were tortured. Many men simply disappeared after being detained by Russian soldiers

or security police; others were shot outright. During an operation in Chechen Aul between 21 May and 11 June, 22 men were killed. The majority were aged 20 to 26; two were 15.

'Since Chechen Aul is considered hostile territory, it has undergone 20 such "mopping-up operations" this year. Usually the raids are conducted by federal armed forces (particularly OMON, the police special forces, and Spetsnaz, its army equivalent) and occur at any time of day or night. Typically a village will be encircled by tanks, armoured vehicles and army trucks, one of which, known as the purification car, is designated for torture. According to Human Rights Watch in New York, torture is a preferred method of gathering intelligence. Cut off and isolated, Russian troops' best hope of discovering guerrilla activity is by grabbing citizens, almost at random, and coercing from them whatever information they might have.

'------------They went to our neighbours' house, the Magomedova family. We heard shots and the screams of 15-year-old Aminat, the sister of Ahmed and Aslanbek. "Let her be!" screamed one of the brothers, "Kill us instead!". Then we heard more shots. Through the window we saw a half-dressed OMON commander lying on top of Aminat. She was covered in blood from the bullet wounds. Another soldier shouted, "Hurry up, Kolya, while she's still warm".'

'Sometimes those who survive wish they were dead, as in Zernovodsk this summer, when townspeople say they were chased on to a field and made to watch women being raped. When their men tried to defend them, 68 of them were handcuffed to an armoured truck and raped too. After this episode, 45 of them joined the guerrillas in the mountains. One older man, Nurdi Dayeyev, who was nearly

blind, had nails driven through his hands and feet because it was suspected that he was in contact with the fighters. When relatives later retrieved his remains, he was missing a hand. The relatives of another villager, Aldan Manayev, picked up a torso but no head. The families were forced to sign declarations that Dayeyev and Manayev had blown themselves up.

'Usually groups of people simply disappear. Shortly thereafter their families begin feverish searches in all the army headquarters and watch posts. If they can track down a missing family member, they might be able to buy him or her back. The going rate for a live person is in the thousands of dollars. For a dead body, the price is not much lower. If they cannot find the person, family members mail letters to Putin (Russia's president) and file petitions with social organisations and rights groups. They post photographs with the caption missing.

'And they wait. Most of the abductees never return and the trail grows cold. Those who do return are often crippled, with bruised kidneys and lungs, damaged hearing or eyesight and broken bones. It is almost certain they will never have children.'

If this is western civilization and what Muslims may expect from it can the Chechens be blamed for not wanting any part of it?

EUROPEAN COLONIZATION

The rest of the Europeans were equally if not more cruel and brutal in their intolerance and barbarity towards people of other religions. In 1502 the Portuguese adventurer Vasco da Gama made his second incursion into the Indian Ocean with a fleet of twenty-five ships. On his way to India he encountered a large ship filled with seven hundred men, women and children returning from pilgrimage in Makka. He confiscated its goods and then set fire to the ship. As the pilgrims jumped overboard to escape the fire Portuguese sailors in boats lanced all of them saving only twenty of the children who were rescued for the Franciscan fathers to be turned into Christians.

When he arrived at the port of Calicut the Zamorin (Hindu ruler) sent a Brahmin to sue for peace with an offer to hand over twelve leading Arab merchants of the city for sacrifice along with a vast sum of money if he would spare the city. All to no avail ----- da Gama imprisoned the envoy and commenced bombarding the city that lasted for three days. He rounded up a score of vessels anchored off Calicut, plundered their cargoes and made prisoners of their 800 or so crews. What followed is reproduced from *'Empires of the Monsoon'*, (p.198) quoting contemporary Portuguese sources:

'He told his men to parade the prisoners, then to hack off their hands, ears and noses. As the work progressed, all the amputated pieces were piled up in a small boat. The Brahmin who had been sent out by the Zamorin as an emissary was put into the boat amid its new gruesome cargo. He had also been mutilated in the ordained manner.

'When all the Indians had been thus executed, he ordered their feet tied together, as they had no hands with which to untie them and in order that they should not untie them with their teeth, he ordered them to strike upon their teeth with staves and they knocked them down their throats; and were put onboard, heaped on top of each other, mixed up with the blood which streamed from them; and he ordered mats and dry leaves to be spread over them, and the sails to be set for the shore, and the vessel set on fire -------- . A message from da Gama was sent to the Zamorin. Written on a palm leaf, it told him to make curry with the human pieces in the boat.

'The bigger ship, engulfed in flames, drifted towards the shore. The families of the men came crying to the beach, trying to put out the fire and rescue any of those still alive, but da Gama had not quite done. He drove off the families, and had the survivors dragged from the boat. Then they were hung up from the masts, and the Portuguese crossbowmen were ordered to shoot their arrows into them that the people on shore might see. The transfixing of men hung in mid-air was the admiral's favourite forms of execution, since it gave his soldiers good practice -------------.

'When yet another Brahmin was sent from Calicut to plead for peace, he had his lips cut off and his ears cut off; the ears of a dog were sewn on instead, and the Brahmin was sent back to the Zamorin in that state. He had brought with him three boys, two of them his sons and a nephew. They were hanged from the yardarm and their bodies sent ashore.

'Keen to win approval, da Gama's captains did their best to match his deeds. One of them, Vincent Sodre, decided to make a special example of an Arab merchant whom he had been lucky enough to capture. This important prisoner,

Coja Mehmed Markar, traded throughout the Red Sea and down the east African coast. His home was in Cairo.

'*The account tells how Sodre had him lashed to the mast by two black sailors, then beaten with tarred ropes that he remained like dead, for he swooned from the sight of blood that flowed from him. When the prisoner was revived his mouth was held open and stuffed with dirt (excrement), despite the pleas from other Arab prisoners forced to look on. Then bacon was fastened over his mouth, which was gagged with short sticks; he was paraded with arms pinioned, then finally set free.*'

The European interlopers repeated similar cruel and barbaric acts, too numerous to include here, in the name of Christianity, wherever they went along the coasts of the Indian Ocean for well over the next two hundred years. They leapfrogged the Muslim world in developing sheer killing power and have been at each other's throats in large conflicts ever since history came to be recorded. It was the Europeans who found justification for large scale genocide and colonization of foreign lands as a state-commercial enterprise. There is nothing in the history of Islam that can even begin to compare with the seizure, annihilation, and occupation of an entire hemisphere?

Such cruel and barbaric acts were repeated along all the coasts of the Indian Ocean by the Europeans for well over two hundred years. The colonization of North and South America, Australia and Africa by the European Christians followed the pattern set by the Portuguese. There are recorded accounts of European Christian men and women going out to hunt aboriginal people in Australia and South Africa for sport, right up to the twentieth century, who were often rewarded by the government depending upon the number of kills. Roman Catholic priests who accompanied the Spanish conquistadors into Mexico, Texas, Arizona and California did not like to waste time. As they approached each Indian village they gave the inhabitants no more than five minutes to make the choice between converting to Christianity or being put to the sword. Until recently, the white governments took away the children of aboriginal peoples in Australia, USA and Canada and handed them over to the churches to be brought up in Christian culture. They were physically and sexually abused by the church official and have been scarred for life as a result.

It is a little known fact that Islam came to America with the slaves from Africa but its practice was banned and it survived only as an oral tradition among them. The tradition is also found among remnants of some Amerindian tribes on the US East Coast giving rise to the intriguing possibility that some Muslims may have visited America before Columbus.

During the westward expansion of America any one could earn five dollars by bringing in the scalp of an Indian be it that of a man, woman or child. When the American army generals had difficulty in persuading the Indians to remain confined to barren and unproductive reserves they took away their only source of sustenance ---- the American buffalo, shooting nearly all of the sixty million that had grazed the western plains, leaving their carcasses to rot in the sun. A flourishing population of twenty million Native Americans was nearly wiped out to make room for the Europeans. Such gross injustices and barbarities were not only condoned but justified by the church through a doctrine known as 'Manifest Destiny' that claimed the Bible as its basis.

We also have records of the European Christians using biological warfare against the American Indians in an effort to exterminate them. The British commander-in-chief in

Canada, Jeffery Amherst (later Baron Amherst of Montreal) ordered a subordinate to spread smallpox among America's native Indians. In 1763, he wrote to Colonel Henry Bouquet, *'Could it not be contrived to set the Small Pox among these disaffected tribes of Indians? We must on this occasion use every strategem in our power to reduce them'*. The colonel replied, *'I will try to inoculate the Indians by means of blankets that may fall in their hands, taking care however not to get the disease myself'*. Amherst approved, *'You will do well to try to inoculate the Indians by means of blankets, as well as try every other method that can serve to extirpate this execrable race. I should be very glad your scheme for hunting them down by dogs could take effect'*. The latter method was a favourite with the Spaniards.

William Trent, the militia commander at Pittsburgh presented smallpox infected blankets from a hospital to some Indian chiefs and then noted in his journal, *'I hope it may have the desired effect'*. Indeed it did. A few months later, more than 100,000 Ottawas, Delawares, Mingos and other aboriginal people lay dead from smallpox. In *'Britain's Colonial Wars, 1688 – 1783'*, Bruce Lenman, Professor of History, St. Andrews University, Scotland writes about Amherst, *'He was rampantly racist, unlike many other servants of the Crown, who tended to be much less than the average American colonist, and he made a bad job of concealing his contempt for the native American peoples. ------- He was openly genocidal'*. (*'The Gazette'*, Montreal, 10th November 2001, by Mark Abley).

A fact, often lost in the current history books, relates to the British occupation of Iraq after the First World War. In an effort to quell the insurgency that ensued, Churchill had ordered the use of poison gas against the rebellious Arab tribesmen. When questioned, he stated that there was nothing morally wrong in killing Arabs using chemical agents if it helped to dissuade them from persisting in their resistance to the British rule.

As mentioned earlier, questions of race have always constituted an important consideration in the European Christian psyche. The machine gun, although it had been available earlier, was deployed in battle for the first time against the spear-carrying Sudanese Muslims at the close of the nineteenth century. Hitherto its use in wars against fellow white men had been considered 'uncivilized' because of its deadly effectiveness against massed troops. Such niceties did not figure in the considerations when it came to killing black people. There is little doubt that without the uninhibited use of this murderous weapon against primitively equipped Africans, European subjugation of the continent could not have been possible in such a short time (*'The Social History of the Machine Gun'* by John Ellis, Judy Piatkus Ltd., London, p. 132). As the poet, Hillaire Beloc wrote at the time:

> *Whatever happens we have got*
> *The Maxim gun and they have not.*

President Truman has admitted in his diary that even if the atom bomb had been ready in time he would not have used it to force Germany's surrender on racial grounds. He had no such qualms about dropping two of them on Japan even though many at the time considered it unnecessary from the military point of view. The Japanese had already started negotiations for unconditional surrender by then (for more on this see *'Hiroshima's Shadow'*, edited by Kai Bird and Lawrence Lifschultz, Central Books, London).

When President George W. Bush exempted the white American Taliban from the inhuman and barbaric laws, enacted in complete disregard of the Geneva Convention concerning prisoners of war, to which the rest of the Taliban are being subjected at Guantanamo Bay, he was simply following a well-trodden path in the western Christian tradition. He also ordered a court martial of the US pilot who dropped a bomb by accident that killed four Canadian soldiers in Afghanistan but took no action against other pilots who fired on wedding parties and other peaceful gatherings, killing hundreds of totally innocent Afghans. The lives of non-whites and Muslims are not the same in his eyes.

During the Vietnam War, US Army's Charlie Company literally wiped out a South Vietnamese hamlet, killing almost everyone the nervous soldiers could find ----- hundreds of women, old men, girls, boys, even infants. The officer in charge, Lieutenant William Calley, undoubtedly guilty of the unprovoked mass murder of unarmed civilians, was convicted and sentenced to life imprisonment. Not long afterwards, his sentence was reduced to 20 years; then to 10. He was eventually paroled after three-and-a-half years. In that period he spent about three days in prison; the rest of the time he was 'confined', along with his girlfriend, at his house inside a military base. His superior officer Captain Ernest Medina, who was present as a participant at the scene of the crime, was acquitted by a jury that took less than 60 minutes to reach a verdict. No one higher up in the chain of command ever faced trial (*'Tell Me No Lies'*, by John Pilger).

In the war against Japan the American soldiers engaged in the grisly practice of boiling the skulls and other body parts of dead Japanese soldiers to obtain clean bones. These were sent back as souvenirs and proudly displayed in their homes. They never did this to the bodies of dead Germans (TV Programme *'History of Photography'*, broadcast by PBS on 15th January 2000). Some medical experiments on syphilis, using black men exclusively, were initiated in the

United States in the 1930s and carried through to the 1970s. Throughout this time these men were kept in the dark and not treated for the disease in order not to jeopardise the experiment.

The cruel and inhuman treatment meted out to the natives in North America and Australia, at the hands of the white governments and churches, well into the twentieth century, could fill a whole book and more on its own. A massive effort is currently underfoot in the United States to compile a data bank of photographs, fingerprints, addresses, jobs, social and other connections, etc. of Muslims living in or visiting the country. Even people who sympathize with Muslim causes are not spared as Robert Fisk of Britain's '*The Independent*' discovered on a recent visit ('*The Independent*', 1st December 2002).

Racial intolerance has historically characterized the actions of nearly all Europeans. The doctrine of 'Manifest Destiny' that used Christianity to justify the dispossession and near extermination of Native Americans in the US was a precursor of Hitler's policy of *Lebenstraum*. In fact the latter was modeled on it. ('*Adolf Hitler*', by John Toland, p. 702 and '*Hitler*', by Joachim Fest, New York, 1975, pp. 214, 650). The majority of American States enacted sterilization laws that remained on the books until the 1950s. Tens of thousands of Americans were forcibly sterilized and the Nazis invoked this US precedent when enacting similar laws in Germany ('*The Nazi Connection*', by Stefan Kuhl, Oxford, 1994). Prohibition of miscegenation in the Nuremberg Laws of 1935 was no different to the segregation and legal disabilities suffered by the Blacks in America ('*Trouble in Mind*', by Leon F. Litwack, New York, 1998 and '*Origins of Totalitarianism*', by Hannah Arendt).

When the Europeans embraced Christianity, it was with certain reservations with respect to its concepts of peace and equality among men, at least on the part of their political philosophers. They seem to have been overly pre-occupied with issues of race in a somewhat complex psychological context. In 1883 German writer Gumplowitcz wrote in the book *'The Race Conflict'*, *'----- The perpetual struggle of races is the law of history, while perpetual peace is the dream of idealists'*. Heinrich von Treietschke wrote in his book *'Politics'*, *'---- War is both justifiable and moral, and the hope of perpetual peace is not only impossible, but immoral as well'*. He preached doctrines of patriotic nationalism and of militarism and war as a means of human progress. Another popular German writer at the turn of the century, Friedrich von Bernhardi wrote in his 1912 book *'Germany and the Next War and Our Future'*, *'------ If it were not for war, we should probably find that inferior races would overcome healthy, youthful ones by their wealth and numbers* (p. 111) *----- We must strenuously combat the peace propaganda ----- We must become convinced that war is a political necessity and that it is fought in the interest of biological, social and moral progress'* (p.105). According to Chancellor Bismarck national independence, political liberty and similar other objectives could only be achieved by 'blood and iron' and not by peaceful discussion. Philosopher Nietzsche contends that it is natural for states to struggle with one another for ascendancy, security, power and wealth ----- war is natural and inevitable ----- the only right is might. As for Christian beliefs, he dismissed these as the 'code of slavish masses' and democracy as 'decadent'.

The Germans were by no means alone in holding such views about race, war and nationalism. In 1890 British scientist, Karl Pearson, lectured *'History shows me one way, and one way only, in which a high state of civilization has been produced, namely, the struggle of race with race'* W.S.

Blunt recorded in 1898 *'patriotism was the imperial instinct of Englishmen, who should support their country's quarrels even when in the wrong'*. He termed such ideas 'scientific humanity' based on an extension of Darwin's survival of the fittest theory, *'At some future period ----- the civilized races of man will almost certainly exterminate, and replace, the savage races throughout the world'*. Rudyard Kipling talked about 'The White Man's Burden' '---- *piously 'sacrificing the flower of white talent'* in the effort to civilise what were, according to him, the inferior races, *'Send forth the best ye breed'* to emancipate the *'Half devil and half child'*. U.S President, Theodore (Teddy) Roosevelt, said diplomacy should be supported by the 'big stick' and 'America should play a great part in the world, and especially ----- perform those deeds of blood, of valour, which above everything else bring national renown' (*'Modern History'* by Carl Becker, Silver Berdett Company, Chicago, 1958, pp. 650-1).

During World War I the tottering Turkish Empire allied itself with Germany and was defeated. The Allies' aims in the war were summed up in the Sykes-Picot-Sazanov Agreement of 1916 signed between Britain, Russia and France ----- to divide the Turkish Empire with Istanbul and the Dardanelles going to Russia; the French taking Syria and Lebanon; the 'Holy Places' in Palestine to come under international administration and the British having their say in the rest. In another arrangement that became known as the *'Balfour Declaration'* Britain gave an undertaking to turn Palestine into a 'National Home' for the Jews.

At this time, Jews constituted only thirteen per cent of the population of Palestine but it meant nothing as Churchill put it in 1937, *'I do not agree that the dog in a manger has the final right to the manger even though he may have lain there for a very long time. I do not admit that right. I do not admit for instance that a great wrong has been done to the*

Red Indians of America or the black people of Australia. I do not admit that a wrong has been done to these people by the fact that a stronger race, a higher grade race, a more worldly wise race to put it that way, has come in and taken their place.' This would hardly seem to cast a flattering light on the civilization that Muslims are supposed to envy, coming as it does, from a man so highly regarded in the West and who never tired of preaching the virtues of western culture and democracy to the entire world all his political life.

Whatever else that may be said of this pronouncement, including the disturbingly striking echoes of the ideology expressed in *'Mein Kampf,'* it constitutes hypocrisy at its worst. Churchill was the Prime Minister of Britain when Europe was liberated from the Nazis. This was when hundreds of thousands of displaced European Jews, instead of being resettled in their own homes in Europe, were shipped to Palestine instead. If he had truly cherished the Jews as much as he had claimed, surely, he and the rest of the European Christian leaders would have done more to settle them comfortably in their own homes rather than have them banished to an inhospitable and unwelcoming land.

There can be little doubt that secretly most if not all of them were glad to be rid of the Jews and even more pleased in the knowledge that henceforward they would be a source of grievous discomfort for the Muslim Arabs. What Churchill expressed was not love and admiration for the Jews so much as visceral dislike and contempt for Islam and the Arabs.

In order to isolate Turkey from Central Asia Britain had proposed the creation of Greater Armenia. It was to include areas of Turkish mainland stretching from the Black Sea to the Mediterranean. As Sir Mark Sykes, the man responsible for Middle East policy at the Foreign Office, explained, *'The Armenian question is the real answer to Pan-Turanism, just as free Arabia is the answer to Turkish Pan-Islamism'*. The fact that Armenians had never lived in much of this part was irrelevant. By the same twisted logic the parts of Armenia that had been occupied by Russia, where the bulk of Armenians had lived, were excluded from the proposed new state. The diabolical double-dealing did not end there. A Greater Kurdistan was proposed for the Kurds at the Versailles Peace Conference that was to consist in large part of the same areas as had been allocated for Greater Armenia.

As if this too were not enough, the British had made similar promises of support to Muslim Tatars who also inhabited some of the same areas (for more on this see British Foreign Office document *'FO371/3300/18464/2150 dated 30th January 1918* and *Eastern Report no. XLVII - Russia: The Bolsheviks and anti-British Muslim Feeling, 20th December 1917')*. To be perfectly fair, the entire blame cannot be put on Britain if people at the receiving end chose to believe in her so implicitly and failed to look after their own interests.

In expectation of the promises made to them by the Allies Christian Armenians in eastern Anatolia had staged a revolt against Turkey and joined hands with the Russians. In reprisal, the Turks deported them to areas in the south of Turkey. This action was termed as the 'Armenian Massacres of 1915' by a commission set up by the allies under James Bryce, a pro-Armenian Liberal politician. Subsequently, the Armenians called it genocide. The well-known historian Arnold Toynbee, who was also a member of this commission, has dismissed the findings of the commission as *'wartime propaganda to further Britain's policy objectives'*. (*'Armenians vs Turks: The View From*

Istanbul,' 'The Wall Street Journal,' 21st September 1983, p.33).

The British aims in the Middle East were summed up in the Government of India memorandum to the Whitehall that read, *'What we want is not a United Arabia: but a weak and disunited Arabia, split up into little principalities so far as possible under our suzerainty ----- but incapable of coordinated action against us, forming a buffer against the Powers in the West'* (*'Britain, India and the Arabs, 1914 - 1921'*, by Briton, Cooper, Busch, University of California Press, Berkeley and London, p. 62). This is how Sir Mark Sykes explained his vision of the future, *'I want to see a permanent Anglo-French entente allied to the Jews, Arabs and Armenians which will render pan-Islamism innocuous and protect India and Africa from the Turco-German combine'* (*'Sledmere Papers, 14th August 1917'*, Weizmann Archives).

Thus it came to pass that the West carved up the Muslim heartland in the Middle East as well as Central Asia into numerous states with artificial and un-natural boundaries that cut across ethnic and tribal lines and planted people of different religions and cultures from Europe in their midst to further its political and economic objectives. In the process it has also ensured that there will be no peace in these lands in the foreseeable future.

There has been no change in this policy since then as stressed by US Senator Larry Pressler at a press conference in New Delhi in 1991. When questioned about the possibility of ex-Soviet Union's newly independent Central Asian Republics forming an association with the other Muslim countries in the area he said, *'We would have to be mad to permit the formation of a block composed of ten Muslim countries'* ----- a position that has been reiterated by the US State

Department on more than one occasion in the past. There is no explanation or reasons given why it is not permissible for the Muslim countries to do the same thing that members of NATO, the European Union, NAFTA, ASEAN and so many other such associations have done around the world.

What was done to the Jews of Europe by the Nazis during World War II was a horrible crime against humanity. The perpetrators of the crime, the Nazis, were not Muslims but church-going European Christians. Any reference to Nazis being Christian is conveniently omitted from all mention of the 'holocaust'. One wonders how it would have played out in the western media if the Nazis had belonged to the Islamic faith? Despite all the vituperation against Islam in the West, the fact remains, that Muslims never conceived of so vile a doctrine in all of their history which must speak something for their religion. Whatever the Nazis did to the Jews was in full knowledge of the Allies ---- Britain, USA and Russia but all of them chose to keep it under wraps at the time.

They also tried to hide the genocide of Bosnian and Kosovar Muslims in the same way a few years ago. The Jews bitterly point out that throughout their ordeal the Roman Catholic Church and Pope Pius XII chose to remain silent in the same way as Pope John Paul II later opted for silence in the two and a half years of genocide in Bosnia. As hundreds of thousands of Jews fled Germany, USA limited the refugees she was willing to accommodate to no more than fifteen thousand and Canada none at all. Words come cheap and actions in the name of compassion are only acceptable at the expense of others.

Nazi contempt and dislike of the Jews is well known as are the brutalities against them. It is also a fact that a substantial number of Jews served in the Nazi army, some of them in quite senior positions. Given the circumstances, why did the Nazis allow the Jews into their armed forces and why did the Jews choose to serve in them? It is a perplexing question that remains to be answered.

The details of Nazi atrocities have been told and retold endlessly the world over. Not a day passes when there is not some mention of the 'holocaust' on one pretext or another. The only purpose is to keep the issue alive and, somehow, keep the world reminded of the guilt. Probably, the Germans executed more Gypsies than the Jews but there is hardly ever any mention of the sufferings of these poor people or the Poles, for that matter. The Jews constituted less than twenty per cent of the population of German concentration camps (*'US Holocaust Museum, 1945- The year of Liberation'*, Washington, 1995, pp. 11 – 35, as quoted by Norman Finkelstein in *'The Holocaust Industry'*, Verso, London, p. 125).

To question the extent of the atrocity or the Jewish claims of the number that died, even the suggestion for a proper scientific investigation of the event for historical purposes, has been made a hate crime in the West, punishable by imprisonment and fines. Professor David Irving, who wrote the book *'Goebbels: Mastermind of the Third Reich'* (Focal Point Publications, London, 1996), after examining eighty thousand pages of Goebbels' diaries, has raised serious questions about these claims. He has been hounded in courts ever since. If what is claimed is true and accurate, why prevent independent investigators from examining the evidence?

One result of all the incessant propaganda about the atrocities against them has been that the Jews themselves have come to define their identity and faith since World War II in relation to the Nazi holocaust. This is something new and politically motivated. It remains to be seen if it will last and what effect it will have on the future of Jewry itself.

Have the attitudes changed in any way since the holocaust? They may have in relation to the Jews but, evidently, not for the Muslims. When the Israeli Army killed nine Palestinian children during a raid in Gaza, President Bush's White House spokesman Ari Fleischer (an Israeli citizen according to Edward Said) described the murders simply as 'heavy-handed' but when a Palestinian killed twelve Israeli soldiers and policemen engaged in shooting unarmed civilians, the same spokesman termed it a 'heinous crime' (Robert Fisk in '*The Independent*', 1st December 2002). In the eyes of the West, Muslim deaths and suffering are clearly not at par with those of the Jews or the Christians.

The attitude of the media is no different. A recent study of *The New York Times*' news coverage of the first year of the current Palestinian uprising (2000 – 2001) and of 2004 by 'If America Knew' indicates significant distortions. For the first year, it reported 197 Israeli deaths in its headlines or first paragraphs whereas only 165 Israelis had died (the discrepancy was due to multiple reporting). During the same period, 233 Palestinian deaths were reported in headlines or first paragraphs whereas the actual number killed was 549. In 2004, it reported 159 Israelis and 334 Palestinians killed as against the actual figures of 107 Israelis and 818 Palestinians. The distortion was much more noticeable in the case of children and did not reflect that the number of Palestinian children killed was nearly nine times greater than those of the Israelis. There were other misrepresentations, for instance, while Israeli deaths were often depicted as innocent victims of Palestinian aggression, Palestinian deaths were generally portrayed as a necessary result of conflict, with the victims frequently identified as combatants.

In the summer of 2002 Hindu mobs went on a rampage of pre-planned murder, rapes and looting of Muslims in Gujrat State with pre-knowledge, connivance and support of the state government. More than six thousand innocent Muslim men, women and children died in the gruesome orgy, many of them burnt alive and the stomachs of pregnant women torn apart. The Prime Minister of India, Bajpai, only reacted after many weeks and then too with the off-hand remark that the incident was 'unfortunate'. The government of the United States dismissed it simply as an 'internal matter' for its ally, India.

The economic, political and cultural effects of western colonization of Muslim lands were diverse as well as profound and continue to colour their relations with the West to this day. Some of these have been examined by Karen Armstrong in an article entitled '*September Apocalypse: Who, Why and What Next?*' in the '*Guardian*':

'-------- *Thus the Suez Canal, initiated by the French consul, Ferdinand de Lesseps, was a disaster for Egypt, which in the end had to provide all the money, labour and materials as well as donating 200 sq miles of Egyptian territory gratis, and yet the shares of the Canal Company were all held by Europeans.*

'*The immense outlay helped to bankrupt Egypt, and this gave Britain a pretext to set up a military occupation there in 1882 in order to protect the interests of the shareholders. Again, railways were installed in the colonies, but they rarely benefited the local people. Instead they were designed to further the colonialists' own projects. And the missionary schools often taught the children to despise their own culture, with the result that many felt that they belonged neither to the west nor to the Islamic world.*

'One of the most scarring effects of colonialism was the rift that still exists between those who have had a western education and those who have not, and remain perforce stuck in the pre-modern ethos.

'To this day, the westernized elites of these countries and the more traditional classes simply cannot understand one another. Even when democratic institutions were established, they could not always function normally. In Egypt, for example, there were 17 general elections between 1923 and 1952: all 17 were won by the popular Wafd party, which wanted to reduce British influence in the country. But the Wafd was only permitted to rule five times; after the other elections, they were forced by the British and the Egyptian king to stand down.

'In Iran, there had been a revolution led by a coalition of secularist Iranians and reforming ulema (in 1906): this resulted in the establishment of a parliament and a constitution, but the British, who wanted to set up a protectorate in Iran after the discovery of oil there, kept rigging the elections.

'Then from 1921, the Pahlavi shahs, backed first by Britain and later by America, set up dictatorships in which there was no possibility of parliamentary opposition. After the second world war, Britain and France became secondary powers and the United States became the leader of the western world.

'Even though the Islamic countries were no longer colonies, but were nominally independent, America still controlled their destinies. During the cold war, the United States sought allies in the region by supporting unsavoury governments and unpopular leaders.

'A particularly fateful example of this occurred in 1953, after Shah Muhammad Reza Pahlavi had been deposed and forced to leave Iran; he was put back on the throne in a coup engineered by British Intelligence and the CIA.

'The United States continued to support the Shah, even though he denied Iranians human rights that most Americans take for granted.

'The Muslim clerics simply could not understand how President Jimmy Carter, who was a deeply religious man and passionate about human rights, could support the Shah after the massacre of Tudeh Square in 1978, when nearly 900 Iranians were killed by his troops.

'Later Saddam Hussein, who became the sole president of Iraq in 1979, became the protégé of the United States, who literally allowed him to get away with murder, even after a chemical attack against the Kurdish population.'

PALESTINE

Long before the Turkish rule in Palestine ended there had been stirrings of revolutionary and nationalistic thought in Europe. It was considered the right of every nation to have an independent country of its own. Inspired by these ideas a number of books were published on the concept of Jewish nationhood in the second half of the nineteenth century. The best known among them was *'Der Judenstaat'* (or *'The Jewish State: An Attempt at a Modern Solution of the Jewish Question'*), written in 1896 by Theodor Herzl, a political journalist from Austria.

Much like the Gypsies the Jews, relegated to an inferior status, persecuted and subjected to frequent massacres and mass expulsions, were never accepted as an integral part of any European nation. It was the insecurity born out of universal rejection that gave rise to the concept of all Jews being a separate nation no matter where they might have lived for the past two thousand years. Measured against any criterion, this diverse group of people, belonging to different lands, speaking a score of different languages and with only their religion as the common link, could hardly qualify to be classified as a nation. It is like all the Roman Catholics or Protestants of the world claiming to be a nation. However, when it comes to religious faith and political expediency, finer points of reason, logic and justice carry no weight or meaning.

If Jews were to be a nation then, logically, there had to be a piece of land that could be designated as their country. With this in mind, in addition to the Rothschilds, a number of other Jewish organisations had been buying up pieces of

land in Palestine for some time for the settlement of Jews
displaced by the pogroms in East Europe. Their numbers
were limited and, by the end of the nineteenth century, their
proportion in the total population was estimated at less than
one or two per cent. Herzl tried to negotiate a deal with
the Ottoman Empire to settle more Jews in Palestine, in
exchange for a large loan, but it fell through.

He then turned to the British who proved more sympathetic.
The lawyer hired to prepare and submit their case, entitled
the 'Charter for the Jewish Settlement', to the British
Government was none other than Mr. Lloyd George who
became the Prime Minister of Britain at a most opportune
time for the Jews thirteen years later. After examining the
possibilities for establishing a Jewish colony in the Sinai,
Libya and Cyprus, the British Government offered 6,000
square miles of territory for their settlement in Uganda. This
was turned down by the World Zionist Congress although
the opinion had been divided. The majority insisted that it
had to be Palestine. The romantic notion found sympathy
among some intellectuals, like George Eliot, as expressed
in his novel 'Daniel Deronda'. An influential political lobby
in Britain looked at the Jewish presence in Palestine as 'a
bridge across the Middle East, to the empire in India and
beyond, held by friendly people'.

There was also a religious element involved. A powerful
mid-nineteenth century evangelical movement within the
Church of England (the Millenarians), led by the Earl of
Shaftesbury, made it its mission to do the Lord's work for
Him by bringing the Jews back to Palestine and converting
them to Christianity, thus hastening the second coming of
Christ, as envisaged in the Bible. This was supposed to usher
in an era of peace and bliss before the world finally came
to an end. Shaftesbury also claimed in his diary that on his
persuasion Lord Palmerston, three times British Foreign

Secretary (1830 - 1851) and later the Prime Minister (1855 - 1865) extended consular protection to Jews in Palestine. As he put it, '*Palmerston had already been chosen by God to be an instrument of good to His ancient people*' ('*The High Walls of Jerusalem: A History of the Balfour Declaration and the Birth of the British Mandate in Palestine*', by Ronald Sanders, Holt, Reinhart & Winston, New York, 1983, p. 5). In the words of Leopold Amery, a member of the British War Cabinet Secretariat, apart from the United States, '*Bible reading and Bible thinking England was the only country where the desire of the Jews to return to their ancient homeland has always been regarded as a natural aspiration which ought not to be denied*' ('*My Political life, vol. 2: War and Peace: 1914 - 1929*' by L. S. Amery, Hutchinson, London 1953, p 115).

The belief, based on the Bible, that the Jews have a God-given right to the Holy Land, including Judea and Samaria, is as much alive today as it had been a century or more ago. Oklahoma Senator James Inhofe recently quoted Genesis itself on the US Senate floor as giving Abraham and his 'seed forever' all the land around Hebron, which is on the West Bank. Such beliefs form a part of the theology of millions of U.S. evangelicals, including Attorney General John Ashcroft and so many other powerful figures in the Republican Party.

Roberta Combs, President of the Christian Coalition, recently led a procession of its members through Washington chanting 'We love Israel' and 'Palestine belongs to the Jews'. This coming together of two diametrically opposed interests is not only opportunistic but also bizarre. Leaving aside all the past historical and theological problems, according to the Bible, the Jews will not only return to Palestine but will also have to convert to Christianity before the Messiah may arrive. In the current atmosphere of bonhomie and mutual support both the sides conveniently overlook this rather awkward detail. The fact that Israel has placed a ban on the observance of Christian religious rites, including carrying of the Cross through the streets and putting up a Christmas tree in Jerusalem, too is diplomatically ignored. The dislike of Christians is so extreme in Israel that Ultra-Orthodox Jews often make a point of spitting on the faces of Christian priests they come across on the streets of Jerusalem.

Christian Palestinians, like their Muslim counterparts, are subject to blatant religious discrimination in Israel. This includes the prohibition of land sale or lease to non-Jews; the denial of government funding to their educational, social or medical institutions; the denial of recognition and government funding for their holy and historical sites; the denial of citizenship rights such as are guaranteed to all Jews under the 'Law of Return'; the impending legislation before the Knesset that would make Christian missionary activity and the possession of Christian scriptures (such as the New Testament) illegal.

Who is fooling whom, one wonders, in this not so holy alliance between Israel and the Christian Right in USA? When theologians engage in such political expediency, hypocrisy and chicanery, it raises a whole host of questions about the kind of religion they profess and preach.

It would appear that there is a fundamental difference in the concept and perception of God between Christianity and Islam. According to the Islamic belief God is omnipotent. He has no needs and does not depend upon human beings to fulfill His wishes. On the other hand, the history of Christian faith is littered with calls for providing help to God so that He may accomplish His tasks. One would have thought that if God wanted the Jews to return to Palestine at some point or to smite the Chechen Muslims He would be quite capable of doing it on His own without the help of some devious, lying, conniving and corrupt politicians, most of whom have precious little regard for God or religion in their personal lives any way. Presumably, such notions creep in only when theologians are unable to perceive God beyond the scope of their own human limitations.

In 1916 Britain and France signed the document, known as the Sykes-Picot Agreement, that laid down how the Turkish Empire in the Middle East would be divided between them after World War I. According to this, France was to take possession of Lebanon and Syria. Palestine had formed a part of Syria but the Jews had eyes on it as well. Under strong pressure from the British and the Americans, the French agreed to issue a declaration, known as the 'Cambon Letter' that expressed sympathy for the Zionist cause in quite vague terms. The Zionists and their friends in the British Government used the Cambon letter to extract a far more firm and meaningful commitment from the British Foreign Secretary, Arthur Balfour, that read in part, *'His Majesty's Government view with favour the establishment in Palestine of a national home for the Jewish people ------ nothing shall be done which may prejudice the civil and religious rights of existing non-Jewish communities.'* Political rights of the non-Jewish inhabitants of Palestine who, at the time, constituted eighty seven per cent of the total population were specifically excluded from this declaration. Lord Balfour further clarified the situation a year later, *'The four great powers are committed to Zionism and Zionism, be it right or wrong, good or bad, is rooted in age-long tradition, in present needs, in future hopes, of far profounder import than the desires and prejudices of the 700,000 Arabs who now inhabit the ancient land'* (*'A History of the Middle East'* by Peter Mansfield, Viking, New York, 1991, pp. 164 - 5). The total number of Jews in Palestine at the time, including the newly arrived settlers from Eastern Europe, was about 80,000 according to British estimates (see Encyclopaedia Britannica) but may have been much less.

There were many arguments presented to justify the British capitulation to the demands of the Zionists at the expense of the Arabs not the least of which was the growing pressure from the United States. The fact that the British Government letter containing the subsequent *'Balfour Declaration'* was addressed to the Jewish banker, Lord Rothschild, and not to the Zionist Federation, gives more than a hint that power of money may have been a more compelling reason. Added to all this was the religious aspect. The men in power believed that in returning the Jews to Palestine, as good Christians, they were helping the Lord carry out His work and, in the process, cleansing Christian lands of the despised race. The satisfaction that came from knowing that it was done at the expense of the Muslims was sweet revenge and the icing on the cake after centuries of defeats and humiliation suffered at the hands of the latter.

There is considerable evidence to indicate the prevalence of widespread anti-Muslim sentiment among the British in particular. This can be gauged from the following comment by Stanley Baldwin, a Conservative backbencher at the time who later became Britain's Prime Minister. It was made shortly after World War I when Turkey was partly occupied but the Allies were being pressed hard by Kamal Ata Turk and the British Prime Minister was trying to start another war. Baldwin told his wife that *'he had found out that Lloyd George had been all for war and had schemed to make his country go to war with Turkey so that they should have a Christian vs. the Mahomedan war and on the strength of that call a General Election'* (*'Baldwin and the Right, in the Baldwin Age'* by Robert Blake, Eyre and Spottiswoode, London, 1960, pp. 37, 41). Lloyd George, for all his Bible thumping, was quite an immoral character. He was known to be a compulsive womanizer and took bribes for bestowing peerages but there is no evidence presently available that could give credence to the possibility that his support for the Jews was motivated by anything other than his religious and political beliefs.

Interestingly, there was never any suggestion to ask the Jews themselves if they really wanted to leave their homes and hearths to settle in the Promised Land that now belonged to some other people. The vast majority of Jews never wanted to be uprooted, from the places where they had lived for the past nearly two thousand years, to start a new life all over in hostile, impoverished and forbidding Palestine. All they were interested in were better conditions for themselves and peaceful acceptance, as more or less equal citizens, in the countries where they lived. This is manifestly evident from the pattern of Jewish immigration to Israel. Very few, almost negligible in number, chose to migrate from countries like the United States and Britain where they have been accepted more readily and treated kindly in recent years.

There is a mistaken belief that the Zionists represented the majority of the Jews. The notion cannot be supported by facts. In 1913 only about one per cent of the world's Jews had signified their adherence to Zionism, as estimated by Leonard Stein in *'The Balfour Declaration',* Valentine Mitchell, London, 1961 (p. 66). Of the three million Jews that inhabited the United States at the time, only 12,000 belonged to the Zionist Federation. In New York itself, the heart of American Jewry, there were only five hundred members. The annual budget of the Zionist Federation never exceeded 5,200 dollars. Prior to 1914, the largest donation it ever received was 200 dollars (*'Justice Louis D. Brandeis: The Zionist Chapter of His Life',* by Ezekiel Rabinowitz, Philosophical Library, New York, 1968, pp 4, 6; *'Brandeis and Frankfurter: A Dual Biography',* by Leonard Baker, Harper & Row, 1984, p 74, and *'Felix Frankfurter and His Times ---- The Reform Years',* by Michael E. Parish, Free Press, New York, 1982, p 135). These figures call into question the entire basis on which British policy with regards to Palestine was formulated ---- if, indeed, that was the basis.

Not all the Jews support the notion even today. This is what the Central Rabbinical Congress of USA & Canada has to say about Zionism, *'The ultimate heresy of Zionism, its denial of Divine Providence over history, was the inevitable outgrowth of an overall rejection of God and Torah which typified the movement's founders. The subsequent history of this bizarre ideology has been a ceaseless record of overt anti-Torah acts'* (*'The Gazette'*, Montreal, 7th March 2001). A Russian-Jewish writer and self-proclaimed 'Spiritual-Zionist', Ahad Ha'am, who emigrated to Palestine in the early days of the last century, saw the injustice of it all when he wrote, *'If this be the Messiah coming, then I don't want to see him arrive'.* The tales of US policy being determined by Zionists, for the benefit of Jews during the First World War, appear to be no more than a myth when viewed under closer scrutiny. It cannot be that the British Foreign Office was not aware of these facts, yet, they proceeded single-mindedly to hand over Palestine to the Zionists.

It is a curious fact that outside of a limited circle there is little evidence of any strong desire or enthusiasm, among the Jews in general at the time, for the establishment of a state for them to live in Palestine. But, whether they liked it or not, there was no lack of apparent sympathy for the cause among the British politicians. In October 1919 Churchill, then Secretary for the Colonies in the British cabinet, declared, *'the Jews, whom we are pledged to introduce into Palestine and who take it for granted that the local population will be cleared out to suit their convenience'.* (*'Winston S. Churchill: Companion Volume, vol. 4, part 2: July 1919 - March 1921'* by Martin Gilbert, Houghton Miflin, Boston, 1978, p. 938).

He also told the Arabs in March 1921, *'It is manifestly right that the scattered Jews should have a national centre and a national home to be re-united and where else but in Palestine with which for three thousand years they have been intimately and profoundly associated? We think it will be good for the world, good for the Jews, good for the British Empire, but also good for the Arabs who dwell in Palestine and we intend it to be so.'*

He was very clear about what the expressions 'national centre' and 'national home' meant to him, *'If, as may well happen, there should be created in our own lifetime by the banks of the Jordan a Jewish State under the protection of the British Crown which might comprise three or four million Jews, an event will have occurred in this history of the world which would from every point of view be beneficial and would be especially in harmony with the truest interests of the British Empire'* (*'Winston S. Churchill: Companion Volume, vol. 4, part 2: July 1919 - March 1921'* by Martin Gilbert, Houghton Mifflin, 1978, pp. 1420, 1028, note 1).

The sentiments expressed by Churchill and others like him were basically intended to justify the creation of a Jewish state in the midst of the Arab world that will forever remain beholden and dependent on Britain for its security and protection and, in the process, provide the excuse for intervention in the Middle East. The true feelings among western politicians about the Jews have never been as sanguine, sympathetic or laudatory. Their inner beliefs are more in line with what George Washington had said, *'They (the Jews) work more effectively against us, than the enemy's armies. They are a hundred times more dangerous to our liberties and the great cause we are engaged in ... It is much to be lamented that each state, long ago, has not hunted them down as pests to society and the greatest enemies we have to the happiness of America.'* ('*Maxims of George Washington*' A. A. Appleton & Co.). Another of America's founding fathers, Benjamin Franklin, was just as explicit, as recorded in the Journal of Charles Pinskey of South Carolina on the *Proceedings of the Continental Convention of 1789* (the *Daily Star* of 22nd December 1968. The original journal is available at the Franklin Institute of Philadelphia, Pennsylvania):

'*There is a grave danger for the USA. This great danger is the Jew, for in every land the Jews have settled they have depressed the moral level and lowered the degree of commercial honesty. They have remained a part unassimilated, oppressed, they attempted to strangle the nations financially as in the case of Portugal and Spain.*

'*I warn you, gentlemen, if you do not exclude the Jews forever, your children and your children's children will curse you in your graves. Their ideals are not those of the Americans and even though they live among us for generations, the leopard can't change its spots. They will imperil our institutions, they should be excluded by the constitution.*'

In all fairness it must be clarified that the Arab leaders during World War I and in particular Husain, Sharif of Makka, who had joined hands with the British and risen in revolt against Turkey, did not raise any serious objections to the British plans for Palestine. His son, Amir Faisal, who was hoping to be made the king of Syria, had practically endorsed these on more than one occasion. According to

Lieutenant Colonel Joyce, Amir Faisal's senior British military adviser who attended the meeting between Faisal and Chaim Weizmann (Zionist leader and the first President of Israel) in 1918, Faisal was willing to accept a Jewish Palestine if doing so would influence the Allies to support his claim to Syria (*'Palestine Papers 1917 - 1922 Seeds of Conflict',* by Doreen Ingrams, John Murray, London, 1972, p. 37 and *'Arab Bureau Papers. Foreign Office 882 vol. 24 Document 105824,'* Public Record Office, Kew). Later, at the 1919 Peace Conference, Faisal went so far as to offer public support for Zionism (*'Brandeis and Frankfurter: A Dual Biography',* by Leonard Baker, Harper & Row, New York, 1984, p. 171). While all this was going on, the only person to show any concern for the inhabitants of Palestine was US President Wilson but no one took any serious notice of his call to respect the rights of the local people.

It is not possible to cover all of the subsequent developments relating to Palestine in these pages. To cut a long story short, after World War I, the League of Nations handed over the territory to be administered as a mandate by the British. In 1947, the UN General Assembly adopted a resolution, which approved partition of the country between the Arabs and the Jews. It gave 47 per cent of the country to the Arabs who now constituted 70 per cent of its population and owned 92 per cent of the land. The rest was given to the Jews.

Unable to maintain peace, the British abandoned the mandate and withdrew their forces in 1948. On 14th May, the state of Israel proclaimed its independence and was accorded instant recognition by the Soviet Union and the United States. In his foreword to late Professor Israel Shahak's book *'Jewish History, Jewish Religion'*, the American dissident and author, Gore Vidal tells the story of how the US came to recognize Israel ----- *'Sometime in the late 1950s, that world-class gossip and occasional historian, John F.*

Kennedy, told me how, in 1948, Harry S. Truman had been pretty much abandoned by everyone when he came to run for president. Then an American Zionist brought him two million dollars in cash, in a suitcase, aboard his whistle-stop campaign train. "That is why our recognition of Israel was rushed through so fast". As neither Jack nor I was an anti Semite (unlike his father and my grandfather) we took this to be just another funny story about Truman and the serene corruption of American politics.'

The neighbouring Arab states promptly declared war on fledgling Israel. This prompted the first Prime Mister of Israel, David Ben Gurion, to disavow the UN plan for the partitioning of Palestine and proclaim that the borders of the Jewish state would be determined by war. The Arabs lost the war and with it a lot more territory. As state policy, Israel cleared out the Arab towns and villages it had occupied through a deliberate campaign of terror, mass murders and burning down villages. Hundreds of thousands of Arabs were pushed out of their homes. They took shelter in refugee camps in Gaza, the West Bank, Lebanon, Syria and Jordan where their children and grandchildren continue to live till this day in extremely cramped, squalid and depressing conditions. The total number of Arab refugees of Palestinian origin scattered all over the world now exceeds four million.

Stateless Palestinians have become pawns in Middle East politics, discriminated against and mistreated by the other Arabs and relentlessly oppressed by Israel. The latter has done every thing possible to prevent them from returning to their homes. Israel's Law of Return allows any Jew from anywhere in the world to migrate to Israel at any time. But the Arabs born in Palestine, that were dispossessed of their land and forced into exile when Israel was formed, have no right of return.

The late Israeli Prime Minister Golda Meir even claimed Palestinians did not exist. An effective campaign has been waged in the United States under the slogan that Palestine was 'a land without people for a people without land,' that has been swallowed hook, line and sinker by the ignorant and the gullible. Any attempt to counter the misinformation is met with howls of accusations and peremptorily labeled as 'anti-Semitic'.

The lands cleared of the Arabs have been settled by the Jews who were not wanted in Christian Europe. Hundreds of thousands of them were shipped to Israel from all over the continent. The money for their settlement was provided by the West. Germany alone has donated over ninety billion dollars so far and the United States an even greater amount. None of this went to the Arab refugees who have survived mostly on the meager subsistence provided by the United Nations.

A state of uneasy truce prevailed until the Suez crisis came to a head in 1956 when Israel, in collusion with Britain and France, occupied Sinai and the Golan Heights. The situation became highly tense when the Soviet Union decided to back the Arabs. This was when irate President Eisenhower ordered Britain, France and Israel to back down. Eleven years later there was another war that proved to be yet more disastrous for the Arabs and they managed to lose both Sinai and the Golan Heights again, in addition to the West Bank, within a matter of six days. In 1973 Egypt and Syria managed to surprise Israel in a coordinated attack that started to look highly menacing for Israel but then the United States came to her rescue with full military support.

This time Egypt decided to break ranks with the rest of the Arabs and negotiated a separate peace deal, under US auspices at Camp David, leaving Israel free to do as she pleased with the rest, one by one. In due course, Israel turned on Lebanon, occupied its southern half and turned out the Palestinian leader Yasser Arafat and his pesky supporters. The brutalities that were committed by the Israelis and their Lebanese Christian supporters against Palestinian refugees in UN camps left twenty thousand dead and shocked most of the world but not sufficiently USA and her allies in the West.

It took nearly twenty years of sustained resistance on the part of the Lebanese to vacate the Israeli aggression from their land. During all this time the conscience of the United Nations and the rest of the western world remained quite undisturbed. A number of resolutions were introduced in the United Nations condemning Israeli aggression both in Palestine and Lebanon. The United States vetoed most of these. Those that did get passed have been contemptuously ignored by Israel. India does the same with the UN resolutions about Kashmir, as does the United States about Cuba. It would appear that these only become enforceable when Muslim countries, like Iraq or Indonesia, are called to account.

Continued Arab frustration led to the formation of a number of extremist groups who committed numerous acts of terror, including the hijacking and destruction of civilian airliners that did little to promote their cause. At one stage, Yasser Arafat's Al-Fatah group was even training terrorists belonging to Al-Zulfikar, an organization run from Kabul by the sons of Pakistan's deposed Prime Minister Zulfikar Ali Bhutto (others were trained in India) to commit terrorism in Muslim Pakistan that had always supported the Palestinians. (For details of Al-Zulfikar's organization, training and operations, etc. please see '*The Terrorist Prince: The Life and Death of Murtaza Bhutto*', by Raja Anwar, Vanguard Books, Lahore, 1998).

Having lost all hope of succour from the outside world Palestinians in the occupied territories started a protest movement of their own that became known as the *'Intifada'*. It mainly involved crowds of Palestinians gathering together after Friday prayers to protest Israeli excesses. When Israeli soldiers tried to disperse them young Palestinians threw stones. In retaliation, the soldiers fired back with live ammunition. When these scenes began to be presented on television worldwide, week after week, Israel and her supporters began to feel uncomfortable.

This is when they offered to negotiate secretly with Arafat, playing on his fears that by missing the opportunity he would run the risk of being side-lined by the new leadership that was taking hold within Palestine. He was presented with an 800-page draft agreement that forty Israeli experts, in nearly as many different fields, had taken two years to prepare. It is not known who examined it and for how long on behalf of Arafat. It could not have amounted to much because the Oslo Accord, as it came to be known, divided the Palestinian land into numerous cantons criss-crossed by Israeli controlled roads. It legitimized the continuation of illegal Jewish settlements on Arab land under Israeli jurisdiction and did not even acknowledge the right of self-determination for the Palestinians. The future of Jerusalem was left to be decided at some time in the future.

It sealed the fate of the Palestinians but Yasser Arafat was made the chairman of the 'Palestinian Authority' and was duly awarded the Nobel Peace Prize. It is rather ironic that there have been more prizes awarded for peace in Palestine than perhaps the rest of the world put together; yet, there has not been any peace in sight in the unfortunate land so far. It is also interesting that the name of Slobodan Milosevic, now under trial for crimes against humanity at The Hague, was also mentioned for the Nobel Prize after signing of the Dayton Accord on Bosnia.

As was only to be expected, the unfair and unjust accord unraveled fairly quickly, the process being helped in no small measure by hardliners in Israel, like Ariel Sharon, who saw little need to make whatever small concessions had been promised to the Palestinians. If there was any hope it lay in the United States' ability to exert pressure on the Israelis. With the election of George W. Bush and his band of ultra-conservative Christian Right supporters this too has flown out of the window. In any case, it is a myth to believe that the US Government can make Israel do anything that she does not wish to do.

If anything, the reverse is much closer to reality. This was demonstrated most clearly when President Bush thundered on television recently, calling on Israel to withdraw her troops from Jenin where they were massacring civilians, '*They must withdraw the troops and I mean now*'. No one took the slightest notice, least of all Ariel Sharon whose troops continue to rampage in the occupied territories committing the worst kind of atrocities and human rights violations. We never heard any thing more about it except when President Bush declared Ariel Sharon, who has been indicted for war crimes, to be 'a man of peace'.

It is difficult to over-emphasize the degree and extent of control that is exercised by the Jews over the politicians and governments in the West, particularly the United States, but this is a different subject. It is only relevant in the present discussion to the extent that both the Jews and the West have political and economic objectives that have come together in their opposition to the Muslims.

It is not the Muslims alone who are persecuted by the Israelis. If anything, the Christian Arabs in Palestine suffer a worse fate but no Church leader in the West dare speak openly about it. Any one interested in the details of how the Jews exercise their influence is advised to refer to three books in particular. The first is entitled, *'They Dare To Speak Out'* by Congressman Paul Findley, Lawrence Hill & Company, Westport, Connecticut, 1985; the others are, *'One Nation Under Israel',* by Andrew Hurley, Truth Press, Scottsdale, Arizona, 1999 and *'The Holocaust Industry: Reflections on the Exploitation of Jewish Suffering,'* by Norman G. Finkelstein, Verso, London, 2000.

To get an idea of what is involved; when Prime Minister Issak Rabin of Israel, a small nation of about four million Jews in the Middle East, was assassinated there was hardly any one among the US politicians and officials to be seen in Washington. All of them, from President Clinton downward, had jumped on any available plane to mark his or her presence at the funeral in Tel Aviv. Each time after being elected President, Clinton, ostensibly the world's most powerful man, personally called at the offices of the America Israel Public Affairs Committee (AIPAC), the Israeli lobbyist outfit in Washington, as an apparent gesture of homage.

As Israeli Knesset member and peace activist, Uri Avnery, describes it in his article *'One Has to Pity This Man, Bush'* that appeared in *'The Times'*, London on 12th June, 2002. *'The Jewish lobby is, of course, one of the strongest in the United States. The Jewish community is highly organized on rigid, authoritarian lines. Its electoral and financial power casts a long shadow over both houses of the Congress. Hundreds of Senators and Congressmen were elected with the help of Jewish contributions. Resistance to the directives of the Jewish lobby is political suicide. If AIPAC (America Israel Public Affairs Committee) were to table a resolution abolishing the Ten Commandments, 80 Senators and 300*

Congressmen would sign it at once. This lobby frightens the media, too, and assures their adherence to Israel.'

According to Washington economist Thomas Stauffer, the US taxpayers have dispensed with $1.6 trillion, in direct as well as indirect terms, to support Israel since 1973 and there is no end in sight (David R. Francis in '*The Christian Science Monitor*,' December 2002). During the run up to the 1992 presidential election a tapped phone conversation became public in which the president of ADL, a powerful US Jewish umbrella organization, was overheard offering support for Clinton to his campaign manager in exchange for giving Israel the right to nominate the next US Secretary of State. There is good reason to believe that it was neither the first nor the last time that such a deal was made. The transcripts of President Nixon's tapes released a few years ago seem to indicate that Henry Kissinger too may not have been his choice as the National Security Adviser.

'*The Palestinian territories today are witnessing the onset of a mass famine; there is a health crisis of catastrophic proportions; there is a civilian death toll that totals at least a dozen to 20 people a week; the economy has collapsed; hundreds of thousands of innocent civilians are unable to work, study, or move about as curfews and at least 300 barricades impede their daily lives; houses are blown up or bulldozed on a mass basis (60 yesterday). And all of it with US equipment, US political support, US finances. Bush declares that Sharon, who is a war criminal by any standard, is a man of peace, as if to spit on the innocent Palestinians' lives that have been lost and ravaged by Sharon and his criminal army. And he has the gall to say that he acts in God's name, and that he (and his administration) act to serve "a just and faithful God". And, more astounding yet, he lectures the world on Saddam's flouting of UN resolutions even as he supports a country,*

Israel, that has flouted at least 64 of them on a daily basis for more than half a century.' (Professor Edward Said in the *'al-Ahram'* 13-19th February 2003).

A group of nine MPs from a number of different political parties in Canada visited Palestine recently and reported on the conditions they found in West Bank and Gaza. One of them, Carolyn Parrish read parts of the report that concluded, *'Palestinians are suffering under sub-human conditions with inadequate water, food and medical care, as well as personal humiliation and deprivation -- -- Palestinian kids can't brush their teeth and can't have shower. There is seventy per cent unemployment. ---- - It's becoming a massive disaster. If this was happening elsewhere in the world, every one would be outraged. There is a huge conspiracy of silence'* (*'The Mississauga News'*, 9th August 2002). The only question is why is no one taking any notice? Could the answer be, because the Palestinians are mostly Muslim?

Mainstream media in the West have been remarkably evasive in covering the Arab side of the story in Palestine. All of its news and editorial coverage is heavily influenced and slanted to reflect only the Israeli perspective. In doing so it has done no service to the people in the West most of whom remain uninformed and ignorant of the real issues. It may serve the purpose of a narrow band of interests but, in the process, it has also widened the gulf of misunderstanding and mistrust that exists between the Muslims and the West today.

IRAQ

Even before the demise of the Soviet Union developments had taken place that were destined to become the basis of western policy vis-à-vis the Muslim countries. The most significant among these was the over-throw of the Shah of Iran and his oppressive regime. He had been a very close friend of the West, in particular, the United States. His removal was regarded as a destabilizing factor for the established order and western vested interests in the area. The Shah's successors were distrustful of the West and their relationship with the latter soured.

Instead of resolving the differences at the political level, western media went into high gear assigning the entire blame to the mullas who now ruled the country and to militancy allegedly inherent in Islam, more specifically, in the Shia sect. It wasn't long before terms like 'militant Islam' and 'Islamic fundamentalism' started to be bandied about and people like Bernard Lewis were writing articles in the *'Atlantic Monthly'* under provocative titles like *'The Roots of Muslim Rage'*. The case of Salman Rushdie, that would have hardly merited a mention in earlier times, was played out for all its worth for years on end. Writers of highly questionable and dubious merit, like Bangla Desh's Taslima Nasreen, were honoured by the European Union's Parliament, it appears, only because in their ignorance and stupidity they had attempted to vilify Islam and its Prophet to ingratiate themselves with the West and offend the Muslims.

The more perceptive among them felt uneasy at the portents that seemed to indicate the West was in search of a new common external enemy to avoid turning on itself, as in its past, and had once more targeted Islam for the purpose. Why else would there be such a sudden increase in interest in Islam? It was not some new development but had been there for well nigh fifteen hundred years. There had been many movements among the Muslims to protest against western excesses in this century alone, starting with the Mahdi in Sudan, the Muslim Brotherhood in Egypt and the wars of independence in Algeria and Tunisia, before the revolution in Iran. These were never portrayed as a common threat to the western civilization and Christendom as a whole.

The sudden outpouring of tendentious writing and media attempts to present the creed in a militant and extremist mode was suspicious particularly to those among the Muslims who tried to question the underlying premise and motives in the onslaught against their religion and were repeatedly denied the opportunity. The people struggling for political and human rights under the UN Charter in Kashmir, Chechniya, Algeria, Palestine, etc. are not described as Kashmiris, Chechens, Algerians or Palestinians by the media in the West but as 'Islamic extremists' and any violence is always attributed to 'Muslim terrorists'. If it is so important to mention the religion of such groups in news reports why omit it when reporting similar occurrences in Sri Lanka, Ireland, the Basque region and other Christian lands? Some one has painstakingly analysed that in the US press the word 'Muslim' or 'Islam' has invariably appeared within three lines of wherever the word 'terrorist' is written. When it happens thousands of times, over a period of decades, one is hard put to dismiss it as unintended or merely coincidental.

Similarly, when people like Samuel Huntington, who should know better, start to lump together over a billion Muslims, living in almost every country of the world in every culture and present them as a single monolith, totally ignoring the obvious differences in society, sect, race, political and economic interest etc. there has to be more to it than meets the eye. In the present context, more important than religion, what most of the Muslims also have in common is that for the past two centuries they have suffered colonial occupation, economic despoliation and relentless exploitation at the hands of the West. To ignore these very significant issues and try to blame their religion for the way the Muslims feel about the West is plain non-sense. To persist in harping on this one flawed theme, while excluding arguments to the contrary, smacks of little more than a propaganda ploy.

This was quite clear by the time Samuel Huntington came out with his '*Clash of Civilizations*' in the summer 1993 issue of the '*Foreign Affairs*' (later published as a book in 1996) ---- not an original hypothesis by any means. As far back as 1963 Professor Northcote Parkinson, author of the classic '*Parkinson's Law*' among others, had outlined a thesis along remarkably similar lines in his '*East and West*' (Houghton Mifflin Company, Boston) but it had gone un-noticed. The only difference between then and now lies in the emergent political need to give the newly selected threat persistent and widespread publicity to condition the minds of the people into a pre-planned mould.

There can be little doubt that propaganda works even with the more sophisticated recipients. In a recent poll, 87 per cent of the Canadians indicated that they were opposed to any war against Iraq. The situation was very different among the Canadians who relied on the US media for their news. More than two-thirds of the latter group were found to be in favour of attacking the country.

'*The whole aim of practical politics,*' according to the American satirist H.L. Mencken, '*is to keep the public alarmed* (and hence clamorous to be led to safety) *by menacing it with an endless series of hobgoblins, all of them imaginary.*' This becomes all too easy when they can have the power of the state to identify a dark and threatening force against which to protect the people. Osama bin Laden and al-Qaida will do for the moment but there is a need for something more substantial and convincing than some rag-tag and bob-tall fugitives in remote caves with a leader on a kidney dialysis machine. This is where Islam comes in.

Reports to the effect that both Huntington and Lewis have known past connections to CIA and MI6 respectively only add credence to the suspicions that the bogeyman of Islam has been resurrected on purpose to replace the earlier perceived threat from the former Soviet Union. We have to keep in mind that all of this had started more than a dozen years before the September 2001 incident and the latter had no bearing on it.

This is how Reich Marshal Hermann Goering explained the process at his trial in Nuremberg after World War II: '*Naturally the common people do not want war, but after all, it is the leaders of a country who determine the policy and it is always a simple matter to drag people along whether it is a democracy, or a fascist dictatorship, or a parliament or a communist dictatorship. Voice or no voice, the people can always be brought to the bidding of the leaders. This is easy; all you have to do is to tell them they are being attacked and denounce the pacifists for lack of patriotism and exposing the country to danger. It works the same in every country.*'

Shakespeare had a prophetic warning of his own about such machinations. '*Beware the leader who bangs the drums of war in order to whip the citizenry into a patriotic fervor, for patriotism is indeed a double-edged sword. It both emboldens the blood, just as it narrows the mind ----- And when the drums of war have reached a fever pitch and the blood boils with hate and the mind has closed, the leader will have no need in seizing the rights of the citizenry. Rather, the citizenry, infused with fear and blinded with patriotism, will offer up all of their rights unto the leader, and gladly so. How do I know? For this is what I have done. And I am Caesar.'*

The need for an external enemy is better understood by looking at the internal make-up of United States. It is not a cohesive nation by any means but a collection of people of different origins that flocked to the bountiful land in search of a better economic future. A combination of talent, hard work, and abundant resources have made her a very wealthy and powerful country but this is not enough to create the sense of cohesion and belonging that characterizes a nation. There are powerful forces, divisions and circumstances within that carry the potential of tearing the country apart. The easiest way to avoid the calamity is to present all the diverse elements with an external enemy as a common rallying point. A somewhat similar situation exists within Europe and between Europe and the United States.

One way to keep these natural competitors from being at each other's throats is to confront them with a common threat. Erstwhile Soviet Union had filled this role admirably but now that it is no longer there a new enemy has to be found. What could be better than the familiar, old and trusted bogeyman that worked so well for so many Popes in the past? There are other benefits as well not the least of which is that it keeps the attention of the people away from their own politicians and problems. Then there is the money to be made in making bombs, guns, missiles, bombers, tanks and ships, etc. Because of the vast disparity in the technological and military capabilities, confrontations with the Muslim countries are like shooting fish in a barrel and virtually free of any risk of adverse internal repercussions. No politician in the West is going to let any issues of morality or justice stand in the way of such opportunities.

As the differences between Iran and the West deepened, Saddam Hussein decided to attack Iran without any provocation whatsoever. There were no resolutions in the Security Council calling for evacuation of the aggression and no demands for military action by the West. All the oil-rich Arab states opened their coffers to him and military supplies and expertise poured in from the West. The United States provided loan guarantees worth billions of dollars to facilitate Iraqi purchases.

Most disturbingly, the West also supplied her with chemical and biological agents and provided experts to help produce the delivery systems for these weapons. The evidence can be seen in the article headed '*Ali Baba's Cave*' by Eric Margolis, columnist for '*The Toronto Sunday Sun*' of 4th April 2002:

'------------- *In 1990, on assignment in Baghdad, I discovered a group of British chemical technicians who told me --- and showed me documents --- that they had been employed until a few weeks earlier at Iraq's top secret Salman Pak laboratories developing or researching germ warfare weapons: anthrax, botulism, Q-fever and tularemia. The British technicians said they had been secretly seconded to Iraq by British Intelligence MI 6 and the Ministry of Defence with the objective of producing biological weapons for use by the Iraqi Army against Iran. ---- Iraq's germ warfare feeder stock came, with full US Government approval, from an American laboratory in Maryland. German firms supplied equipment and training for Iraq's chemical weapons manufacturing, in the full*

knowledge of the US, British and German governments.'
The contents of this article have not been disputed or denied todate by any of the named governments or their agencies.

The United States supplied chemical and biological agents not only to Iraq but to Israel as well. The Israeli El-Al Boeing 747 aircraft carrying one such deadly cargo crashed into a housing complex in Amsterdam shortly after take off in October 1992. Hundreds of its poor inhabitants have died since then and many of the survivors are still showing symptoms similar to those of nerve gas poisoning. It was not until the Dutch daily *'Handelsblad'* obtained and published copies of permits issued by the United States to Pennsylvania based Solkatronic Chemicals for the export of dimethyl methylphosphate, a chemical used in the production of Sarin nerve gas to Israel's Chemical and Biological Institute outside Tel Aviv that an enquiry was ordered by the Dutch Parliament (Associated Press and *'The Washington Post'*, 7th October 1998). Its proceedings and findings have not been made available to the public as yet. While still on the issue of proliferation of weapons of mass destruction, it is also a matter of record that the white regime in South Africa bartered semi-processed uranium and nuclear weapons technology that it had acquired from Israel, for Iraqi oil during the embargo in 1980s.

Saddam Hussein did produce and use chemical weapons against not only Iran but also the Kurds in his own country. When some reporter questioned the then Director of CIA (Robert Gates?) on the issue he replied, *'We know Saddam is a son of a bitch but he is our son of a bitch'* (TV programme *'Paying the Price'*, by John Pilger aired by ITV in England in March 2000).

The US State Department's assessment of Saddam at the time was that 'he is a man we can do business with'. There was good reason for them to believe so because during his exile, before the coup that made him the president of Iraq, he had been a regular visitor to the US embassy in Cairo. A steady stream of US Senators and Congressmen, among them the present Secretary of Defence Donald Rumsfeld, were lining up in Baghdad to pay homage to him. Democratic presidential candidate Al Gore's running mate in the 2000 race, Jewish Senator Joseph Lieberman, described him as 'a good dictator and a friend of America.' This friendship and tributes lasted only as long as Saddam was waging war on Iran.

In a diabolical act of double-dealing that would have left Machiavelli green with envy, with the full involvement of the United States, Israel sold $5 billion worth of US arms to Iran, a country she had described as a 'terrorist state' and 'enemy of the Jewish people', to help sustain her war with Iraq. The only western purpose in this appears to have been that the war between the two Muslim powers should continue for as long as possible. It lasted eight years and cost the lives of at least a million young men, possibly more, and the expenditure of countless billions of dollars. During all this time neither the United Nations nor any one else was allowed to bring about a cease-fire and mediate peace between the warring nations. The U.N Security Council stood idly by as if it were a matter of little concern.

Soon after the end of the utterly pointless and wasteful war that achieved nothing but misery and tragedy on both sides, Saddam decided to invade and occupy Kuwait, having first obtained assurances from the US Ambassador, April Gillespie, that they would treat it as simply an 'intra-Arab' issue. US Secretary of State, James Baker too declared, 'Our dog is not in that fight'. Obviously, Saddam had learnt nothing from his past dealings. Sadly, he is not alone nor will he be the last among tin-pot dictators, in the tradition

of Panama's Manuel Noriega, to court disaster for his nation
by taking the West at its word. He had served his purpose
and it was time for the West to move on to its next objective,
which happened to be the elimination of Iraq itself as a
military power in the region.

The US position had been that as long as they got the oil
it did not matter to them who owned the land. This soon
changed under the powerful influence of the Jewish lobby
and relentless persuasion by Britain's Mrs. Thatcher. With
her newly acquired military and industrial capability Iraq
had become a potentially serious threat to western and
Israeli interests, a situation that was not to be tolerated.
Suddenly, President Bush was calling America's erstwhile
friend 'Hitler' or worse and leaning upon the rest of the world
to join him in vacating the aggression, under the banner of
the United Nations ----- an organization whose dues USA
had refused to clear for years. Bush was by no means alone
in his desire to destroy Iraq. There was a memorable TV
interview in Britain at the time in which David Frost asked
the Archbishop of Canterbury, Dr. Robert Runcie, how he
knew that the war with Iraq was going to be a 'just war'?
Lost for an answer and refusing to be drawn into the point
any further, the Archbishop could only repeat, *'One knows'*
---- whatever that may mean.

The Gulf War of 1991 was paid for, probably twice over, by
the rest of the oil-producing Arab countries as well as oil
consuming countries like Japan. Saudi Arabia alone claims
to have doled out eighty billion dollars for a war that USA
said cost only sixty-one billion (Reuters, 27th Sep. 2002).
No one knows how many billions Kuwait, the United Arab
Emirates, Japan and the rest of them paid to USA. Whatever
oil money was left over the Arabs spent it on buying vast
quantities of arms and other equipments like Boeing and
Air-Bus airliners from the West at grossly inflated prices.

They also dropped the price of oil to record low levels, which was of immense help to the western economies but left very little in the Arab coffers. It is estimated that in real dollar terms, after allowing for inflation, the Saudi income was reduced close to ten per cent of what it had been in the hay days of the seventies. Her per capita income dropped from $ 28,600 in 1981 to $ 7,200 in the year 2000.

The war also cost the lives of hundreds of thousands of Iraqi Arabs. At the end, Saddam was still left in place as a threat to the neighbouring Arab states and, on that excuse, the US got to station her troops, ships and planes in Saudi Arabia, Qatar, Bahrain and Kuwait on a permanent basis.

In the name of the United Nations, economic sanctions were imposed on Iraq whose sole purpose was to destroy her economy and industry. Over and above, USA and Britain have continued to bomb Iraqi installations and facilities, even flocks of sheep, for the past twelve years to cripple her economy with no let up in sight. Radiation from depleted uranium munitions used by the western forces has caused an alarming rise in the incidence of cancer in the country. In an article in '*The Guardian*' of 21st December 1998 Maggie O'Kane claims that the western forces discharged one million such shells that fragmented on impact. The Iraqis lack the means to clean up these widely dispersed sources of radiation that could remain lethal for up to four thousand years. The problem is horrendous in its implications.

It was the same in Vietnam where US forces sprayed Dioxin to defoliate trees and killed half a million Vietnamese in the process. As an after effect, women still give birth to children who are blind, mentally retarded or have no hands, feet or limbs (the US Government have compensated their own personnel for injuries caused by Dioxin but refuse to accept responsibility for the Vietnamese). The total number of Vietnamese killed in the war is estimated to be between three and five million. Indiscriminate and irresponsible use of such lethal weapons that keep killing innocent people forever has to be a crime against humanity, regardless who uses them.

UNESCO, the Red Cross, the Food and Agricultural Organization, the World Health Organization, the U.N. Development Program, Human Rights Watch and others have catalogued in detail the horrors of Iraqi sanctions. They have noted, for example, that since the imposition of sanctions, Iraq *'has experienced a shift from relative affluence to massive poverty.'* Infant mortality rates in Iraq are now among the highest in the world, chronic malnutrition affects every fourth child under 5 years of age, only 41 per cent of the population have regular access to clean water, and 83 per cent of all schools need substantial repairs.

USA and Britain have been, among other things, systematically bombing and destroying all of Iraq's water and sewerage treatment plants and facilities long after the war was over. Under the UN sanctions she was not allowed to import replacement parts and machines to repair the systems nor was she permitted to import or manufacture chlorine to purify drinking water. As a result, UNICEF has estimated, 4,500 children under the age of five died each month from diarrhoea, pneumonia and malnutrition. Current estimates suggest that between 1 million and 1.5 million Iraqis have died from the sanctions, around a third of them children, or 500 Iraqis for every American who died in the World Trade Centre. This is more than five times the number that were killed in Hiroshima. Many people have now taken to calling the UN sanctions a 'weapon of mass destruction.'

Three successive U.N. humanitarian coordinators for Iraq have denounced the sanctions ----- Denis Halliday, his successor, Hans von Sponeck, and Jutta Burghardt, head of the World Food Program in Baghdad. When he resigned his post in utter disgust, Halliday termed the sanctions '*genocidal*', noting that '*we are in the process of destroying an entire society.*' No one cares; Iraqis are Muslim and they are not white; as such, they don't count. By comparison, UN sanctions against Serbia that had perpetrated genocide were lifted immediately after she signed the peace accord at Dayton and there was even talk of nominating indicted war criminal, Serbian President, Slobodan Milasovic, for the Nobel Peace Prize.

In 1997, UNICEF reported that some 4,500 Iraqi children under the age of five were dying each month from hunger and disease as a direct result of the US-led economic sanctions; one in four children in the same age group was chronically malnourished and one in eight died before his fifth birthday. When questioned by CBS' Leslie Stahl on the TV programme '*60 Minutes*', US Secretary of State Madeline Albright, blandly asserted that this was 'a price worth paying' for the achievement of US objectives (John Pilger on ITV). One really wonders if she would have said the same thing had the children belonged to the white race and Christian or Jewish faiths. No one in the administration or the western media condemned her for the outrageous comment or called for her resignation.

Although all the military capability of Iraq has been destroyed the persecution has not stopped. The reason for it lies in the fear and expectation that if she could acquire it once she could do it again. The potential still exists ----- Iraq has vast reserves of oil, a literacy rate close to 100 per cent and per capita more PhDs than perhaps any other country in the world. It is a potential that cannot be destroyed by war alone, hence, the never ending sanctions.

Thanks to the US manipulation of the UN committees, out of the $60 billion in oil sales since the Gulf War, Iraq has so far received less than $20 billion, while the other $40 billion of its money has been siphoned off to pay compensation to Kuwait and western firms and to finance UN inspections and other operations. Iraq is allowed to spend only about 49 cents per person per day to sustain the life of its citizens ----- less than half the daily per capita income of Haiti, the poorest country in the western hemisphere and far below the amount the UN spends on food for dogs used in de-mining operations in northern Iraq. Amusingly, US Secretary of State Colin Powell recently stated that after the planned new war with Iraq the country's oil would be 'held in trust for the benefit of the Iraqi people.' It defies credulity that after what they have been doing to the people of Iraq the West still expects the world to swallow such hypocritical non-sense.

As recognised by UNESCO, the education system in Iraq was unparalleled in its scope in that it had allowed a child born even into an illiterate poverty stricken family to receive free high-quality education right up to the university level and join virtually any profession of his or her choice. Even graduate courses abroad were paid for by the Iraqi government.

Under the UN imposed sanctions the supply of all educational materials, including blackboards, pencils, pens, course books, medical journals, computers, even paper, was halted. According to Felicity Arbuthnot, British journalist and activist, when the UN weapons inspectors (UNSCOM) raided the science laboratory of Baghdad's once lavishly equipped university they threw out what few scientific books still remained in its library. (This is something the Pakistanis who, at the behest of the West, crusaded in favour of signing CTBT would do well to remember). It also raises grave questions about the role being played by the UN in the systematic destruction of Muslim societies.

The results of these vicious attempts to deprive the Iraqis of all scientific and technological capability are already evident. Teachers and scientists who were being paid more than $300 per month now get the equivalent of $2 per month and are forced to sell whatever they possess in order to survive. Pointedly, under the renewed sanctions Iraq has been asked to provide the names and addresses of all the scientists in the country any of whom can be taken out of the country to be 'questioned' by the West on behalf of the UN. At this rate it will not be long before Iraq loses all her ability to recover and is reduced to the level of the rest of the Arab countries in terms of scientific and technological capabilities.

During his recent visit to Cairo to attend an international anti-war conference Denis Halliday, head of the UN Mission in Iraq, was asked if he thought that the sanctions were ever meant as a method of bringing Iraq back into the international fold? He told the *'al-Ahram'*, *'No, I think the Gulf War, the invasion of Kuwait ---- which was supported by the United States and encouraged by the United States ----- was all part of a plan to crush Saddam Hussein, and crush Iraq ----- perhaps the only country showing leadership potential in the Arab world. Sanctions were a part of this. They built on the destruction of the war ----- the use of depleted uranium, the bombing of civilian targets, the destruction of water systems and electrical power. It was horrific back in 1991 and I think we have all deliberately been genocidal in our endeavours since then until today.'*

As USA and Britain gear up for another war on Iraq many questions come to mind. For example, why was it right for the UN to attack Iraq when she invaded Kuwait and not when she invaded Iran? Also, why is it right for the UN to force Iraq to destroy her weapons of mass destruction and not do the same to Israel? One of the reasons given for a renewed campaign against Iraq is that Saddam is a brutal dictator who has killed his own people but at the time when these crimes were committed the West not only did not take any action but continued to provide generous aid to him. USA and her cohorts have already killed a thousand times more Iraqis than Saddam ever did and now they want to kill more of them, by attacking once again, to free Iraq from Saddam's clutch. It makes one wonder as to who is the real homicidal maniac in this bizarre and grotesque saga?

Commenting on the excuses given by the US in calling for a UN attack on Iraq, Professor Edward Said wrote in the '*al-Ahram*' (13-19 February 2003), '*But what is so monumentally hypocritical about the official US position is that literally everything Powell has accused the Ba'athists of has been the stock in trade of every Israeli government since 1948, and at no time more flagrantly than since the occupation of 1967. Torture, illegal detention, assassination, assaults against civilians with missiles, helicopters and jet fighters, annexation of territory, transportation of civilians from one place to another for the purpose of imprisonment, mass killing (as in Qana, Jenin, Sabra and Shatilla to mention only the most obvious), denial of rights to free passage and unimpeded civilian movement, education, medical aid, use of civilians as human shields, humiliation, punishment of families, house demolitions on a mass scale, destruction of agricultural land, expropriation of water, illegal settlement, economic pauperisation, attacks on hospitals, medical workers and ambulances, killing of UN personnel, to name only the most outrageous abuses: all these, it should be* noted with emphasis, have been carried on with the total, unconditional support of the United States which has not only supplied Israel with the weapons for such practices and every kind of military and intelligence aid, but also has given the country upwards of $135 billion in economic aid on a scale that beggars the relative amount per capita spent by the US government on its own citizens.'

In a bitterly critical article in the online '*Times*' of London (23rd January 2003), well-known novelist, John le Carre writes, '*America has entered one of its historical periods of madness; but this is the worst I can remember: worse than McCarthyism, worse than the Bay of Pigs and in the long term potentially more disastrous than the Vietnam War.*

'----------------- *What Bush won't tell us is the truth about why we're going to war. What is at stake is not an Axis of Evil ---- but oil, money and people's lives. Saddam's misfortune is to sit on the second biggest oilfield in the world. Bush wants it, and who helps him get it will receive a piece of the cake. And who doesn't won't.*

'---------------- *Baghdad represents no clear and present danger to its neighbours, and none to the US or Britain. Saddam's weapons of mass destruction, if he's still got them, will be peanuts by comparison with the stuff Israel or America could hurl at him at five minutes' notice. What is at stake is not an imminent military or terrorist threat, but the economic imperative of US growth. What is at stake is America's need to demonstrate its military power to all of us ----- to Europe and Russia and China, the poor mad little North Korea, as well as the Middle East; to show who rules America at home, and who is to be ruled by America abroad.*

' --------------- *The imminent war was planned years before bin Laden struck, but it was he who made it possible. Without bin Laden, the Bush junta would still be trying to explain such tricky matters as how it came to be elected in the first place; its reckless disregard of the world's poor, the ecology and a raft of unilaterally abrogated international treaties. They might also have to be telling us why they support Israel in the continuing disregard for UN resolutions.*

'But bin Laden conveniently swept all that under the table. ----- Now 88 per cent of Americans want the war we are told. The US defence budget has been raised by another 60 billion dollars. A splendid new line of nuclear weapons is in the pipeline, so we can all breathe easy. Quite what war 88 per cent of Americans are supporting is less clear. How Bush and his junta succeeded in deflecting America's anger from bin Laden to Saddam Hussein is one of the great public relations conjuring tricks of history. But they swung it. A recent poll tells us that one in two Americans now believe Saddam was responsible for the attack on the World Trade Centre. But the American public is not merely being misled. It is being browbeaten and kept in a state of ignorance and fear.'

As to the real purpose behind the proposed new crusade against Saddam, Conservative activist and presidential hopeful Pat Buchanan has cited an account of a disturbing conversation between Congressman Tom Lantos, ranking Democrat on the House International Affairs Committee and Colette Avital, a visiting Israeli Knesset member. Lantos gave this assurance to Avital, *'My dear Colette, don't worry. You won't have any problem with Saddam. We'll be rid of the bastard soon enough. And in his place we'll install a pro-western dictator, who will be good for you and good for us. This pro-western dictator will rule for five or six years and after America gets rid of all the regimes of evil, it will go straight to Syria and tell young Assad that's what will happen to him if he doesn't stop supporting terrorism'*

(Dr. Ahmed Faruqui in '*The Daily News*', 19th November 2002). What should one make of these champions of western democracy who never tire of extolling its virtues in sermons to the public while secretly conspiring to bring about regime changes to install dictators of their choice in the Muslim countries?

Just as during the run up to the attack on Afghanistan when US Secretary of Defence Donald Rumsfeld was crediting al-Quaida with the ability to manufacture nuclear bombs and launch satellites, Iraq is being accused of concealing weapons of mass destruction of all kinds without proof of any believable kind. They don't even seem to care how it makes them look and whether any one believes them or not. Such is the corruption of power.

While Bush tells the world that Iraq possesses weapons of mass destruction and has links with al-Quaida, the Director of CIA, George Tenet, insists that there is no proof to support either of these allegations. In his 2002 State of the Union address to the US Congress, Bush claimed that Iraq clandestinely imported uranium from Niger in 1980s for making nuclear bombs knowing that it was based on false information. US Ambassador Joe Wilson, who had investigated the affair, went public in an article in the '*New York Times*' that there was no proof and that Bush was misleading the nation. This was denounced as treason and he was made the object of a smear campaign that included revealing the identity of his wife as a CIA agent, putting her life at risk.

'*The Washington Post's*' Dana Milbank wrote that for George W. Bush, '*facts are malleable*' and that statements on Iraq's military capability are '*dubious, if not wrong.*' The CIA's former head of counterterrorism notes with greater candour: '*Basically, cooked information is working its way into high-level pronouncements.*' At a recent antiwar rally at Ruskin College in Oxford, England, a packed audience cheered as Ken Nichols O'Keefe, a former U.S. Marine, described the United States as '*the most despicable and criminal nation in the world*' ('*The Washington Post,*' 11ᵗʰ February 2003). A German cabinet minister recently compared Bush's political tactics to those of Adolf Hitler. Francine Ducros, political advisor to the Canadian Prime Minister Jean Chretien, went so far as to describe George W. Bush as 'a moron' in a briefing to the reporters at the meeting of NATO heads of government. If this is the opinion, expressed in public, by its own people about the leader of the much-vaunted western civilization what faith should the rest of the world repose in him and his actions?

While addressing the Cairo international conference on Iraq (18th – 20th December 2002), Denis Halliday, ex-UN Mission chief in Iraq, denounced the US administration's war plans as 'obscene.' '*It's criminal*', he said, '*and I believe it's indictable*'. Asked if US policy was solely determined by oil, he said: '*Well, it's certainly not about weapons, because there is no threat from Iraq. We know that in this neighbourhood, and the Americans know it perfectly well. It's a game being played by Mr. Bush, a very dangerous, nasty game ----- So it's about oil. But it is also about oil and Israel, Israel's position, Israel's representation of American interests in the Middle East ----- it's also about this desire for influence and power and presence throughout the world, including the Middle East ----- And it gets back again and again to the need to control oil reserves, which are of such importance to the survival of the economy of the United States.*

'*And I think that Washington is very insecure in its relationship with Saudi Arabia; they are not at all sure what's going to happen in the years ahead, and they want a reserve* tank. And the reserve tank, unfortunately, is called Iraq. It's sitting on a 120 billion barrels, its cheap and easy to obtain, and all it needs is a friendly regime in Baghdad that will kow-tow to American interests and American demands, and I think that's the name of the game of the attack, the war, the bombing, the invasion (and) the occupation of Iraq that Mr. Bush clearly has in mind. It's part of a strategy to dominate world globalization that is designed to support and enhance the lifestyle of Americans.'

Colonel Scott Ritter, the UN weapons inspector in Iraq from 1992 – 1998 wrote in the '*Guardian*' of 7th October 2002, '*The Bush administration's actions lay bare the mythology that this war is being fought over any threat posed by Iraqi weapons of mass destruction. It has made it clear that its objective is the elimination of Saddam Hussein. And this is where I have a fundamental problem. The UN charter prohibits regime removal. The US constitution states that international agreements entered into by the United States carry the force of law. The US has signed the UN charter. Regime removal is not only a violation of international law, it is unconstitutional.*

'*There is a way to deal with the need to change a regime deemed to be a risk to international peace and security, and that is through the UN. If President Bush truly wanted to seek regime removal in Baghdad, then he would push for an indictment of Saddam Hussein and his senior leadership in the international court for crimes against humanity, something that should not prove hard to do, given the record of the Butcher of Baghdad (and something other members of the UN would clearly support as an alternative to war). But seeking judgment through the international court requires a recognition by the US of the primacy of international law, something the Bush administration has been loath to do.*'

There are also a large number of other more frustrated and angry westerners who, feeling impotent and unable to influence events in any other way, express their rage through the Internet, like Mark Morford who wrote thus under the heading '*Happy Imbeciles at War*' on 10th January 2003, '*Perhaps you wonder just where in the hell is the spineless major media in all this, as they watch the chicken-hawk Shrubster himself, between golf swings, announce how tens of thousands of American troops are being sent to the Gulf alongside an enormous billion-dollar military build-up and imminent gobs of heaping death raining down upon a paltry oppressed nation and coming up next on CNN, we interview that dumb guy from "Joe Millionaire." Perfect.*

'*Perhaps you wonder where is the national TV coverage of all those huge anti-war protests, hundreds of thousands of people, all over the world, from Spain to Berlin to New York to San Francisco?*

'*Perhaps you wonder where are all the "serious" journalists, the risk-taking news agencies pointing up the absurdity of it all, the imminent horror, the outrage. Could it be these news agencies are owned by major conservative corporations? Could it be they're all terrified of losing ratings, of saying something unpopular, of invoking Cheney's wrath, of losing advertiser dollars and that ever-precious, ever-dwindling dumbed-down audience? One guess.*

'*And besides, who needs a reason for a massacre anymore? This is the age of the pre-emptive strike, screw-you Bush regime. Who needs, for example, the Monroe Doctrine, that crusty old rag stating how America will go to war only as a last resort, as a defensive measure, and won't become embroiled in unwinnable foreign wars that are none of our business?*

'Who needs every precedent ever set by international law? Who needs the U.N. Charter? Who needs confused congressional approval? Who needs ethical integrity?'

Eric Margolis is a veteran Canadian journalist who volunteered to join the US Army during the Korean War. Later, he spent many years in the Middle East, Afghanistan and Pakistan covering the Soviet invasion and the struggle in Kashmir and wrote a book called *'War at the Top of the World'*. Like most good men he feels outraged and angry at what the Bush administration is doing to the world. While he has little confidence in the Arabs, his observations and advice to them are interesting (*'Whither Arab countries?'* in the *'Toronto Sunday Sun,'* 2nd February 2003):

'Never has the old maxim "hang together or be hanged separately" been more fitting than for the Arab states now quailing in fear before President George W. Bush's evangelical crusade against Iraq. The Arab world's startling weakness and subservience to the West has never been more evident than in its open or discreet cooperation with Bush's plans to invade 'brother' Iraq.

'Though 99.99 per cent of Arabs bitterly oppose an American-British attack on Iraq, their authoritarian regimes, which rely on the US for protection from their own people and their neighbours, are quietly digging Iraq's grave. Every Arab leader knows the US will crush Iraq, so none will support unloved megalomaniac Saddam Hussein and risk ending up on Washington's hit list.

'In order to deflect the coming fury of their people over the almost certain invasion of Iraq (barring a last-minute coup against Saddam Hussein), Arab rulers have ordered their tame media to launch broadsides against Iraq and lay blame for the impending Gulf War II on Saddam. Never has the Arab world's chronic disunity, back-stabbing, and

petty tribalism been more pathetically on display. ---------

'*If ever Mideast regimes have shown an utter lack of legitimacy, it is now. Arab governments are ferocious at internal repression, but fainthearted and inept when it comes to facing external threats.*

'*In contrast to Israelis, who are clever, organized and determined, Arab rulers appear a frightened, dithering bunch of hand-wringers, whose interests rarely transcend personal power, wealth and extended family.*

'*What could Arabs do to prevent a war of aggression against Iraq that increasingly resembles a medieval crusade?*

'*Form a united diplomatic front that demands UN inspections continue. Stage an oil boycott of the US if Iraq is attacked. Send 250,000 civilians from across the Arab world to form human shields around Baghdad and other Iraqi cities. Boycott Britain, Turkey, Kuwait and the Gulf states that join or abet the US invasion of Iraq.*

'*Withdraw all funds on deposit in American and British banks. Accept payment for oil only in Euros, not dollars. Send Arab League troops to Iraq, so that an attack on Iraq is an attack on the entire League. Cancel billions worth of arms contracts with America and Britain. At least make a token show of male hormones and national pride.*

'*But the Arab states won't. They will cringe, temporize, then join the vultures who will feed on Iraq's bleeding carcass, while vying to prove their loyalty to Washington. The brutally efficient Arab security forces will crush popular uprisings caused by the US attack on Iraq, particularly in Egypt, Morocco and Jordan. The Arab states will continue torturing and executing those who protest their craven policies. Self-proclaimed Arab champions, like Libya and Syria, have gone mute. No wonder Osama bin Laden remains so popular.'*

Iraq is not a 'fundamentalist' Muslim state, it never has been one nor is there any proof of its having any links with terrorist organizations. The only plausible reason for destroying the country lies in its scientific and technological potential that could enable her to threaten western hegemony in the region at some future date. It is a given that sooner or later, one way or another, this potential will be destroyed.

During the war in Vietnam there were daily protests on American streets and campuses led by Students for Democratic Society (SDS) and other organizations. A group calling itself 'The Weathermen' carried out a bombing campaign within the United States for years during the 1970s. The passions were so high that in sympathy with the Buddhist monks, who had doused their bodies with gasoline and burnt to death, some Americans went so far as to immolate themselves but it did not put a stop to the war. What put an end to the American aggression was when they decided that the cost of continuing with the war had become unacceptable. This should be a poignant reminder to those who are naïve enough to believe that the present campaign against Muslim countries will somehow end on its own either before or after Iraq.

Appeasement of an aggressor only whets his appetite for more and invites further aggression. There is only one way to put a stop to it and that is by raising the stakes high enough for the West. Since those who are in a position to do so have lacked the necessary will so far, there is no reason to believe that aggression against the Muslim countries will end any time soon. After all, if aggression pays and they can get away with it why should they stop?

Oil has proved to be a curse for the Arabs in particular and the Muslims in general. Only the West derives all the benefit from it out of which it doles out a little to ensure that pliant surrogate regimes in the oil producing countries remain in place. It is not inconceivable that this realisation will sometime dawn on the Arabs as well. That will be the time when the chicken hatched by western greed will come home to roost. The implications for the precarious oil-centric western as well as the world economy are horrendous. In their crass arrogance and mindless misuse of power George W. Bush and his cohorts have sown the seeds of a storm that will continue to lash the future generations all over the world for a long time to come. It is a storm that western installed surrogates, like Hamid Karzai, will not be able to prevent or stop. Had wiser counsel prevailed to curb the zeal of the avenging crusaders in the West in time, the world might have been able to look to a more sanguine future with greater optimism.

KASHMIR

World War II had exhausted Britain in many different ways. Finding herself no longer in a position militarily and financially to continue the occupation of her colonies she decided to give independence to India in 1947. The settlement called for the partition of the country, with contiguous areas of majority Muslim population forming the new state of Pakistan and the rest going to India.

It was a perfectly fair and simple formula to implement but not as far as the British Government was concerned. It first decided to bifurcate the two largest Muslim majority provinces, Bengal and Punjab, and hand over the districts that had majority of non-Muslim populations in them to India. None of the provinces in which the non-Muslims were in majority were divided on these or any other grounds. Apart from this, referendums were held in North-West Frontier Province and the district of Sylhet in Assam Province, that were overwhelmingly Muslim, to make certain that the people really wanted to join Pakistan. No such procedure was allowed for any of the non-Muslim areas despite pleas by the leader of the Muslims, Mohammed Ali Jinnah.

Worse was yet to come. A British judicial commission, under Lord Radcliffe, gave away a huge chunk of territory comprising of four Muslim-majority districts in Punjab Province ---- Gurdaspur, Amritsar, Jullunder and Ferozepur to India. The blatantly perfidious act was designed to provide her with over-land access to the overwhelmingly Muslim state of Kashmir and facilitated its annexation by India.

Having done the black deed Lord Radcliffe burnt all his records to deny future historians any access to them. British civil servants, who were in the know, were sworn to secrecy and official historians told to *'skirt around the issue'* (*'Eminent Churchillians'* by Andrew Roberts, Weidenfeld & Nicholson, London, 1994, pp. 92, 101, 107). Access to British government documents and files relating to matters concerning Kashmir at the time of independence is still denied to researchers on one pretext or another.

It was left to the Secretary to Radcliffe Commission, Christopher Beaumont, a remarkable man of admirable conscience, to do the honourable thing. In a sworn affidavit lodged with the warden of All Souls College, Oxford, he has exposed how the award by the commission had been manipulated and altered to the detriment of Pakistan. (The writer was acquainted with Mr. Beaumont for many years and hopes to make available to the public his correspondence on the subject with this very noble Englishman in the near future. The affidavit itself can be seen in chapter 12 of *'The Pathans of Jullunder'*, by K. Hussan Zia).

The unprecedented orgy of killing that followed these shenanigans and gerrymandering by the British lasted for four long months in the newly independent Indian state of East Punjab, from August to November 1947. More than one million Muslims were killed by Sikhs, Hindus and the armies of princely Sikh states like Patiala, Nabha and Kapurthala. Approximately thirteen million Muslims were driven out of their homes to resettle in Pakistan. All official protection for them was withdrawn and the joint Boundary Force set up to ensure the safety and security of minorities was disbanded at the express demand of the Indian leaders Pundit Nehru and Sirdar Valebhai Patel. The killings did not stop until the province had been cleansed of all the Muslims (for some eye witness accounts of the holocaust see '*The Pathans of Jullunder*', chapter 9). Britain and rest of the world turned a blind eye to the plight of these people just as they had done when the Jews were murdered and dispossessed in Europe and would do so again during the genocide of the Muslims in Bosnia and Kosovo.

In 1949 both India and Pakistan accepted a United Nations resolution to stop the fighting that had broken out and allow the people of Kashmir to decide which of the two countries they would like to join. It was agreed that a plebiscite, under the auspices of the United Nations, would be held to ascertain their wishes. Since then India has found one excuse after another not to honour this commitment and continue with her military occupation of the state. Tired of inaction on the part of the United Nations and prevarication, exploitation and excesses by the Indians, the people of Kashmir have risen in revolt to claim their rights.

Since then the Indian security forces have murdered more than eighty thousand Kashmiris, the vast majority of them in cold blood while in custody. Countless others have been tortured in brutal ways and thousands of Kashmiri women gang-raped by unruly and ill-disciplined Indian soldiers. The United Nations has felt no compunction at its inability and unwillingness to enforce its own resolutions that would allow the Kashmiris to exercise their rights under its own charter. Muslims have also noted that, at the same time, the UN acted with remarkable alacrity to push through a referendum in East Timor in 1996 that separated the region from Muslim Indonesia, nor did it experience any difficulty in mustering more than half-a-million-strong military force to attack Muslim Iraq in 1991.

The West has gone one step further by branding any one fighting for the rights of Kashmiris as a 'terrorist' but not the Christian Nagas who are engaged in a similar struggle against India in the northeast of the country ('*statement by Mr. Blackwill, the US ambassador to India*' on 12th January 2003). It is leaning heavily on the military regime in Pakistan to give up the demand for the plebiscite in Kashmir as promised by the United Nations and, in effect, to accept the Indian occupation against the wishes and demands of the Kashmiri people. It is as George Orwell stated in his '*The Animal Farm*', some animals are more equal than the others and Muslims are simply not 'equal' in a world dominated by the West. When it comes to the Muslims, no matter where they might be, it feels as if open season had been declared on them long before 11th September, 2001.

The people fighting for the rights of Kashmiris are not terrorists regardless of any assertions to this effect made by any ambassador or any one else. They are fighting and dying for the rights promised to all the citizens of the world under the UN Charter. These rights are not automatically extinguished if the affected individuals happen to be Muslim. If any one is to be blamed and taken to task for the present situation in Kashmir it is the Indians and the United Nations who have prevaricated and failed to fulfil their commitments and obligations to the people of Kashmir for so long.

The issue of Kashmir lay dormant for fifty years and the West showed no proclivity in resolving it until recently. The reasons for the renewed interest, ostensibly, have to do with the concern about the possibility of nuclear conflagration in the sub-continent. These cannot be taken at their face value. Pakistan knows that it cannot win any war with India, nuclear or conventional. If there is ever such a war it will most likely result from some gross miscalculation by the Looney-Toons with half-baked ideas in the Indian government who are making a habit, most irresponsibly, of bragging about their ability and intentions 'of teaching Pakistan a lesson' and 'winning a nuclear war.'

Any nuclear war between India and Pakistan might involve, at the most, a hundred or so moderate sized explosions. While these will lay waste to the two countries themselves the effect on the rest of the world would be minimal. This is borne out by the fact the United States alone has conducted over twelve hundred nuclear tests, more than three hundred of these above ground, including some with extremely powerful hydrogen bombs. Add to these all the tests carried out by the Soviet Union, Britain, France and China and the world still remains intact, with its population nearly doubled since the first tests. If anything, a nuclear war between India and Pakistan would help to resolve one of the prickliest issues facing the western powers today. As the two countries destroy each other, in the process, they would also remove two of the most worrisome sources of nuclear proliferation for the West.

However, this is a far-fetched possibility, with too many imponderables, that is neither convenient nor easy to bring about. In any case, the West is not too concerned about India's nuclear capability; just as it is not bothered by the two hundred or more nuclear warheads in the possession of Israel. Its primary concern is Pakistan, a Muslim state and the new-found interest in Kashmir is to be viewed in this light. If she could be snared into an agreement that gives arbitrary powers to the West, it might just provide the leverage needed to divest her of the capability without having to resort to the more aggressive means with their accompanying risks.

A complex arrangement negotiated through western mediation and phased over an extended time-scale, while giving the illusion of a settlement, would put Pakistan securely at the mercy of the West as the guarantor. It will be made conditional on Pakistan giving up any leverage she might have by assuming responsibility for the Kashmiri freedom struggle. Given the situation, it is next to impossible for Pakistan to ensure peace inside Kashmir. All that will happen is that, on one pretext or another, there will be unending demands on her to make concessions, not to the Indians so much as to the West itself. Just as with Arafat, there will be no going back for her after the lobster is securely in the pot.

When an issue has been festering for too long impatience tends to set in to cloud the vision. There are indications of this happening in Pakistan. General Musharraf's bizarre trip to Agra and the most peculiar proposition made to visiting US Congressmen by his Minister for Interior, Moinuddin Haider, as reported in '*The Dawn*,' to settle the issue if India were to make some territorial concessions, appear to confirm the suspicion. The minister may or may not have realized it but, apart from anything else, his statement legitimizes India's illegal occupation by default while denying the people of Kashmir their fundamental rights ----- the very basis of Pakistan's principled position on the issue.

Kashmir is not a land dispute but an issue of people's rights. Any settlement that does not meet with the wishes of its people will be a constant irritant that will keep poisoning the relations between India and Pakistan forever. It is infinitely better to wait for a more opportune time rather than entering into an unsatisfactory settlement under pressure from vested interests at this stage. When it comes to issues of national interest, considerations of time assume a different scale and may extend to scores and even hundreds of years.

The Kashmiris may not have to wait that long. Despite the deployment of more than six hundred thousand troops for over twelve years and having carried out the worst atrocities that included rape, torture and murder of over eighty thousand innocent people, the Indians have not been able to extinguish the Kashmiri's desire for freedom. It has cost the Indians dearly and not only in monetary terms either. The morale of the Indian Army is abysmally low as is its state of training and operational readiness because of the demands placed on it by continual deployment under the most trying conditions. This was made graphically evident in an article published in '*The Daily Telegraph*' of 5th May 2002 entitled '*Indian Army Finds Inflatable Answer to Low Morale*', By Mark Chipperfield in New Delhi. According to this, among all the other hardships suffered by the Indian soldiers in Kashmir, there is now an alarming increase in cases of impotence. It is so widespread that the army is now resorting to large scale use of penal implants to relieve the distress of its fighting men.

The fact that the Indian Army, supported by the air force, failed to dislodge five hundred or so lightly armed mujahids from Kargil, even after four months of desperate attempts, is a clear indication of the degradation of its fighting capabilities. It does not take a genius to work out that at this rate, even if the Indian Government does not, the Indian Army will be pressing for a political settlement of the dispute. It appears that the BJP Government is trying to get the best possible deal by calling upon the West to lean on the generals in Pakistan. Since nothing comes free in this materialistic world, even the Indians must be aware that the West will extract a price for any such favour.

It is a paradoxical situation for the West. On the one hand, it would not like to see Muslim Kashmiris succeed in their struggle, especially, at this point in time. It will set the wrong example and act as a source of inspiration and encouragement for the oppressed Muslims in other parts of the world. At the same time, the West would like to avail of the opportunity and oblige India, without any cost to itself, at the expense of Pakistan. However, by helping to resolve the Kashmir issue, even if it is in India's favour, it would run the risk of losing the leverage it presently enjoys in the area provided by the continuing dispute between the two countries. As things stand at the moment, both India and Pakistan vie with each other, 'gyrating their hips furiously,' in the words of the Indian writer Arundhati Roy, to win favour with the West.

The choice for Pakistan is more clear. Giving in to pressure, from any source, would only provide hope and succour to the Indians and encourage them to prolong the agony in Kashmir for longer than may be they would otherwise. Ultimately, Pakistan has to negotiate with the Indians but it should be done from a position of strength when the time is right. It is infinitely better to wait rather than rush in prematurely and suffer the same sorry fate that has befallen Yasser Arafat. Pakistan has survived without Kashmir for more than half a century and it can happily do so for much longer. Waiting for the right time can make a world of difference in the kind of settlement one is able to achieve. It is important that any negotiations with the Indians, no matter how arduous and trying, be carried out directly without the involvement of any so-called honest brokers. When the choice is between India and Pakistan there will be no such animal readily available.

There is no logical basis for the assumption that relations between India and Pakistan will be any better after the Kashmir issue has been settled. There are a whole host of critical issues that would still remain to vitiate the climate. Uppermost among these is India's political need to keep the bogey of Muslim Pakistan alive to maintain her internal cohesion and rally the myriad diverse elements that constitute India. Without the existence of a manifest external threat there is every possibility of history taking its course and the country breaking apart. This has become particularly relevant since the emergence of the virulent fundamentalist Hindu nationalism that rends the fabric of her body politic. Peace in Kashmir and a settlement with Pakistan carry the inherent risk of depriving it of much of its raison d'etre.

Chauvinist Hinduism is not alone in its need to keep the pot of India-Pakistan hostility boiling. The West too has a vested interest for more reasons than can be included here. As stated earlier, amity between the two nations will take away much of the justification for western influence and interference in the area. It is unthinkable that any western adventure in Afghanistan would have been possible if the two countries had not been at such loggerheads with each other. It costs the West virtually nothing to play one country against the other to get what they want. Most of the time, all they have to do is to make appropriate noises that the Indians like to hear in India and then do the same in Pakistan to keep both of them licking at their boots. Since the West has greater interest in India at the moment, as a prospective proxy in its conflict against the Muslims and China, it finds it convenient to keep her happy by leaning more against Pakistan.

It is to be hoped that, sooner or later, saner heads will prevail and India will realize that with 130 million Muslims in the country it is not exactly wise for her to be an over-enthusiastic member of the western league at this point in time. The belligerent stance towards Pakistan may be politically expedient for parties like BJP in the short term but it does far more harm to the country's interest as a whole. The issues that are there must be resolved directly and peacefully, through dialogue, no matter what and how long it takes.

Any talk and threats of war with Pakistan are unadulterated madness and downright dangerous given the potential for destruction that exists with both the countries. Equally forlorn is the hope that the West can, somehow, be enticed or manipulated into doing India's dirty work vis-à-vis Pakistan for her. The circumstances are entirely different and she does not possess the same leverage as Israel to try and emulate the latter.

The issue of Kashmir has been like a running sore in the relations between the two countries. It has to be resolved before any stable relations can be established. Unless and until a solution acceptable to the people of Kashmir is found, they will keep protesting. This will, inevitably, become the source of constant mutual suspicions and irritation and peace and amity between the two countries will remain hostage to it.

The indiscriminate use of violence and undue force, to suppress the Kashmiris in the past twelve years, has been a great mistake. The atrocities by the Indian security forces have been so widespread and excessive that these will not be forgotten or forgiven, perhaps, forever. If there was ever any hope of the Kashmiris becoming a part of India willingly, it has been dashed permanently by the senseless campaign. To persist in the disastrous policy can only cause more misery, suffering and discontent.

Getting the West to put pressure on Pakistan has little meaning. Neither Pakistan nor any one else can persuade the Kashmiris, after all that they have suffered, to give up their struggle and become loyal subjects of India. The situation is irretrievable and needs to be accepted as such and faced realistically, more for the sake of India's future than anything else. In the long run, it will be infinitely better for her to allow the Kashmiris to exercise their free will in a UN supervised referendum than to look for some unsatisfactory settlement with unrepresentative elements within the community or with Pakistan alone, to the exclusion of the Kashmiris as a whole. The time is running out for India. The sooner she comes to terms with this reality better it will be for all concerned.

THE BALKANS

The history of the Balkan states is replete with myths. The telling and re-telling of these, particularly in the western media in recent times, has only helped to muddy the real issues almost beyond recognition. Briefly, the area had been under Serbian rule when the Turks invaded it towards the end of the fourteenth century. Many colourful stories have been written since then, embellished a little more each time, about the heroic defeat suffered by the Serbs at the battle of Kosovo Polje (Field of the Blackbirds) in 1389 in the defence of Christianity.

The truth is that it was fought for little more than imperial expansion and acquisitive purposes. It was neither the beginning nor the end of some epic struggle between Christianity and Islam nor was there any question of Serb nationalism involved. This should be clear from the fact that ethnic Serbs formed a substantial part of the Turkish army. There is no credible proof or record of the Turks engaging in any butchery or forced religious conversions after the battle. As with the other parts of East Europe, they left the Serbs to be ruled over by their Christian masters after the battle, requiring only that they should henceforward pay tribute to the Sultan in Turkey.

More or less this is how matters remained until the dying days of the Turkish Empire. The European powers that had been waiting in the wings instigated a revolt among the Serbs in 1875. When that failed, Russia invaded Turkey forcing the Sultan to withdraw from the region. Under the treaty signed at San Stefano in 1877 that was modified a year later, the area was taken away from Turkey and split into a number of principalities. These included Serbia, Bosnia-Herzgovina, Macedonia, Croatia, Slovenia, Kosovo, Montenegro and Macedonia that were eventually banded together into a decentralized confederation to be called Yugoslavia.

The Soviet forces liberated the Balkans, including Yugoslavia, from the German rule in 1944. The British Prime Minister, Winston Churchill, felt that he could use the Balkans as a trading device in his attempts to secure a better working relationship with the Soviet leader, Josef Stalin. At Churchill's suggestion, it was agreed that the U.S.S.R. would have dominant influence in Romania and Bulgaria while the West would enjoy the same advantage in Greece. Yugoslavia and Hungary were to be shared equally, and Albania was not even mentioned. These were the conditions under which the charismatic resistance leader Josip Broz, popularly known as Marshal Tito, kept Yugoslavia together until his death in 1980.

After Tito's death Serbian nationalism started to reassert itself in a particularly vicious form. In 1986 the Serbian Academy of Sciences released a document whose paranoid and bellicose text talked of 'historic injustices' done to the peace-loving Serbs by the other groups such as the Croats, Slovenes, Montenegrans, etc. and accusing them of victimization and threatening genocide. Milosevic, a particularly unscrupulous leader of Serbia's Communist Party, taking advantage of the increasing uncertainty and unrest, gained power in Belgrade in 1989 with the slogan, *'To hell with Yugoslavia ---- we'll make a Greater Serbia'*. He then unleashed a massive propaganda campaign that portrayed the Serbs as innocent victims of foul play by their villainous neighbours.

One of his first acts was to disband the parliament in the autonomous region of Kosovo that was ninety per cent

Muslim and replace it with an apartheid style government run by Christian Serbs who constituted less than eight per cent of its population. No Muslim was allowed to hold any government office or job, which meant the end of employment for them since there were no private jobs as such under the communist system. The use of Albanian, the language of Muslim Kosovars, was banned in schools, offices and universities. The net effect was that ninety per cent of the population in Kosovo could not hold any job or attend any public school or university simply because they were not Christian but Muslim Slavs. Any mention of these excesses was scrupulously excluded from the western media until the situation boiled over in March 1998 and could no longer be kept under wraps.

To a lesser degree, Muslims living in the West are generally having to face similar problems and grappling with the same cultural issues that Jews did before them: integration or isolation, tradition or reform, intermarriage or intra-marriage. They, like Jews, often dress differently and cannot eat some of the food of the host countries. Like the Jews of the past, they are now seen as parasites on the social body, burdened with a uniform and unreformable law, contributing little, scheming in ghettoes, and obscurely indifferent to personal hygiene.

Cartoons of Arabs seem little different to the caricatures of Jews in German newspapers of the Nazi period. In the 1930s, such images ensured that few found the courage to speak out about the possible consequences of such a demonisation, just as few today are really thinking about the anti-Muslim rhetoric of the extreme-right parties across Europe and the United States. In fact, the calls for placing restrictions on the civil rights and liberties of Muslims in the West are met with widespread approval and acceptance. Muslims in general and Arabs especially, have become the new 'other' but in the Balkans the local Muslims, in addition to religious prejudice, are also burdened by the legacy of mostly fanciful history.

The declaration of independence by Roman Catholic Slovenia signalled the break-up of Yugoslavia in the summer of 1991. This was followed shortly afterwards by a similar declaration by the other Catholic Republic of Croatia. Under pressure from Germany, the European Union and USA, both these republics were admitted as members of the United Nations. Encouraged by this Bosnia and Macedonia followed suit. The event passed without any trouble in Slovenia and Macedonia and the fighting that broke out in Croatia was soon brought under control.

It was a different story in predominantly Muslim Bosnia. In April 1992, Serbian Army under General Ratko Mladic occupied northern Bosnia while Radovan Karadzic set himself up as the president of the Serb republic in Pale. One of their first acts was to jam satellite television transmissions and impose censorship on newspapers. Muslim Serbs were removed from all positions of authority in the administration and the military and replaced with Orthodox Christian Serbs.

Serb militias, backed by the army, commenced a systematic campaign to exterminate the unarmed and unprotected Muslim population in the villages first. In a typical operation the Serb Army would surround a village or town and bombard it with artillery. The militia would then move in shooting and killing any one they came across. Any survivors that were left alive were herded into one or more houses and hand grenades thrown in among them. Those that managed to escape were either rounded up and shot or herded into Nazi style concentration camps to be molested, tortured and starved to death. The dead were bulldozed into mass graves and their farms and houses taken over by the Serbs. The same grisly and inhuman scenes were enacted in towns and villages that numbered in the thousands.

Photographs taken by the United States U2 spy planes have revealed the existence of mass graves in close to 3,000 Bosnian villages. Almost all mosques, some more than five hundred years old, were razed to the ground and the land turned into parking lots. Those left standing were converted into prisons, slaughterhouses and morgues.

It is estimated that in the region of three hundred thousand Muslim men, women and children were murdered and two and a half million forced to flee their homes. The neighbouring European countries, including Germany, Austria, Hungary, Slovenia and Croatia, effectively closed their borders, in blatant violation of the 1948 Universal Declaration of Human Rights, obliging the refugees to seek shelter in Muslim controlled areas within Bosnia that were shrinking by the day as the Serb army advanced ('*A Witness to Genocide*', by Roy Gutman, Macmillan Publishing Company, New York, P. 104). It was the second incidence of genocide, based purely on religious intolerance and hatred in Christian Europe, the cradle of the much touted 'superior' culture and civilization, within a short period of fifty years. In each case, the rest of the western powers had watched and allowed the extermination of innocents to proceed without attempting any intervention.

It is too distressing to narrate all the details of the barbarism and depravity inflicted upon the Muslim population of Bosnia. Any one interested in these may like to refer to Pulitzer Prize-winning author Roy Gutman's '*A Witness to Genocide*'. Here only one or two incidents, typical of the thousands of such acts committed all over Bosnia in the years from 1992 to 1995, are reproduced.

'*According to the victims, preparations for the mass rape began early in the morning of June 17* (1992) *when Serb soldiers in army uniforms and masks piled out of their minivans and rounded up the Muslims of Brezovo Polje for ethnic cleansing. They loaded the able-bodied men from 18 to 60 onto buses and sent them for interrogation to Luka, a notorious Serb-run detention camp in nearby Brcko where nine in 10 prisoners were slaughtered, according to a survivor interviewed by* 'Newsday'.

'*Then they packed about 1,000 women, children and old people into eight buses, drove them round the countryside for two days and held them under armed guard for four terrifying nights without food or water in a parking lot in the nearby town of Ban Brdo, the victim said. Serb soldiers returning from the front invaded the buses every night and led off women and girls to an unknown location at knife point, recalled Senada, 17. "They threw them out in the morning, and their clothes were torn, and they were covered in blood", she said.*

'*Finally the group arrived in Caparde, where about 50 Serb irregulars, bearded followers of a warlord named Zelko Arkan, robbed the mothers and forcibly separated them from their daughters. The mothers were taken by bus and deposited in a war zone. Meanwhile, in the Osnovo furniture house in Caparde, where the daughters were held, the men, mostly with long beards in the style of the World War II Serbian royalist force known as Chetniks, selected what one the rapists said were the 40 prettiest young women of Brezovo Polje and raped them in groups of ten*' (p. 70). According to the European Union's investigations the total number of Muslim women subjected to mass rape in Bosnia exceeds twenty thousand. This does not include the women who were murdered after being raped which was the norm.

'-------------- *In Novo Selo, a village near Zvornik, Serb troops rounded up 150 women, children and old people, and forced them at gunpoint into the local mosque. In front of the captives they challenged the local community leader, Imam Memic Suljo, to desecrate the mosque, Akim said, quoting eyewitness accounts. They told him to make the sign of the cross, eat pork and finally to have sexual intercourse with a teenage girl. Asic said that Suljo refused all these demands and was beaten and cut with knives. His fate is unknown.*

'*In Bratunac, about 30 miles south, Imam Mustafa Mojkanovic was tortured before thousands of Muslim women, children and old people at the towns soccer stadium, according to a sworn account by witnesses quoted by the Imam of Tuzla, Efardi Espahic. Serb guards also ordered the cleric to cross himself, Espahic said. When he refused, "they beat him. They stuffed his mouth with sawdust, poured beer in his mouth and then slit his throat," Espahic told 'Newsday'* (p. 80).

All of the thousands of such outrages were in the full knowledge of not only the western governments and the United Nations but also humanitarian organisations like the Red Cross and Amnesty International. None of them made any attempt to protest let aside intervene. The entire western news media blacked out coverage of the genocide pretending as if nothing was happening. The systematic mass murders went unreported for four months before reporters from Britain's Channel Four TV and '*The Guardian*' stumbled across the concentration camps set up by the Bosnian Serbs at Omarska and Trnopolje and decided to break the news.

There was no limit to perfidy and deceit. The US State Department had been receiving volumes of detailed information from dozens of sources but, on Secretary of State Lawrence Eagleburger's orders, told the press that 'it had no information to confirm the existence of concentration camps or the atrocities associated with them'. Eagleburger also dispatched the Assistant Secretary of State to Capitol Hill on 4th August 1992 to tell the Senate Foreign Relations Committee that 'there was no information of any kind to confirm the existence of the camps or the atrocities' (*'Bosnia; The Secret War'*, by Ed Vulliamy in *'The Guardian'*---- there are a total of twelve articles that cover the entire conflict). Disgusted with the cover-up and the refusal to save innocent lives, a number of honourable men, like Marshall Harris at the US State Department, resigned in protest but it made little difference.

Samuel Huntington viewed the situation in a different and more revealing light in his *'Clash of Civilisations'*. When, after more than two years of killing, the US could not put off the intervention any longer, he felt it was a mistake, *'American idealism, moralism, humanitarian instincts, naiveté and ignorance concerning the Balkans thus led* [the U.S.] *to be pro-Bosnian and anti-Serb.* ----- ------ *By refusing to recognize the war for what it was, the American government alienated its allies, prolonged the fighting, and helped to create in the Balkans a Muslim state heavily influenced by Iran.* --------- *The Spanish Civil War was a prelude to World War II. The Bosnian War is one more bloody episode in an ongoing clash of civilizations'.* In other words, the American government realising the 'civilizational demands', as perceived by him, should have allowed the genocide to take its course. It might well have. The only trouble was that the Serbs had ceased to make headway and were by then beginning to suffer reverses.

Eagleburger was by no means alone in refusing to acknowledge what was happening in Bosnia. As early as 15th May, the Bosnian ambassador to the UN Mohammed

Sacirby informed the Secretary General Boutros Boutros Ghali but said 'he was not taken seriously'. Louis Gentile, the head of UNHCR's Banja Luka office agonized that what the world had allowed to happen in Bosnia could never be forgiven. According to Marrack Goulding, head of the UN peace-keeping operations department, the UN troops in Bosnia (UNPROFOR) were only there 'to protect humanitarian activities' ---- in a war being waged by Bosnian Muslims wielding a few hunting rifles against the Serb army supported by tanks, heavy artillery and aircraft.

As David Rieff puts it in his book '*Slaughterhouse --- Bosnia and the Failure of the West*' (Simon Schuster, New York, pp. 139, 140). ' ------ *If all the United Nations intended to do was to bring in food and medicine, didn't this just amount to keeping people alive longer so the Serbs would have more chances to kill them? Wasn't it incongruous that UN soldiers and UNHCR convoy drivers risked and sometimes lost their lives to bring in food to isolated areas, but steadfastly refused to silence the guns that were causing the emergency? It seemed unimaginable that the United Nations would be content to go on in this way indefinitely.*' Fred Cuny, a veteran UN aid worker from Texas quipped at the time, '*If the UN had been around in 1939, we'd all be speaking German.*' After this, for any Muslim to repose his faith in the UN, amounts to nothing more than self-delusion.

Yet it was the same UN that a few months earlier had mustered half a million strong army to vacate Iraqi aggression against Kuwait that involved no genocide or any other such crimes against humanity, killing hundreds of thousands of Iraqis in the process. It is twelve years since Kuwait was liberated but the bombing of Iraq continues and UN sanctions against her remain in place while all sanctions against Serbia were lifted and western aid started to pour in the day she signed the Dayton peace accord. The only visible difference between the two situations is that in one case the aggressor was a Muslim Arab state and in the other a European Christian one. It is sad but true that the United Nations no longer stands for the ideals that led to its formation but is becoming more and more an instrument for the establishment of a new form of colonialism in the service of one or two states.

The main reason for evasion and cover up in Bosnia was that the United Nations charter calls for intervention, by force if necessary, in cases involving genocide. For domestic political considerations none of the western nations was keen to intervene against fellow Christians who were engaged in clearing out Europe of the Muslims. At first, it was attempted to present the affair as a military conflict. When that appeared less and less plausible the genocide was inventively labelled as 'ethnic cleansing' to forestall any calls for international action under the UN charter. US Secretary of State, Lawrence Eagleburger, heaved and squirmed in his chair before TV cameras in the Charlie Rose Show more than once refusing to accept that it was either genocide or a religious war. Britain and France joined hands in calling it a 'humanitarian crisis' as if it was the result of an earthquake and then proceeded to direct more than sixty per cent of the aid to the Serbs who were perpetrating the atrocities. While Muslim masses every where fretted and worried, barring Turkey, their governments took little action.

When procrastination and reluctance to save the victims dragged into months and then years it became clear that they were only waiting for the Serbs to complete their grisly work and then declare it a fait accompli. At one stage, to divert domestic and world attention away from Bosnia, President Bush all of a sudden decided that Somalia posed a more urgent problem and marched UN troops into the country but then pulled them out in a hurry when a few US marines got killed and others had to be rescued by a contingent of the Pakistan army. Since then Somalia has dropped from the western radar screens, as suddenly as it had appeared, never to be heard of again.

In all this time the killings went on unhindered in Bosnia under the noses of UN troops. Serbs were by no means alone in this. The Croats were in it as well, along with volunteers from other Christian lands. There was a bizarre case in which the Serbs apprehended a Canadian UN soldier, tied him to a pole and threatened to kill him. The man doing the threatening happened to be one of these volunteers also from Canada.

While still on Canada, the man in charge of the UN military contingent in Bosnia and now the deputy leader of the Progressive Conservative Party, Major General Lewis Mackenzie, unabashedly sympathized and sided with the Serbs going so far as to suggest that the Bosnian Government was shelling its own people in order to malign the Serbs (see his book *'Peacekeeper'*, p. 293). On investigation it was found that this was a fabrication and Mackenzie had been in Belgrade and nowhere near the scene when the incident happened. On return from Bosnia, at his first press conference, he declared it a mistake for NATO to have threatened intervention and claimed if things had been allowed to continue as they were for another six months the problem would have resolved itself. This part of the interview was excised from all the subsequent broadcasts in Canada (personal information). Grateful Serbs in the United States quoted him in newspaper advertisements and arranged a generously funded speaking tour for him.

This is what Daniel Kofman, who teaches political philosophy at Oxford, had to say on the subject in *'The Montreal*

Gazette', '*Given what the Canadian officials and officers were stating in public, one shudders to imagine how they were privately instructing their troops. Would it be any wonder if soldiers, "peacekeeping" during a genocide that their commanders were denying, lacked a serious moral commitment?*' These fears were found to be true not only for Canada but also for Britain, France and the United States on numerous occasions. The attitude of other UN Commanders in Bosnia like Britain's General Michael Rose, France's Briquemont and US' Wesley Clark was not much different to that of Lewis Mackenzie.

The United Nations had established a number of so called 'safe havens' to protect refugees from the marauding Serbs. The one at Srebrenica was run by the Dutch troops. When the Serbs advanced on it, amid cries of protest, two US fighter planes were sent to deter the Serbs. They reported inability to find any targets and returned to base but the US Secretary of Defence William Perry said, '*That mission was satisfactorily carried out*'. Indeed, a few hours later the Dutch disarmed all the Muslims and handed over the 'safe haven', without offering any resistance, to the Serbs. In the butchery that followed eight thousand Muslim men and boys, who had entrusted their lives to the United Nations, were separated from their families by the Christian Serbs, systematically slaughtered and buried in mass graves around Screbrenica. Abdication of responsibility by the UN of this kind was only evident where Muslim lives were involved. When the Croat Army threatened to over-run a contingent of the Serb Army at Medak, the UN did order its Canadian troops to intervene and save the Serbs. The operation was kept out of public eye until ferreted out by a Canadian reporter many years later.

As with the Israelis, when they entered UN-run refugee camps in Lebanon along with their Christian Phalangist allies and murdered thousands of Palestinians, no serious effort has been made to find the perpetrators of crimes against humanity in Bosnia and bring them to justice. Writing in '*The Washington Post*' of 21st April 2002 under the heading '*Bystanders to Mass Murder*', Samantha Power describes the attitude in Washington:

'*In July 1995 the safe area* (Srebrenica) *became the most dangerous spot on earth when Bosnian Serb Gen. Ratko Mladic strolled into town. After meeting little resistance from Dutch soldiers on the ground or NATO bombers overhead, Mladic presided over a 10-day killing spree, systematically executing every Muslim man and boy he could lay his hands on ---- more than 7,000 in all. ----------*

'*But on this side of the ocean, the move was greeted by silence ---- a silence that is in fact the trademark of American policy before, during and after genocide. Neither the United States nor any of the Security Council powers that ordered the creation of the safe areas and then abandoned Srebrenica's civilians in their hour of need have stepped forward to shoulder their portion of the blame for the massacre. ---------*

'*I spent several years investigating the Clinton administration's response to Srebrenica, analyzing an ad hoc assortment of declassified documents obtained through the Freedom of Information Act and conducting some 50 interviews with U.S. officials involved in shaping this country's Bosnia policy. Even this unofficial inquiry yielded startling evidence of extensive American knowledge of the peril to Srebrenica's Muslims:*

• *Senior Clinton administration officials knew the safe areas were likely to come under attack. Indeed, several expressed private hope that the Muslim territory would fall into Serb hands, because it would facilitate the partition of the country.*

• *Once Mladic seized Srebrenica on July 11, 1995, American policymakers were keenly aware that the men and boys were being separated from the women and children, that Dutch soldiers were barred from supervising the "evacuation," and that the Muslims' fate lay in the hands of Mladic, the local embodiment of "evil."*

'*U.S. officials received hysterical phone calls from leading members of the Bosnian government who pleaded with Washington to use NATO air power to save those in Mladic's custody. One July 13 classified cable related the "alarming news" that Serb forces were committing "all sorts" of atrocities. On July 17 the CIA's Bosnia Task Force wrote in its classified daily report that refugee reports of mass murder "provide details that appear credible." In a July 19 confidential memorandum, Assistant Secretary of State for Human Rights John Shattuck described "credible reports of summary executions and the kidnapping and rape of Bosnian women."*

'*Yet, despite this knowledge, neither President Clinton nor his top advisers made the fate of the men and boys an American priority. The president issued no public threats and ordered no contingency military planning. Spokesman Nick Burns told the Washington press corps that the United States was "not a decisive actor" in the debate over how to respond. The most powerful superpower in the history of mankind had influence only "on the margins," in Burns's words.*

'*Because more intimate knowledge of Mladic's designs would have been inconvenient, senior U.S. officials ordered neither a change in the flight pattern of American satellites snapping images overhead nor the reassignment of intelligence analysts. Toby Gati, assistant secretary of state for intelligence and research at that time, recalls: "We weren't analyzing these pictures in real times for atrocity; we were analyzing whether NATO pilots were vulnerable." Another official remembers, "Once the men were in Mladic's custody, we forgot about them because we knew we could no longer address their futures."*

'*Three precious weeks passed after the safe area's fall before a senior official ordered a sustained review of satellite images gathered the previous month to confirm rumors that Srebrenica's Muslims had indeed been murdered. By then virtually all of Mladic's captives were dead and (hastily) buried.*

'*After the massacre, neither the Clinton team nor Congress looked back. I have found no evidence that Clinton commissioned an internal after-action review of the U.S. response to Srebrenica. The Senate had individual members ---- Joseph Biden, Bob Dole, Joseph Lieberman, John McCain and others ---- who took principled stands throughout the Bosnian war, urging intervention. But Congress never summoned Clinton administration officials to Capitol Hill to publicly answer for being bystanders to mass murder.*

'*When the United Nations conducted its own Srebrenica inquiry in 1998, its investigators say, Clinton administration officials did not return their phone calls. The U.N. team was granted access only to a group of hand-picked junior and midlevel officials who revealed next to nothing. Dutch investigators complained that they met a similar stone wall in Washington.*'

By this time the Serbs were in possession of 72 per cent of Bosnian territory and the European leaders were insisting that since they had 'won the war' the Bosnian Muslims should accept whatever they were offered. In the forefront of this appeasement were mediators like US President Jimmy Carter, Britain's Lord David Owen (once described in the US Congress as 'a de facto proponent of Serb genocidal interests'), Foreign Secretary Douglas Hurd and Prime Minister John Major who reportedly once said that he will not accept the establishment of a Muslim state in Europe. One would like to believe that their motives were honourable and the bit of news in *'The Daily Mail'* of 8ᵗʰ April 1999 on page 15 about Douglas Hurd having *'received at least one million pounds from NatWest Markets, of which he was deputy chairman, for the one billion pounds contract he signed with Yugoslavia's Slobodan Milosevic* (an indicted war criminal) *in 1997'* -----, even if true, has no relevance to the case.

Whatever the case, beleaguered as they were, the Bosnians stuck to their guns. Soon they were getting some help from Muslim volunteers from different parts of the world. This kind of resistance was new to the Serbs and soon they were losing territory and on the run. Before it could get any worse for them the western powers stepped in and pushed through a peace settlement at Dayton that gave 49 per cent of Bosnia to the Serbs who constituted 30 per cent of its population. It was amazing how all the people, like Secretary of State Lawrence Eagleburger, who had crusaded so vigorously against any intervention so far, suddenly forgot the reasons and excuses they had been putting up and now turned in favour of intervention. These arguments had only been valid as long as the Serbs were winning. In a rare acknowledgement the US mediator, Richard Holbrooke, went on record to say that but for the help rendered by the 2,000 or so foreign volunteers the fate of Bosnia's Muslims was sealed.

Since then warrants of arrest have been issued against some of the perpetrators of genocide in the Balkans. Among the prominent names only Slobodan Milosevic has been apprehended and put on trial. The primary villains, Radovan Karadzic, president of the Bosnian Serb Government and his military chief Ratko Mladic cannot be found despite more than seven years of 'intensive' search and all the means and powers at the disposal of the United Nations, USA, the European Union and NATO. If some people can believe this then they must also believe that fairy tales are true as well. Significantly, no one in the West calls for 'bombing Serbia into the Stone Age' for not handing over these indicted criminals to the International War Crimes Tribunal in stark contrast to the shrill cries raised against Afghanistan which only asked to negotiate the surrender of Osama bin Laden. Again, there is truth in the words of George Orwell's pig in his *'Animal Farm'* when it proclaimed, 'Some animals are more equal than others' ----- at least in the eyes of the West.

Another equally disturbing aspect of the Balkan tragedy is that, with a few honourable exceptions, all one heard from the Christian church luminaries at the time was deafening silence. What we do know for certain is that Eastern Orthodox priests routinely blessed Serbian soldiers and paramilitaries before they went on shooting rampages to kill badly beaten and starving detainees of Serb concentration camps (BBC). If there were any cries of protest, condemnation and calls for action against the abomination by Reverend Jimmy Swaggert, Pat Robertson, Franklin Graham and other champions of Christian civilization these must have come in very faint whispers for most of us never heard them. Pope John Paul II, when he did speak, did so only to advise the twenty thousand or more Muslim women, who had become pregnant as a consequence of being gang-raped by the

Serbs and survived (most were killed), not to abort their pregnancies.

The concern was touching and one only wished that it had been extended to stopping the grotesque and brutal tragedy while it happened in the first place. The photo ops of John Major visiting a couple of wounded Bosnian children under treatment in a hospital on British TV, day after day, were just as hurtful knowing that he was a major obstacle to bringing equitable peace to the hapless nation and the saving of lives of thousands of other Muslim Bosnian children.

Worst of all was, perhaps, the indifference and inaction on the part of the Muslim states, barring a few like Turkey, Iran and Malaysia, to the plight of the Muslims in the Balkans. This was particularly galling considering that some of them had so readily agreed to sending large army contingents to join the war against Iraq but did so little to alleviate the suffering of fellow Muslims in Europe.

The tragedy of the Balkan Muslims is by no means over. Millions of refugees who had fled their homes to look for safety in other areas have returned to find their homes destroyed and jobs non-existent. Both the Red Cross and the Red Crescent organizations have reported that there is very little aid forthcoming from donor countries. The killing may have stopped but the humanitarian crisis resulting from the 'ethnic cleansing' continues to cast a dark shadow over the region.

The situation in Bosnia was not provoked by the United Nations but it could certainly have ended it much sooner than it did and saved hundreds of thousands of innocent lives. The killing need not have been allowed to go on and on. There was also a systematic attempt at misleading the world as to the full extent and nature of the tragedy involving not only by the western governments but also the Red Cross,

Amnesty International and various UN organizations like
UNHCR and UNPROFOR. In the words of David Rieff,
'----- *the UN was providing the world community with a
fig leaf both for the inability of some states, like the United
States, to muster the will to act, and for the failure of others,
like Britain and France, to come clean to their own publics
about their decision to allow the murder of Bosnia to
proceed*' ('*Slaghterhouse*', p. 192).

To that extent the UN was guilty of moral dereliction. If it
could act with such admirable zeal and alacrity to protect
the strategic interests of a few member states in the Persian
Gulf it should also have done more, in the name of humanity,
to save hapless Bosnian Muslims from genocide. The same
goes for all the permanent members of the UN Security
Council and the Secretary General, Boutros Boutros Ghali.
There is a valuable lesson in this for the Muslims, in places
like Palestine and Kashmir, in particular. It would be a folly
for them to pin their hopes on either the UN or the West to
help find an equitable solution to their problems. Burying
their heads in sand and pretending that the UN or any one
else will help to restore their rights will get them nowhere.
Ultimately, they will have to rely on their own united efforts
without which there can be no hope.

AFGHANISTAN

On Christmas Eve 1979 Soviet forces seized Kabul, gunned down the country's President Hafizullah Amin and installed their own man Babrak Karmal in his place. It took them less than a week to over-run the rest of the country. According to Moscow the action had been undertaken to 'liberate' Afghanistan from the control of its 'medieval feudal rulers' and 'Islamic extremism' and to clear the 'nests of terrorists and bandits'. They also vowed to liberate Afghan women from the oppressive veil, do away with all 'backward' Islamic customs and bring the country into the 'civilized' world of the twentieth century.

It proved a little harder than they had imagined. The Afghans did not take kindly to this intrusion and mounted armed resistance that lasted ten years. The Soviet Union brought in more and more troops, tanks and planes to suppress the Afghan struggle for freedom. In the process they committed the most brutal and barbaric atrocities, bombing entire villages out of existence and torturing and killing tens of thousands of young men in jails. By the time the 'civilizing' zeal of the Soviets had run its course ten years later, the entire land had been devastated, more than one million Afghan men, women and children lay dead and over five million had left the country to seek shelter in refugee camps across the border in Iran and Pakistan. This accounted for more than a quarter of the total population of the country.

Since the Soviets were enemies of the West at the time and the Afghans were fighting against them, sympathies in the West lay with the Afghan struggle for freedom.

What are called 'extremists', 'terrorists' and worse today were described as 'freedom fighters' then and welcomed as honoured guests in the White House and other such places. After all, by keeping the Soviet Union engaged in a ruinous and un-winnable war they were providing an extremely valuable service at very little cost to the West. When one listens to the epithets used to describe the same Afghan mujahids today in such virulent and hateful terms in the West, inevitably, one is reminded of George Orwell and his *'1984'*. Looking at the recent developments in the United States in particular, he appears to have come close to being a prophet of sorts.

Ultimately, unable to subdue the Afghan spirit and realizing the harm they were doing to themselves, the Soviets retreated, leaving behind a chaotic and devastated land strewn with over ten million land mines, unexploded cluster bombs and other munitions that continue to maim and kill Afghans till this day. There were over half a million children alone that had been left maimed by these munitions before George W. Bush decided to add his share to this number, following his merciless bombardment of the already devastated land in October and November 2001. First the Russians and now the new champions of western civilization have added their share to the millions of utterly poor and innocent people, killed and maimed as they claim, to civilize the Afghans and 'liberate' them from their 'medieval feudal rulers' and 'Islamic extremism' and to clear the 'nests of terrorists and bandits.' If this is civilization then God help the human race.

After the Soviets left, the country broke into absolute anarchy in the absence of any legitimate and acceptable central authority. Rapacious warlords, each with his own army, set up little domains in which they plundered and brutalized people at will. The international community watched with total disinterest leaving the country and its hapless people to their own devices. Even the United Nations cut food and other aid to the refugees to less than half because of continually decreasing donations from member states. As far as the western powers were concerned, the Afghans had served their purpose after being used as pawns in the struggle against the Soviet Union. There was no further interest left in Afghanistan for the time being.

It was left to impoverished Pakistan and Iran to take care of the millions of refugees as best as they could. Thousands of volunteers who had flocked to fight for the Afghan cause from other Muslim countries were left stranded when their governments refused to take them back for fear that they may bring back contagious germs of freedom with them. This was particularly true of the regimes in Egypt and some of the other Arab countries.

After six years of chaos Taliban emerged to impose order in the name of Islam. Most of them were unlettered, unsophisticated and unfamiliar with the ways of the rest of the world. In their own way they were sincere to Islam and meant well for Afghanistan. The Afghans understood and accepted them as such. More importantly, contrary to all the western propaganda, they were effective in bringing peace to an extremely troubled land at a fraction of the cost in human tragedy as compared to what the West has done. Considering the limitation of resources and the handicaps that they suffered it was by no means an insignificant achievement.

This is more than can be said for any regime before or since Taliban. Their rule may not have measured up to western standards but to say that they were evil is a gross distortion. It is true they resorted to methods that would be considered Draconian in other parts of the world but such are the laws of 'Pakhtoon-wali', the traditional code of tribal jurisprudence in the country. The code is not based on Islam, as is generally believed, but predates it by at least a thousand years if not more.

Shortly after Taliban came to power Osama bin Laden, a Saudi dissident millionaire who had been associated with the United States in fighting the Soviets but had now fallen foul of them, moved to Afghanistan in May 1996. Previously, he had lived in Sudan but was no longer welcome there because of his alleged anti-West activities. It was not long before Taliban also started to feel uneasy with his presence in the country. Under considerable pressure from Saudi Arabia, but always mindful of the strict Pakhtoon-wali tradition that does not permit the betrayal of a guest, they agreed to extradite him provided justification could be found for it in Islamic law. At this time Osama bin Laden and his rag-tag band of a few hundred Arab and other volunteers had little support even within Afghanistan and were not in any position to pose a serious threat to any one. To suggest that al-Quaida was developing nuclear and chemical weapons and preparing to launch satellites, as US Defence Secretary Donald Rumsfeld did, is plain ludicrous, putting it mildly.

There have been suggestions from many sources that bin Laden had contacts with CIA at least until mid-July 1998 when he was hospitalized in Dubai (Alexandra Richard in '*Le Figaro*', 31st October 2001). If any one is surprised at this, there is a lot more. The financial assets of Saudi bin Laden Group (SBG) are managed by the Carlyle Group in the United States, presided over by former deputy director of CIA and Secretary of Defence, Frank Carlucci. Among his associates are people such as one time Secretary of Treasury and State James Baker, former British Prime Minister John Major and President George Bush Senior.

The more you delve into this aspect the murkier it gets but it is something that does not concern us here.

In April 1998, a high level US delegation led by the Energy Secretary Bill Richardson visited Kabul for talks with Taliban on the construction of a pipeline to transport oil and gas from Central Asia through Afghanistan to the Arabian Sea. Apparently, they also discussed the extradition of bin Laden. The details of the meeting are extremely sketchy but a deal was made for UNOCAL to build the pipeline. According to Saudi chief of intelligence, Prince Turki, Taliban had agreed to set up a joint commission of Islamic scholars to formulate the justification for bin Laden's extradition (Allan Cullison and Andrew Higgins in '*The Globe and Mail*', 3rd August 2002).

The US embassies in Kenya and Tanzania were bombed in August 1998 for which al-Quaida was blamed. In retaliation, President Clinton fired eighty missiles into Afghanistan. Most of these hit schools, mosques and villages, some of these in Pakistan, killing a number of innocent civilians. It was an outrageous and stupid act that was to have highly significant far-reaching consequences. Many a cynic has suggested that Mr. Clinton had reacted in this way primarily to divert public attention away from the Monica Lewinsky sex scandal that was beginning to make life very uncomfortable for him. It is interesting that in one of the transcripts of his telephone conversations with Miss Lewinsky, produced during his trial, Clinton tells her of his conviction that Israelis were 'bugging' all the phones in the White House. What a curious statement coming as it does from the president of the most powerful country in the world!

The digression aside, Taliban were understandably furious and called off the deals about the pipeline as well as the extradition of bin Laden. They were not alone, the overwhelming majority of Muslims in all parts of the world, aggrieved by the callous highhandedness, sympathized with the Afghans. It also made Osama bin Laden a household name in the Muslim world in particular. Volunteers and donations poured in as he came to be looked upon as the lone symbol of Muslim resistance to the excesses of the West. It also dug his grave because he was now a prime target for the United States.

A year later Karl Inderforth, US Assistant Secretary of State, called on General Pervez Musharraf, who had installed himself as the supreme ruler of Pakistan, and asked him to intercede with Taliban. According to Inderforth, Musharraf said, *'He would go to Kandahar and stay until Mullah Omar agreed to curb Mr. Bin Laden even if this means taking a backpack and sleeping on the floor'* (*'The Globe and Mail'*, 3rd August 2002). We do not know what compulsions were involved but this was an extra-ordinary statement coming as did from the ruler of a third country against whom the United States was leaning extremely hard at the time and had imposed a whole host of very tough economic and other sanctions. Since the general never went to Kandahar, it would appear, Taliban were not convinced of where exactly he stood in this affair. Still feeling outraged by the uncalled for US attack they negotiated a new and much more profitable deal for the oil and gas pipeline with an Argentine firm in preference to UNOCAL.

This is when, according to some reports, the US decided to attack Afghanistan. Former Pakistan Foreign Secretary Niaz Naik confirmed in September 2001 that he witnessed officials of the U.S. government threatening Afghanistan with military strikes just before the terrorist attack against the U.S. The British newspaper *'The Guardian'* quotes Naik reporting on a conversation with U.S. representative

Tom Simons, former ambassador to Pakistan. Naik asked why an attack would be any more likely to be successful in killing bin Laden than it had been in August 1998, when Americans killed 20 Afghanis and many more Pakistanis but missed bin Laden? The ambassador replied, '*This time they were very sure. They had all the intelligence and would not miss him this time. It would be aerial action, maybe helicopter gunships, and not only overt, but from very close proximity to Afghanistan.*' According to Naik the Pakistanis passed this message to Taliban.

Before any of this could materialize, some airliners crashed into the World Trade Centre in New York and the Pentagon in Washington on 11th September 2001. There is no evidence to suggest this was orchestrated to provide the excuse for what followed but the manner in which the tragedy was managed in the initial stages has left a very large number of questions unanswered. Some of these will be raised here but any one interested in getting more details is advised to read the veteran Canadian journalist William Thomas' book '*All Fall Down: the Politics of Terror and Mass Persuasion*'. If the facts relating to the attacks on the World Trade Centre and the Pentagon are different from those put forward by the US authorities then the implications extend far beyond the actions that have thus far been contemplated and Muslims in general have far more to worry about.

According to the official story four airliners taking off from different locations were hijacked in mid-air by 19 young Arabs, some of whom had attended flying schools in the US, with the help of box-cutters with quarter-inch blades. Three of these were flown into the above buildings while the fourth broke up in mid-air and crashed in Pennsylvania with its parts falling in two widely separated locations. The names of the hijackers were announced within forty-eight hours, along with the identity of their ringleader and links to al-Quaida, although none of these appeared on the airline passenger lists. The indestructible 'black boxes' with all the flight data were claimed not to have survived the crashes and cockpit conversations during the hijacking could not be released.

From the very beginning, the incident was handled in a most unusual manner. To start with, it was a criminal act which required first and foremost, as in all such other cases, an enquiry to investigate all the circumstances related to it. It was only after such an enquiry that the criminals involved could be properly identified, their motives established and charges laid. All of these legal requirements were dispensed with and instead the Bush administration, on its own and without any known legal process, decided who the perpetrators were and also their motives and then got ready to wage war on Afghanistan. This is how Professor Noam Chomsky argues the situation:

'-------- *When IRA bombs were set off in London, there was no call to bomb West Belfast, or Boston, the source of much of the financial support for the IRA. Rather steps were taken to apprehend the criminals, and efforts were made to deal with what lay behind the resort to terror. When a federal building was blown up in Oklahoma City, there were calls for bombing the Middle East, and it probably would have happened if the source turned out to be there. When it was found to be domestic, with links to the ultra-right militias, there was no call to obliterate Montana and Idaho. Rather, there was a search for the perpetrator, who was found, brought to court, and sentenced, and there were efforts to understand the grievances that lie behind such crimes and to address the problems. Just about every crime, whether a robbery in the streets or colossal atrocities, has reasons, and commonly we find that some of them are serious and should be addressed.*

'There are proper and lawful ways to proceed in the case of crimes, whatever their scale. And there are precedents. A clear example is the one I just mentioned, one that should be entirely uncontroversial, because of the reaction of the highest international authorities' (Interview with *Hartford Courant*, 20th September 2001 reproduced in (*'9 – 11'*, Seven Stories Press, New York, p. 24).

President Bush asked that no public enquiry be carried out to establish the details of the tragedy. The commission of enquiry that was eventually instituted, after fourteen months of persistent lobbying by the families of the victims, has very restricted terms of reference which exclude any investigation into the actual circumstances of the event. Basically, all it has been asked to determine is if there had been a lapse in providing timely warning of the attacks and to suggest improvements in the existing intelligence set-up. It will not examine any details of the crime itself or those related to its alleged perpetrators. At the end, we are unlikely to be any wiser and all we shall have is the US administration's version of events surrounding the tragedy.

Similarly, President Bush and Vice President Cheney leaned on the House Majority Leader, Tom Daschle, to severely circumscribe the extent of any congressional investigation as evident from this CNN report aired on 29th January 2002, *'President Bush personally asked Senate Majority Leader Tom Daschle Tuesday to limit the congressional investigation into the events of September 11, congressional and White House sources told CNN.*

'The request was made at a private meeting with congressional leaders Tuesday morning. Sources said Bush initiated the conversation. He asked that only the House and Senate intelligence committees look into the potential breakdowns among federal agencies that could

have allowed the terrorist attacks to occur, rather than a broader inquiry that some lawmakers have proposed, the sources said.

'Tuesday's discussion followed a rare call to Daschle from Vice President Dick Cheney last Friday to make the same request.

'The vice president expressed the concern that a review of what happened on September 11 would take resources and personnel away from the effort in the war on terrorism," Daschle told reporters'.

The longer the delay in instituting a proper investigation the greater will be the chances of vital evidence getting lost or corrupted. It is not doing the image of USA or the administration any good. Bush and a number of influential members of his cabinet are particularly vulnerable to criticism because of their past connections to the oil business. If the US Congress can order a full enquiry to be carried out to determine the circumstances one day after the break up of space shuttle Columbia, it makes no sense to withhold such an investigation into the 11th September attacks indefinitely.

The issue is not lost on the American people by any means. The families of the victims of the attacks on the World Trade Centre have been consistently lobbying for a full and independent enquiry into the incident. Others have set up web sites to collect all relevant information concerning the event. A couple of these, that are fairly representative of similar other domains can be accessed at: *http://www.911review. org/* or at the site *http://www.freedomunderground.org/ memoryhole/pentagon.php#main.*

'The Independent' in London questioned how Bush could claim, in two separate public appearances, to have seen the

first plane hit the first tower long before any such TV footage was broadcast? The paper also asks why he continued sitting with elementary school students after the second tower was hit and he had been told, *'America is under attack.'* It is mysterious indeed when the standard procedure for such a situation is to whisk the president away to safety ----- unless he knew something others did not that morning. As *'The Independent'* asked, *'What television station was HE watching?'* The pictures that Bush claimed to have been watching were not released until thirteen hours after the time he said he saw them (*'9 / 11 – The Big Lie'*, by Thierry Meyssan, Carnot Publishing Ltd. London, 2002, p. 38).

In the days before the attacks, there was unusually heavy trading on the stock market in airline and related stocks using a market tactic called a 'put option' that essentially bets that a stock will decline in value. An unusually high number of put options were purchased in early September for the stocks of AMR Corp. and UAL Corp., the parents of American and United Airlines, each of which had two planes hijacked. There was an in-house (not independent) investigation ordered into the suspicious trading in 38 companies directly affected by the events of September 11 but it did not find any proof of wrongdoing.

In Germany, a former minister of technology, Andreas von Buelow, made headlines when in an interview he dismissed the U.S. government's explanation that Osama bin Laden's al-Quaida network is responsible for the attacks. His own explanation implicated the White House. *'I wonder why many questions are not asked,'* von Buelow said. *'For 60 decisive minutes, the military and intelligence agencies let the fighter planes stay on the ground; 48 hours later, however, the FBI presented a list of suicide attackers. Within 10 days, it emerged that seven of them were still alive.'* Doubts continue to persist. In *'The Observer'*, London of

27th October 2002 celebrated American author Gore Vidal in an article entitled '*The Enemy Within*' argues that 'Bush junta' used the terrorist attacks as a pretext to enact a pre-existing agenda to invade Afghanistan and crack down on civil liberties at home.

When questioned as to how the details had been established so expeditiously it was explained that the passport belonging to one of the hijackers had flown out of the aircraft window at the time of the crash and was found in a nearby street! Why would a man on a suicide mission be carrying a passport in his pocket on an internal flight? How does a passport survive a crash that destroyed the indestructible 'black boxes' and melted huge steel girders that supported the World Trade Centre structure?

It is impossible to understand that hundreds of passengers and crew, who would have surely realised at some point that they were facing certain death, did not attempt to overpower a few men armed with nothing better than almost harmless box cutters and regain control of the aircraft.

Details about who was on the flights when they took off and what happened on board were tightly held by airlines, airport and security officials. All of them said that the FBI had asked them not to divulge details. In Washington, FBI took away films from the two security cameras that would have recorded the occurrence, one on the highway and the other at a gas station next to the Pentagon, within minutes of the strike.

There were also reports that prior intelligence warnings of impending attacks were ignored. The head of the World Trade Centre arson investigation is said to have reported the presence of 'explosive devices' in the buildings.

Why did the plane that crashed in Pennsylvania break up in two in mid-air before hitting the ground with its wreckage scattered in two widely separated areas?

The damage to the outer Pentagon face where the Boeing 757–200 allegedly hit is only 19 meters wide whereas the aircraft's wingspan is twice as much. No sizeable aircraft parts, not even the huge engines, could be found at the site of the crash. It has never happened like this in any of the other cases where airliners have crashed into buildings. From the pictures the damage looks suspiciously similar to a Tomahawk missile hit. This is consistent with the accounts of a number of individuals present near the scene at the time.

The air traffic controllers on duty are trained and required to instantly query the slightest discrepancy in assigned altitude or heading. It is something that could not have been missed by four different controllers for better part of an hour. Written procedures specify notification of the North American Air Defense command that keeps armed fighters at instant readiness to intercept any unidentified or suspicious air contacts. What actions were taken at NORAD when four big 'bogies' in different locations made drastic departures from flight plans and airways as rigidly regulated as embedded tracks in the sky?

Then there was the anthrax scare that was talked of no more after it was revealed that the strain found in the 'letter bombs' could only have come from the government laboratories in USA.

There is also the bizarre case of the so called Israeli 'art students'. In a four-part series on Fox's 'Special Report With Brit Hume' that aired 11–14 December 2001, correspondent Carl Cameron reported that federal agents were investigating the 'art student' phenomenon as a possible arm of Israeli espionage operations tracking al-Quaida operatives in the United States. One investigator told Cameron that *'evidence linking these Israelis to 9/11 is classified. I cannot tell you about evidence that has been gathered. It's classified information.'*

According to Cameron, some 60 Israeli nationals had been detained in the anti-terrorism sweeps in the weeks after the attacks on 11th September and at least 140 Israelis, identified as 'art students', had been detained or arrested earlier. *'Some of the detainees failed polygraph questions related to their alleged surveillance activities against and in the United States.'* A number of them had been on active military duty. Cameron noted, however, that there was *'no indication that the Israelis were involved in the 9/11 attacks'*.

There is more. As the World Trade Centre burned and crumpled, five men were seen dancing and celebrating on the banks of Hudson River in New Jersey. A fearful housewife, who asked not to be identified except as 'Maria', reported it to the police, *'They seemed to be taking a movie. They were like happy, you know ----- they didn't look shocked to me. I thought it was strange.'* Police Chief John Schmidig said: *'We got an alert to be on the lookout for a white Chevrolet van with New Jersey registration and writing on the side. Three individuals were seen celebrating in Liberty State Park after the impact. They said three people were jumping up and down.'*

The men were soon apprehended and identified as Israeli nationals working for a New York company called 'Urban Moving'. Vince Cannistraro, former chief of operations for counter-terrorism with the CIA, says the red flag went up among investigators when it was discovered that some of the Israelis' names were found in a search of the national intelligence database. Cannistraro says many in the US intelligence community believed that some of the Israelis were working for Mossad and there was speculation over whether Urban Moving had been *'set up or exploited for the purpose of launching an intelligence operation against radical Islamists'*.

The men remained in the custody of FBI for two and a half months. Little is known of the information that might have been obtained from them. All of them were released and allowed to proceed to Israel at the end of November 2001. Whatever the details, the question that comes upper most to mind is how did these men come to document the event unless they knew beforehand that it was going to happen?

Tied in with all this is the confusion over the number of Israelis killed at the World Trade centre. The Jerusalem Post reported on 12th September 2001 that *'the Foreign Ministry in Jerusalem had so far received the names of 4,000 Israelis believed to have been in the areas of the WTC and the Pentagon at the time of the attack ---------- ---------.'* In his address to the Congress, Bush specifically mentioned that 130 Israelis had died in the attack.

The story in the New York Times of 22nd December 2001 reads in part, '------ *But interviews with many consulate officials Friday suggested that the lists of people they were collecting varied widely in their usefulness. For example, the city had somehow received reports of many Israelis missing at the site and President Bush in his address to the country on Thursday mentioned that about 130 Israelis had died in the attacks.*

'But Friday, Alon Pinkas, Israel's consul general here said that lists of the missing included reports from many people who had called in because, for instance, relatives from New York had not returned their phone calls from Israel. There were only three Israelis who had been confirmed as dead:

two on the planes and another who had been visiting the towers on business and who was identified and buried.' Later, this too proved to be incorrect reducing Israeli casualties at WTC to zero.

There were reports indicating that Israeli citizens working in the vicinity of WTC had received prior warnings to keep away from the site. A news item by Brian McWilliams under the heading, *'Instant Messages to Israel Warn of Immediate Attack'* in the *Newsbytes* (messaging service of the Washington Post) dated 27th September 2001 read, *'Officials at instant-messaging service Odigo confirmed today that two employees received text messages warning of an attack on the World Trade Centre two hours before the terrorists crashed planes into the New York land marks'.* This was also reproduced in the *Ha'aretz* in Jerusalem on 29th September. These are all issues that need thorough and public investigation. Unless and until this is done, doubts will remain and we shall never learn the whole truth of exactly what happened on that infamous day.

One possible explanation that could satisfy most of these questions is given by Thierry Meyssan in his book *'9 / 11 – The Big Lie'* (p. 34). *'The professional pilots we talked to confirmed that few amongst themselves could envisage performing such an operation and completely ruled it out in the case of amateur pilots. There is, however, one infallible method of achieving this result: the use of radio beacons. -------- It was not necessary in fact to have any hijackers onboard at all, as there was no taking of hostages: by hacking into the planes' computers before take-off, it would have been possible to take over the aircraft in flight, thanks to the Global Hawk technology perfected by the Department of Defense. The Boeings would have been under remote control, like a drone --- a plane without a pilot.'*

When interviewed by CNN on 15th September 2001 Egypt's President Hosni Mubarak expressed very similar reservations '---------- *something like this done in the United States is not an easy thing for some pilots training in Florida, so many pilots go and train just to fly and have a license, that means you are capable to do such terrorist action? I am speaking as a former pilot. I know that very well, I flew very heavy planes, I flew fighters, I know that very well, this is not an easy thing, so I think we should not jump to conclusions for now*' ('*9 / 11 – The Big Lie,*' p. 26).

It is curious that in all of the media coverage of the episode in the United States in particular hardly any aviation experts were called upon to give their opinions on the problems associated with totally inexperienced amateur pilots handling very large aircraft in the unfamiliar and unusual circumstances that were involved in navigating, locating the targets, identifying and then homing on to them, without faltering and with such unerring accuracy. It appears all but an impossible proposition unless manual controls had been disabled and the aircraft were under some form of autonomous external guidance.

All such doubts could easily have been set at rest by ordering an immediate public enquiry into the incident and basing any future actions on its findings. This is not how the Bush administration was thinking. On their own they decided that it was the work of 'Islamic' terrorists working on orders from Osama bin Laden. At times the situation was quite bizarre and full of confusion. On 20th September 2001, FBI expressed doubts about the identity of some of the hijackers. On the same day Bush said, '*We know exactly who these people are and which governments are supporting them.*'

It is a fact that there is no credible evidence of bin Laden claiming responsibility for the attacks on 11th September

2001 nor did he issue any demands. His alleged operatives, most unprofessionally, used their own Muslim names and left a clear trail for the FBI to follow. Their leader, the pilot of Flight 11 (north tower), even left his car at the Boston Airport in which the FBI found a suicide note and a copy of the Koran. There was a second document in his luggage that did not make it to Flight 11. The same note was carried by one of the hijackers on Flight 93 and it survived the crash even though the airplane itself was totally destroyed along with the indestructible 'black boxes'. Why would people bent on committing suicide, take passports and luggage with them? What is the probability of not a single 'black box' surviving among all the four aircraft involved in the incident? Why did the hijackers resort to writing suicide notes when other Arabs have recorded messages on video tapes in similar circumstances? Lastly, why would Osama bin Laden, who had so little to gain and every thing lose, mastermind such a dastardly act?

When asked, the US Secretary of State, Colin Powell, promised to produce a white paper 'within one month' that will clearly prove that al-Quaida was responsible for the attacks. That was the last we have heard of the white paper. Instead, a garbled video tape of Osama bin Laden has been played on TV channels in Arabic all over the world that allegedly shows him claiming responsibility for the criminal acts. The Arabic speaking individuals who have listened to the tape are unable to make any sense out of it as the speech is garbled and quite unintelligible. In the absence of an independent, open and public investigation, it all boils down not to impartially and legally established facts but to allegations that the US administration claims are facts.

Given its past history, this is hardly a reliable yardstick. Before unleashing the war against Iraq in 1991, the Pentagon had claimed they had satellite photographs of 250,000 Iraqi troops and 1,500 tanks poised for attack along the Saudi border. This information was presented to the Saudis who then invited the US- led coalition to defend them against Iraqi aggression. What the western media never reported was that the Soviet Union satellites at that very time showed no Iraqi troops on the Saudi border. The photographic evidence claimed in its possession by the Pentagon was never made public.

Similarly, it is now well established that the alleged naval attack by the North Vietnamese boats on *USS Maddox* in August 1964 in the Gulf of Tonkin was a complete fabrication to justify the US going to war and carrying out horrendous bombing of that country. There is also documentary evidence to prove that the US, Britain and Holland deliberately provoked Japan into attacking Pearl Harbour in December 1941, by disrupting her oil supplies, to provide the excuse for the US' entry into the war. The US had prior knowledge of the attack but kept it secret from the Pacific Fleet for fear that any defensive preparations might cause the Japanese to abort the attack.

In an article headed '*The Algebra of Infinite Justice*' in '*The Guardian*' Arundhati Roy commented, '*In his September 20 address to the US Congress, President Bush called the enemies of America enemies of freedom. Americans are asking, "Why do they hate us?" He said, "They hate our freedoms our freedom of religion, our freedom of speech, our freedom to vote and assemble and disagree with each other." People are being asked to make two leaps of faith here. First, to assume that The Enemy is who the US government says it is, even though it has no substantial evidence to support that claim. And second, to assume that The Enemy's motives are what the US government says they are, and there's nothing to support that either.*'

All voices of caution and reason were drowned in the drumbeat for war and revenge. The media went into high gear of frenzy. A so-called liberal US TV commentator now working for Fox, Geraldo Rivera, announced, *'I'm feeling more patriotic than at any time in my life, itching for justice, or maybe just revenge. And this catharsis I've gone through has caused me to reassess what I do for a living.'*

It was revenge that Bush and his men seemed to be looking for. The unthinkable had happened; fortress America had been breached and Americans had been killed. Some one was going to pay for this audacity committed against the mightiest power on earth. Bush, for his political survival if for nothing else, needed to be seen to be wreaking vengeance worthy of the great power that had been violated. Instituting an enquiry to establish the true nature of the crime and identity of its perpetrators would take too long and possibly not fit the bill in the end. It would be seen as too timid a response. There was an immediate need to identify the culprits and strike them with overwhelming military power. If the culprits were already dead or could not be found then strike any one, as the Israelis did, taking care first that the designated enemy was not in a position to retaliate and cause further American casualties.

Afghanistan fitted the bill perfectly for such a role. The fact that none of the alleged hijackers happened to be from Afghanistan was a minor detail. It was enough that the country was ruled by Taliban who harboured Osama bin Laden and al-Quaida. It was left to the spin doctors of the administration and the media to demonise and dehumanise them in the eyes of the people as evil Islamic tyrants, militants, terrorists, oppressors, etc. that deserved to be exterminated like vermin. The essence of propaganda is repetition. It can turn any illusion into reality by simply repeating it often while carefully excluding all contradictory in-puts.

'It is the absolute right of the State to supervise the formation of public opinion.

'If you tell a lie big enough and keep repeating it people will eventually come to believe it.

'The lie can be maintained only for such time as the State can shield the people from the political, economic and / or military consequences of the lie. It thus becomes vitally important for the State to use all of its powers to repress dissent, for the truth is the mortal enemy of the lie, and thus by extension, the truth becomes the greatest enemy of the State.'

—Dr Paul Joseph Goebbels, Hitler's Minister of Propaganda.

How the decision to strike Afghanistan was made has been described in *'Bush at War,'* by Bob Woodward (Simon & Schuster, New York, pp. 82 – 84, 99): *'Afghanistan's history nagged at the president's advisors. Its geography was forbidding and its record of rebuffing outside forces was real. Despite the options that had been presented earlier that morning, several advisors seemed worried. Bush asked them: What are the worst cases out there? What are the real downside risks?*

'One was triggering chaos in Afghanistan that could spill over into Pakistan. Rice and Cheney in particular viewed this as a great danger. ---------- President Musharraf is taking a tremendous risk, the president said. Let us make it worth his while. We should help him with a number of things, including nuclear security. --------- Another risk they faced was getting bogged down in Afghanistan. ---------- Should they think about launching military action elsewhere as an

insurance policy in case things in Afghanistan went bad? They would need successes early in any war to maintain domestic and international support. ---------

'*Rice asked whether they would envision a successful military campaign beyond Afghanistan, which put Iraq back on the table.* ------------ *Wolfowitz seized the opportunity. Attacking Afghanistan would be uncertain. He worried about 100,000 American troops bogged down in mountain fighting in Afghanistan six months from then. In contrast, Iraq was a brittle, oppressive regime that might break easily. It was doable.* ---------

'*When the group reconvened, Rumsfeld asked, Is this the time to attack Iraq? He noted that there would be a big build-up of forces in the region and he was still deeply worried about the availability of good targets in Afghanistan.*

'*Powell objected. You are going to hear from your coalition partners, he told the president. They are all with you, every one, but they will go away if you hit Iraq. If you get something pinning September 11 on Iraq, great* ----- *let's put it out and kick them at the right time. But let's get Afghanistan* -----------

'*As for Saddam Hussein, the president ended the debate. "I believe Iraq was involved, but I am not going to strike them now. I don't have the evidence at this point* ------------'.

This discussion that took place at Camp David on 15th September 2001 seems almost surreal. There was no talk about proof of involvement or guilt but only about which victim would be 'doable', acceptable to coalition partners and provided suitable targets. Why were they even considering attacking Iraq when, as they claimed, it was al-Quaida that was responsible for the destruction of the World Trade Centre? How does one assign guilt without having any evidence? After this, what should one think about the leaders of the so-called civilized world who decide to rain death and destruction upon innocent people, mostly women and children, simply because it is 'doable'?

Seeing the writing on the wall and in an effort to save her people from the terrible fate that awaited them, Afghanistan offered to hand over Osama bin Laden. Writing under the heading *'War on Terror – False Victory'*, in *'The Mirror'*, John Pilger reports, *'The guilty secret is that the attack on Afghanistan was unnecessary. The "smoking gun" of this entire episode is evidence of the British Government's lies about the basis for the war. According to Tony Blair, it was impossible to secure Osama bin Laden's extradition from Afghanistan by means other than bombing. Yet in late September and early October, leaders of Pakistan's two Islamic parties negotiated bin Laden's extradition to Pakistan to stand trial for the September 11 attacks. The deal was that he would be held under house arrest in Peshawar. According to reports in Pakistan (and the 'Daily Telegraph'), this had both bin Laden's approval and that of Mullah Omar, the Taliban leader.*

'The offer was that he would face an international tribunal, which would decide whether to try him or hand him over to America. Either way, he would have been out of Afghanistan, and a tentative justice would be seen to be in progress. It was vetoed by Pakistan's president Musharraf who said he "could not guarantee bin Laden's safety". But who really killed the deal? The US Ambassador to Pakistan was notified in advance of the proposal and the mission to put it to the Taliban. Later, a US official said that "casting our objectives too narrowly" risked "a premature collapse of the international effort if by some luck chance Mr. bin Laden was captured". And yet the US and British governments insisted there was no alternative to bombing

*Afghanistan because the Taliban had "refused" to hand
over Osama bin Laden.*

*'What the Afghani people got instead was "American justice"
----- imposed by a president who, as well as denouncing
international agreements on nuclear weapons, biological
weapons, torture, and global warming, has refused to sign
up for an international court to try war criminals: the one
place where bin Laden might be put on trial.*

*'The "war on terrorism" gave Bush the pretext to pressure
Congress into pushing through laws that erode much of the
basis of American justice and democracy. Blair has followed
behind with anti-terrorism laws of the very kind that failed
to catch a single terrorist during the Irish war. In this
atmosphere of draconian controls and fear, in the US and
Britain, mere explanation of the root causes of the attacks
on America invites ludicrous accusations of "treachery."
Above all, what this false victory has demonstrated is that,
to those in power in Washington and London and those who
speak for them, certain human lives have greater worth
than others and that the killing of only one set of civilians
is a crime. If we accept that, we beckon the repetition of
atrocities on all sides, again and again.'*

President Bush and his Defence Secretary Donald
Rumsfeld disdainfully declared that there were to be
no negotiations. The need of the hour was not to put bin
Laden on trial but to put together an 'international effort'
for attacking Afghanistan. As far as the British and rest of
the British 'white' Anglo-Saxon commonwealth countries
are concerned, when America says 'jump' they do not ask
why? They only respond, 'How high, master?' Australians
were among the first to volunteer their armed forces for the
attack to 'liberate' Afghanistan while at home their ships

were using force to prevent destitute Afghan refugees from entering the country.

The crime had been committed in USA but, curiously, the British government seemed equally if not more concerned and eager for revenge. This was explained as being a part of the 'special relationship' that supposedly existed between the two Anglo-Saxon countries. This special relationship seems to have been very one-sided for during the twenty years when Britain faced a continuous wave of IRA terrorism most of the financial and material contributions to the terrorists came from USA.

Itching to avenge their earlier humiliation and hoping to isolate the newly independent Muslim Central Asian Republics the Russians hardly needed an excuse to join the war against Afghanistan. According to Arundhati Roy, ' ------ *the Indian government was furiously gyrating its hips, begging the US to set up its bases in India rather than Pakistan.*' The details of how the generals in Pakistan capitulated have been spelt out by Bob Woodward in *'Bush At War.'* Some relevant extracts from the book are reproduced below:

'Woodward says that in the immediate aftermath of 9/11, Powell decided that Pakistan was bound to be the linchpin if the US was to take on the Al Qaeda on its turf. He and his deputy Richard Armitage then draw up a list of seven demands from Pakistan.

1. Stop Al Qaeda operatives at your border, intercept arms shipments through Pakistan and end ALL logistical support for (Osama) bin Laden,

2. Blanket overfreight and landing rights,

3. Access to Pakistan, naval bases, air bases and borders,

4. Immediate intelligence and immigration information,

5. Condemn the Sept 11 attacks, curb all domestic expression of support for terrorism against the United States, its friends and allies,

6. Cut off all shipments of fuel to the Taliban and stop Pakistani volunteers from going into Afghanistan to join the Taliban, and

7. Break diplomatic relations with the Taliban and assist us to destroy (Osama) bin Laden and his Al Qaeda network.

'In so many words,' says Woodward, *'Powell and Armitage would be asking Pakistan to help destroy what its intelligence service had helped create and maintain: The Taliban.'*

Ironically, Woodward writes that the bearer of this bad news for Musharraf would be his intelligence supremo Gen Mahmood Ahmed. By sheer coincidence, the ISI chief was visiting Washington at the time of the 9/11 attacks and was called into to the CIA headquarters.

At a meeting with CIA Director George Tenet and his deputies, Mahmood defends Taliban leader Mullah Omar, saying he is a religious man, 'a man of humanitarian instincts, not a man of violence, but one who had suffered greatly under the Afghan warlords.'

'Stop!' Tenet's Deputy Jim Pavitt says. *'Spare me. Does Mullah Omar want the United States military to unleash its force against the Taliban? Do you want that to happen? Will you go and ask him?'*

Later, Deputy Secretary of State Richard Armitage invites Mahmood to the State Department to crank up the heat. He begins by saying that it is not yet clear what the US would ask of Pakistan, but the requests would force 'deep introspection'.

'Pakistan faces a stark choice, either it is with us or it is not. This is a black and white with no gray,' Armitage tells him.

Mahmood, sounding utterly defensive, says his country had faced tough choices in the past but Pakistan was not a big or mighty power. *'Pakistan is an important country,'* Armitage cuts in.

After Armitage has softened up Musharraf through his emissary, Secretary of State Powell calls him up in Islamabad. *'As one general to another, we need someone on our flank fighting with us,'* he says, and then adds meaningfully: *'Speaking candidly, the American people would not understand if Pakistan was not in this fight with the United States.'*

To Powell's surprise, says Woodward, Musharraf promises to support the US with each of the seven actions.

An elated Powell then conveys his achievement at a National Security Council meeting in the White House Situation Room, saying: *'I'd like to tell you what we told the Pakistanis today,'* before loudly and proudly reading out the seven demands. When he finishes, he tells the meeting that Musharraf has already accepted them.

'It looks like you got it all,' Bush says. Others in the room ask for a copy of the US charter of demands (pp. 47, 59, 61).

Woodward's book also reveals that the US and Indian intelligence agencies work closely and exchange information on a regular basis not only on this but on most other issues as well.

The Americans were fortunate in finding Pakistan under the autocratic rule of a single individual. In a democratic set-up, answerable to the people and their representatives, it is highly doubtful if such sweeping and unpopular concessions, evidently contrary to national interest, could have been made in such indecent haste and with so little in return for the country itself. When you make concessions on international issues, without any quid pro quo, it is a clear sign of weakness. The process never ends at that and more often than not there is a cascade of further demands that follows. It is always wiser to visualize where it will all end before you decide to take the first step on the slippery road to concessions. Evidently, Musharraf never considered this. He could have asked for time to consult his cabinet or the rest of the generals but he didn't. It remains a mystery why he buckled under and capitulated so readily. Most likely, he simply lost his nerve, driven by an over-whelming sense of self-preservation.

His discomfiture became painfully evident when the US bombing of Afghan towns and villages continued into the Muslim holy month of Ramazan. It was particularly awkward and embarrassing for Musharraf, as the ruler of a Muslim nation, who had thrown his lot with the West. In an effort to relieve his discomfort he appealed for a halt in the bombing until the end of the month. His request was peremptorily, almost disdainfully, brushed aside by the Secretary of Defence, Donald Rumsfeld. Having surrendered all the bargaining chips and leaving himself with little or no leverage, he should not have expected any thing else. The Northern Alliance rounded up hundreds of Pakistanis in Afghanistan and is holding them for ransom. In return for all the assistance provided to the US, Musharraf has not even managed to get them released not to speak of the Pakistanis being tortured in Guantanamo's Camp X-Ray, unlike the British Prime Minister Tony Blair, whose government seldom misses the opportunity to pressurize the US in support of the Britons held there.

There could hardly be a greater irony than for USA and Pakistan that had supported the Afghan freedom struggle to join forces with Russia, that had occupied and brutalized Afghanistan for ten years, in mounting an attack on the desperately poor and starving Afghans whose only crimes were that they were weak and wanted to live their lives in their own way. It appears that subsequent to making the above concessions Pakistan gave away further substantial ground to the Americans. In addition to providing bases in Baluchistan for US army, navy and air force operations, according to news published in '*The Dawn*', even while India had threatened war by massing her army along the border to attack Pakistan, a substantial number of her troops remained deployed, not facing the Indians, but combing the western hills looking for al-Quaida fugitives for the Americans. Please see Annex for details of the assistance and facilities provided by Pakistan --- taken from CENTCOM's web site before these were removed by the latter at the request of the Pakistan government.

Mrs. Shirin Mazari of the Institute of Strategic Studies, Islamabad bemoans that US agencies like the FBI have been given free run of the country without getting anything in return ---- not even a let up in pressures by the West against Pakistan or the release of thousands of Pakistani hostages held for ransom by the war lords allied to the US in Afghanistan. Of all the people she must know that promises made in war are not for keeping and gratitude is the most unreliable currency in the world of international politics. The same applies to Musharraf and Prime Minister Jamali when they express the hope that Pakistan's co-operation in America's wars would save the country from aggression by her at a later date. USA has national objectives and interests vis-à-vis Pakistan that are not going to change simply because her rulers agreed to assist in the destruction of Afghanistan. At best, these will be kept on hold until a more opportune time.

There had been a similar situation earlier in Pakistan's history when excessive reliance on the US by another army dictator, Yahya Khan, played a critical role in the 1971 break-up of the country. This is how Mr. Sultan M. Khan, the then Foreign Secretary, has recalled it in his book *'Memories and Reflections of a Pakistani Diplomat'* (The Centre For Pakistan Studies, London, 1997, p.404) ' -------------- *the situation escalated out of Yahya Khan's grasp and he could no longer control it. From then on he was merely reacting to the developing situation and had lost all initiative. I wish I knew what he had been promised by the US Ambassador. When he* (Yahya Khan) *told him of "being led up the garden path" and about "promises made which had not been kept"* (US Ambassador) *Farland avoided looking at him'.* Unfortunately, Yahya died without revealing what he had been falsely promised and Farland, being a loyal American, will never tell. The tragedy then and now is the generals do not understand that foreigners look after the interests of their own countries first and foremost even when these are at the expense of Pakistan. When they put their faith in the promises of functionaries of a foreign state they do so at Pakistan's peril.

There is no rule in international relations under which cooperation in the past is rewarded by providing dispensation in the future. Any future action by USA against Pakistan will be based solely on America's further aims and objectives in the area. When the US refused Pakistan's request for arms sales and declined to enter into any long-term commitment, it was abundantly clear that the current arrangement was a temporary expedient and held no guarantees for the future.

Whatever the reasons for the abject and total surrender by the Pakistani generals it sealed the fate of the Afghans. According to UN estimates one million of among them, fearing the worst, left their homes to look for protection in Pakistan and Iran only to find the borders closed. This is how India's Anudhati Roy explained the situation in '*The Guardian*', '*Witness the infinite justice of the new century. Civilians starving to death while they're waiting to be killed. In America there has been rough talk of bombing Afghanistan back to the stone age. Someone please break the news that Afghanistan is already there.*'

The non-stop bombardment started on 6th October and continued for over six weeks during which more bombs were dropped than during five years of World War II. Most of the bombing was initially concentrated on Taliban's frontlines facing the Northern Alliance ---- a motley collection of criminal warlords, guilty of the worst human rights violations well documented by the United Nations, Amnesty International and others, who had now agreed to sell their souls to the invaders for bagfuls of greenbacks. They became the West's new allies, friends, partners and standard-bearers in bringing the shining light of western democracy and enlightenment to the Afghans. Despite earlier promises that these murderous criminals would not be allowed to enter Kabul, the occupying powers gave them the controlling share in the post-Taliban Government.

On Sunday, 14th October, a week after the commencement of the attack on Afghanistan, London's Independent Television (ITN) was still broadcasting the news every hour that FBI doubted if al-Quaida was involved in the World Trade Centre incident. It surprised no one that rest of the media chose neither to repeat nor deny the news. It was simply allowed to die a quiet death while the murderous bombing of innocents continued unabated.

Since the bombs were released from a great height, to avoid any danger to the planes, the effect was minimal. There was growing anxiety, bordering on despair, in Washington at the lack of progress, according to '*The Washington Post's* Bob Woodward. The policy was then changed and the bombing shifted from the front lines to towns and villages. Innocent families sleeping peacefully in their homes were suddenly blown into smithereens by powerful bombs, without any warning, at the dead of night. The diabolical cluster bombs that spread hundreds of little bomblets, each exploding at a different time, were dropped indiscriminately on population centres.

It had a terrible effect. There was widespread panic as frightened people emptied towns and villages and took to the hills for safety. Those who are familiar with Afghanistan will know the people are so poor that they cannot afford any protective winter clothing and rely on the sun in daytime and fire at night to keep warm. Since lighting any fire was out of the question, sleeping in the open, entire families froze to death in the bitterly cold winter nights on the hills. British reporter Christina Lamb of '*The Sunday Telegraph*', among others, has written horrific accounts of such tragedies that she witnessed in western Afghanistan. These are too distressing to be reproduced here. When US helicopter gunships repeatedly machine-gunned a remote farming village, killing as many as 93 civilians, a Pentagon official was moved to say, '*The people there are dead because we wanted them dead.*'

Worse still, it was sowing time and no crops could be sown, raising the prospect of famine the following year. The United Nation's Food and Agriculture Organization had warned the world only ten days before the start of the bombing that seven million people would face starvation in Afghanistan if the military action was initiated. These and other such warnings were disdainfully and contemptuously ignored along with the suffering and looming tragedy for the Afghans.

All of this went unreported in the US media, in particular, partly due to inbuilt bias but mostly because of 'news management', a euphemism for media control, by the Pentagon. Commenting on this Robert Fisk wrote under *'Hypocrisy, Hatred and the War on Terror'* in *'The Independent'* of 8th November 2001, *'Infinitely more shameful and unethical were the disgraceful words of Walter Isaacson, the chairman of CNN, to his staff. 'Showing the misery of Afghanistan ran the risk of promoting enemy propaganda', he said. 'It seems perverse to focus too much on the casualties or hardship in Afghanistan ----- we must talk about how the Taliban are using civilian shields and how the Taliban have harboured the terrorists responsible for killing close to 5,000 innocent people.'*

'Mr. Isaacson was an unimaginative boss of "Time" magazine, but these latest words will do more to damage the supposed impartiality of CNN than anything on the air in recent years. Perverse? Why perverse? Why are Afghan casualties so far down Isaacson's compassion list? Or is Isaacson just following the lead set down for him a few days earlier by White House spokesman Ari Fleischer, who portentously announced to the Washington press corps that in times like these "people have to watch what they say and watch what they do."

Indeed, Fisk makes a highly pertinent point. If it was a crime to kill innocent people at the World Trade Centre, why was it justified to kill equally innocent people in Afghanistan? What was done to Afghanistan was a crime against humanity, plain and simple, committed by powers that never tire of lecturing others about human rights, democracy and the rule of law.

There is also clear evidence of war crimes and gross violations of the Geneva Conventions relating to prisoners of war committed by the US and British troops. Some of these have been documented in a British film under the title, '*Massacre at Mazar.*' It describes how thousands of Taliban troops were rounded up at Kunduz in late November 2002 and transported in sealed shipping containers to Sheberghan prison in northwestern Afghanistan, a jail under US control. Most of the prisoners suffocated to death during the journey. The drivers of the vehicles testified that upon arrival at Sheberghan they were ordered to drive the trucks to the desert of Dashte Laili where the prisoners that were still alive were shot and their bodies left to rot in hastily dug shallow mass graves.

Speaking at the film's showing in Berlin, Andrew McKntee, ex-President of Amnesty International UK and human rights lawyer, described it as 'very credible evidence and one that raises questions that will not go away' ('*New Film Accuses US Army of War Crimes in Afghanistan*' article in '*The Guardian*' of 13th June 2002 by Kate Connolly and Rory McCarthy).

In a similar action the United States Air Force mercilessly bombed five hundred bound and blind-folded Taliban prisoners of war at Kila Jangi near Mazare Sharif for three days until the last of them had been killed. The atrocity was the reaction to a prisoner revolt against CIA interrogators who shot any prisoner in cold blood whose answers to their questions they found not to their liking. This is an excerpt from chapter 10 of William Thomas' book, '*All Fall Down*', about the treatment meted out to Taliban prisoners after they had surrendered to the US and her allies in the Northern Alliance:

'*This is a haunted place. Entering a prison near the first town retaken by the Northern Alliance, journalists and Red Cross workers encountered "a horrific scene of carnage". Nearly 800 Taliban prisoners lay slaughtered after a three-day massacre directed by US Special Forces and CIA operatives.*

'*From the Center for Research on Globalization, Jerry White wrote that most of those killed died from US air strikes on the prison compound. "At least 30 bombing attacks were carried out by US warplanes and helicopter gunships, whose targets were pinpointed by Special Forces at the prison."*

'*Stunned witnesses stumbled across the dismembered corpses of hundreds of Taliban prisoners "strewn amidst the rubble and still burning buildings, the blasted parts of dozens of dead horses and bullet-raked vehicles."*

'*An Associated Press photographer found the corpses of 50 prisoners, executed with their hands tied behind their backs with black scarves. The dead were mostly Pakistanis, Chechens, Arabs and other non-Afghans who surrendered Nov. 24, after the Taliban's northern stronghold fell to alliance militias.*

'*According to the Times of London, resistance by panicked Taliban prisoners began only after CIA provocateurs shot and killed at least five unarmed POWs. German television footage showed alliance soldiers firing over the walls into the mass of prisoners inside.*

'*The carnage ended when "US and British special forces set fire to oil poured into a shelter where three Taliban prisoners remained. A Northern Alliance tank then drove over the bodies of several Pakistani and Arab Taliban volunteers and fired three rounds at a range of 20 yards, obliterating the building and killing the last holdouts."*

'*The prisoners had been brought to the fortress under an agreement between the Taliban commander and Northern Alliance leader General Rashid Dostum to surrender the city. Dostum's troops had just finished massacring Taliban prisoners in Kunduz - "stomping on faces of captured Taliban and shooting others as they lay wounded," according to AP.*

'*President George Bush had just finished saying he preferred to see Taliban prisoners killed...*'

A number of international human rights organizations have demanded investigation into these crimes. Mary Robinson, the UN High Commissioner for Human Rights had also backed these demands for an urgent inquiry but all of these have fallen on deaf ears. Such is the state of impotence of this supposedly august body called the United Nations.

The total number of Afghans killed in the war will never be known for no effort has been made to make an accurate count. The Pentagon claims the figure to be about 3,500. The basis for this calculation is not known. Most experts regard it as gross under estimation. Carl Conetta, the director of The Project for Defence Alternatives in the Commonwealth Institute in Massachusetts, basing his figures on a January 2002 survey of 2,000 families in the central Afghan highlands, feels the number of casualties from both direct and indirect action would more likely be in the region of fifty thousand dead. More than sixty per cent of them would be women and children. For those interested, his report is available at www.comw.org.

It is worth reproducing here what Robert Fisk wrote in '*The Independent*' about the entire issue, including subsequent developments, in general and the western attitude in particular:

'*Over the past 50 years, we sat on our moral pedestal and lectured the Chinese and the Soviets, the Arabs and the Africans, about human rights. We pronounced on the human-rights crimes of Bosnians and Croatians and Serbs. We put many of them in the dock, just as we did the Nazis at Nuremberg. Thousands of dossiers were produced, describing - in nauseous detail - the secret courts and death squads and torture and extra judicial executions carried out by rogue states and pathological dictators. Quite right too.*

'*Yet suddenly, after 11 September, we went mad. We bombed Afghan villages into rubble, along with their inhabitants - ---- blaming the insane Taliban and Osama bin Laden for our slaughter ----- and now we have allowed our gruesome militia allies to execute their prisoners. President George Bush has signed into law a set of secret military courts to try and then liquidate anyone believed to be a "terrorist murderer" in the eyes of America's awesomely inefficient intelligence services. And make no mistake about it, we are talking here about legally sanctioned American government death squads. They have been created, of course, so that Osama bin Laden and his men should they be caught rather than killed, will have no public defence; just a pseudo trial and a firing squad.*

'*It's quite clear what has happened. When people with yellow or black or brownish skin, with Communist or Islamic or Nationalist credentials, murder their prisoners or carpet bomb villages to kill their enemies or set up death squad courts, they must be condemned by the United States, the*

European Union, the United Nations and the "civilised" world. We are the masters of human rights, the Liberals, the great and good who can preach to the impoverished masses. But when our people are murdered ----- when our glittering buildings are destroyed ----- then we tear up every piece of human rights legislation, send off the B-52s in the direction of the impoverished masses and set out to murder our enemies.'

The atrocities against the Afghans did not end with the bombing. Hundreds of Taliban and al-Quaida prisoner of war, including the Afghan ambassador to Pakistan, were gagged, bound with duct tape, strapped to stretchers and flown in that condition to the US military facility at Guantanamo Bay in Cuba. Included among them were many eleven and twelve year old boys and aged Afghans well into their seventies. A 90-year-old detainee was released from the prison recently after being detained in a small solitary cage in the open, like an animal, and tortured for more than eleven months. There are widespread reports, including fears expressed by such organizations as Amnesty International, of torture and brutality committed against these prisoners who remain in solitary caged confinement with no communication to the outside world, in complete violation of all international conventions concerning prisoners of war.

The released inmates speak of cruel and mindless torture and humiliation at the hands of their US captors. During the long flight from Kabul to Cuba each prisoner was bound by the hands, feet and stomach and had his eyes and face covered. All food, water and bathroom visits were denied. On arrival at Guantanamo they were placed in darkened isolation cages for thirty days. There was just one small hole through which food was thrown to them and they were allowed outside for just fifteen minutes every three days. The temperature inside the cage was alternately raised and lowered to unbearable levels. Loud music blared through speakers and guards threw rocks against the cages to disrupt any sleep.

The prisoners were interrogated at all hours and during these sessions in smoke filled rooms their faces and bodies were smeared with excrement and blood. They were stripped naked and made to lie on cold concrete slabs sometimes for two or three days. Guards made a habit of stepping on the prisoners shackles that cut through to the bone. Prisoners were also hung on a wall by their shackles and remained in that position for as much as four days. Presumably in an attempt to humiliate, their private parts were repeatedly photographed and probes inserted into their anuses. They were denied access to religious rituals and copies of the Koran were deliberately desecrated before them.

Under special laws enacted for the purpose by President Bush all normal legal safeguards and provisions have been denied to them. The Geneva Convention that calls for POWs to give only their names and serial numbers under interrogation and requires them to be released immediately after the war has been contemptuously ignored. Under the Bush law they can be detained indefinitely and denied access to all legal help. If and when they are put on trial for any alleged crimes, it will be before some kangaroo courts set up specifically for the purpose in which hearsay, among other things, will be permitted as evidence. It will not be justice but cruel and gross vengeance that will be seen to be done.

This is the treatment meted out to prisoners taken in a foreign war by the champions of western civilization. As compared with this we have the story of Yvonne Ridley, the *Sunday Express* correspondent, who entered Afghanistan illegally and was taken prisoner as a spy by the Taliban. In her book '*In the Hands of Taliban*' (Robson Books, London, 2001) she details the decency, courtesy and kindness with which she was treated, even at the height of the inhuman murderous bombing of the Afghan towns and villages, and eventually safely released by the people so viciously portrayed in the West as primitive and barbaric savages. It is a story that the western media have chosen to ignore altogether because it does not fit the pattern depicted by them for propaganda purposes.

Islam, that has been described by George W. Bush's religious mentor, Reverend Franklin Graham, as '*a very evil and wicked religion,*' demands that Muslims treat their opponents humanely. It is unlawful for them to take prisoners, except during the fighting of a regular war. Prisoners must not be ill-treated and should be released after hostilities have come to an end. If no ransom is forthcoming, the prisoner must be allowed to earn money to pay the sum himself, and his captor is urged to help him out of his own pocket ('*The Koran 8:68, 47:5, 24:34, 2:178*').

A tradition records the Prophet of Islam's directions about the treatment of captives in these terms: '*You must feed them as you feed yourselves, and clothe them as you clothe yourselves, and if you should set them a hard task, you must help them in it yourselves.* When Messers Bush, Blair and Berlusconi compare different civilizations with their own one wonders if the standards they apply to each of them are always the same?

The atrocious conduct of the US military in Afghanistan is not new. The malaise is deeply rooted. It had acted in much the same fashion during the war in Vietnam. One of the returning veterans had testified before the Senate Foreign Relations Committee at the time that his compatriots in Vietnam had 'raped, cut off ears, cut off heads, taped wires from portable telephones to genitals and turned up the power, blown up bodies, randomly shot at civilians [and] razed villages in a fashion reminiscent of Genghis Khan.' None of this would almost surely have taken place if the enemy had belonged to the white Caucasian race.

The debate about what Pakistan and the rest of the Muslim world could and could not have done to save Afghanistan from the rape and devastation will go on forever. Whatever the conclusion, this chapter of Muslim history will always be remembered as one of betrayal, ignominy and shame ----- not so much because they did not prevent the disaster but because they did not make the effort. At the behest of the US, the military rulers of Pakistan even cut off the trucking of food and other supplies to Afghanistan ('*The New York Times*, 16th September 2001). What they got in return for helping to overthrow pro-Pakistan Taliban in Kabul was a government led by traditionally hostile Tajik, Uzbek and other warlords supported by India and Russia.

The picture of Saudi Prince Walid rushing off to present a cheque to the mayor of New York for the relief of the World Trade Centre victims, only to have it contemptuously thrown back in his face, while hundreds of thousand of innocent fellow Muslims were abandoned to their fate in Afghanistan, freezing and starving to death, will remain as an indelible reminder of what has become of the Muslims. It is a far cry indeed from the days when Prince Abdul Rahman in Spain had threatened war on his Christian neighbour on learning about the mistreatment of a solitary Muslim woman. If Pakistan and the others could not prevent the attack on Afghanistan the least they could have done was to try and alleviate the suffering of her people by organizing some humanitarian relief efforts. They did not even do that much.

After Taliban gave up resistance to save the country from further genocidal US bombing, the West installed a puppet regime in Kabul. At one stage when its nominated president Hamid Karzai, a man who had been on the pay roll of UNOCAL, expressed some dissatisfaction with the composition of his government, US Secretary of Defence, Donald Rumsfeld, bluntly stated in public that if he did not accept what he was told, they would find some other Afghan to replace him. The popularity of Hamid Karzai is such that after a number of attempts on his life he is unable to find even half a dozen loyal Afghans that he can trust to guard his life. A contingent of US military personnel now protects him from his own people.

Not only Hamid Karzai but all of the western occupying force in Afghanistan is living under a state of siege, mostly in and around Kabul. Hostility among the masses, particularly against the United States, is increasing by the day. Fearful of further troubles, Britain, Canada and some other countries have already pulled their ground troops out of the country. As the casualties begin to mount, it is inevitable, questions will also be raised in the United States as to its purpose in the land. Already, they have started blaming Pakistan for not doing enough to help stabilize the situation in Afghanistan. Having done what the US has to the Afghans, it is lunacy to expect them to feel charitable towards any westerners. The long haul that George Bush had warned the American people about has only just started.

The writ of Karzai government does not extend beyond the limits of the city of Kabul. The control in the rest of the country has passed into the hands of criminal and rapacious warlords who are committing the worst possible excesses against the people with no one to check them. The cultivation of opium that had been virtually eradicated by Taliban has reached record levels but such awkward facts are seldom mentioned by the media. What little news is allowed to leak out of Afghanistan is not good, to say the least. There is little employment, no law and no security for the common man. It is a far cry from the days of the much maligned Taliban. Only a small portion of the so called 'aid' promised by the western countries has actually been delivered and even less of it has reached the Afghans themselves.

After one year of occupation the West has not been able to come up with any solution to the situation. It is highly doubtful if they have the will and the inclination to find one either. At this rate, it is only a matter of time before they start to look for a face saving way out, knowing perfectly well from the Soviet experience what might happen if they decided to stick it out. Looking at the portents the future holds little cheer for the poor Afghans after the West has finished with them.

The question still remains as to the real reasons for the American invasion of Afghanistan. The country is situated in a region full of vast unexploited oil, gas and mineral reserves. According to the 10th September 2002 issue of '*The Oil and Gas Journal*,' Central Asia represents one of the world's last great frontiers for geological survey and analysis, offering opportunities for investment in the discovery, production, transportation, and refining of enormous quantities of oil and gas resources. It is estimated that by 2050 Central Asia will account for more than eighty per cent of the oil consumed in the US. There is more oil and gas in the Caspian Sea area ----- six trillion dollars' worth at current prices ----- than in Saudi Arabia, but you need a pipeline through Afghanistan to get it out.

There is another secondary reason for getting control of Central Asia's energy reserves. China is a growing power with an increasing thirst for oil and gas. An effective way to assert political control over her would be by controlling her energy supplies in the same way as is done with Japan. Laying claim to Central Asian fossil fuel reserves at this early stage would pre-empt China and, apart from ensuring continuation of future supplies for America, also provide a strangle-hold on China's economic and military capability.

On 31st January 2002, even before the bombs stopped falling and there were any signs of pacification in the country, the U.S. government quietly announced it would support the construction of the trans-Afghanistan oil pipeline. A month later, the Afghani puppet Karzai and Pakistan's Musharraf announced their agreement to build a proposed pipeline from Central Asia to Pakistan, via Afghanistan. There could hardly be a stronger and clearer indication of the real western motives in the war against Afghanistan.

Musharraf government's decision to build a new port at Gwadar, on the western extremity of the coast, to serve as the oil terminal for Central Asia's oil and gas exports is quite significant in this context. Gwadar is presently not connected by road or rail nor are there any links to electricity, gas and telephone lines in the rest of the country. All of these would need to be built over distances extending hundreds of miles in some of the most inhospitable environment on earth. Worse still, there is not enough fresh water available in the entire region to support a sizable population.

Pakistan already has surplus port capacity and does not require any new ports for its own use. The distances from Central Asia to Gwadar are the same as to Port Qasim where extensive facilities already exist for the handling of ships. Almost all of the needed road and rail communications and other infrastructure necessary for accommodating Central Asian exports too are already in place. In the face of this it makes little economic sense to incur a huge expenditure to build a new port next to nowhere and connect it to the rest of the country with new road, rail, electricity and gas lines at prohibitive cost when the existing facilities can easily meet any future needs. It makes even less sense for Pakistan to pay for something out of her own meager resources that will basically serve the political and economic needs of western oil interests and Russia.

There are other implications as well that may be less obvious. Any country transporting Central Asian resources through Pakistan will, of necessity, remain dependent upon her goodwill. Pakistan is a large Muslim nation with nuclear capability and may not always lend itself to manipulation by outside influences. The situation will remain at the top of the West's list of worries as long as she continues to maintain this capability. One way to resolve these matters would be to politically separate the part of the country that provides the link to Central Asia from the rest and turn it into a banana republic. What could be better from the western point of view, in that event, if the breakaway part already has a built-in deep-sea port?

The notion is neither so outlandish nor altogether inconceivable. Publish a few articles about how poor deprived Baluchis were being discriminated against and denied their national aspirations by the domineering and insensitive 'Punjabi establishment'. Leave it to the media to give it continuous exaggerated coverage. Then find a few gullible Baluchi youth and tribesmen, smuggle a few arms to them and you are more than halfway to creating a new Bangladesh. The scenario may or may not play out in this precise manner but, given the circumstances, Pakistan cannot be sanguine or unmindful of the possibility, especially, in the light of her past history and experiences. It is a consideration that must remain paramount in all strategic planning. Perhaps, the best way to guard against any such adventurism would be by ensuring that the West's economic ambitions and links with Central Asia remain tied to a united Pakistan and the existing facilities at Port Qasim.

ESSENTIAL WEST

Just as many in the West treat the Muslim world as a single monolith, there is also a corresponding tendency among the Muslims to regard the entire western world in a similarly mistaken light. The West is by no means a homogenous political or religious entity having a uniformly unfriendly attitude towards Islam. It is composed of many different countries each with its own peculiar interests that may come together on some issues but not on others. In the recent past they had closed ranks because of fears of the communist expansion but with that danger now having evaporated political consensus on other issues is becoming more difficult.

What binds the western countries together more than anything else is economic interest ----- not national so much as corporate interest. This is an age of 'globalization' and expanding corporate culture which now takes precedence over national interest although, for various reasons, most politicians are loathe to admitting this fact. Whenever one hears any mention of democracy in the West these days, almost invariably, it is in association with capitalism even though there is, strictly speaking, no relevant connection between the two.

The driving force in the West is not democracy but capitalism. In essence, capitalism involves the exploitation of human as well as material resources to generate profits for the investors. These are greater whenever the scale of production is large which, in turn, calls for accumulation of further capital for investment in greater industrial capacity and marketing. The survival of capitalism depends upon constantly increasing consumption and growth. Without this, economic stagnation will set in and prosperity come to an end. The solution lies in creating greater demand as well as consumption that in turn requires ever increasing numbers of consumers as well as resources and raw materials.

Profits also increase if the costs of raw materials are low and the prices of manufactures as high as possible. Control over the capital market can help to eliminate competition and establish monopolies by denying access to investment resources to others. The West also maintains a tight control over the supply and cost of raw materials most of which originate in the third world and Muslim countries. The control of these markets ensures prosperity for the West at the expense of the weaker and poorer nations.

There is an ever-increasing demand for raw materials to fuel the western economies. Unbridled growth in the West, coupled with the increasing appetite of new economic powers in East Asia and dwindling supplies, has given rise to fears of shortages in the future. It is compelling US economic interests in particular to lay exclusive claims to as many areas that produce industrial raw materials as possible. This is specifically true for oil. Unexplored regions of Central Asia as well as the existing sources in the Middle East are coveted jealously. This is the underlying basis for the aggression or the 'civilizational clash', as Huntington calls it, that we are witnessing. Cultural and religious differences have little to do with it. These are little more than obfuscation and a ruse to justify the use of otherwise unjustifiable force in the eyes of the American and European people.

The US military operations in the Persian Gulf have little to do with a clash of culture, civilization, terrorism or the spread of democracy. It is all about oil ----- to ensure not only its uninterrupted flow but also that the price paid to the producing countries is as little as possible. The case of East Timor is typical. Under overwhelming pressure from western powers, the UN organized a referendum that resulted in the oil rich region becoming independent from Indonesia not so long ago. It remains the world's poorest country, with an unemployment rate close to ninety per cent. Most of its oil and mineral resources are exploited by Australia. The Australian Government under John Howard has had no qualms in defying International Maritime Law to withhold East Timor's badly needed dues of oil and gas revenues worth eight billion US dollars ('*The Other Tsunami*' by John Pilger in the '*New Statesman*', 10th January 2005). Altruism has no place in the scheme of corporate or national interest of the western powers. It is the weak that have to pay the price.

The significance of oil is not simply as a commodity. It powers the military machine. As such, its control ensures international power for the nation that possesses it and crippling vulnerability for any one lacking this vital resource. The control of oil is in itself a powerful weapon in international politics.

As an example of how capitalism works in favour of the West, the price of cotton produced by Pakistan has remained almost constant, in real US dollar terms, for the past fifty years while the price of aircraft manufactured in the West has increased almost a thousand times. The cost of actual materials in an aircraft that sells for $100 million, like aluminum, rubber, polymers, etc. obtained from developing countries is less than one million dollars; the rest is simply added value. A western middle man pays less than $2 for a T-shirt from Bangladesh that includes the cost of materials, labour, packaging, freight and insurance and sells it for $20 in a shop in New York. The price of oil in real terms, after correction for inflation, has been less recently than it was

40 years ago. The prices of other produce from undeveloped nations like sugar, cocoa, coffee, rice, palm oil have fallen fifty per cent in the past twenty years. The end result of all this has been that wealth has continually drained into the western coffers in ever increasing amounts.

Capital always flows into places that afford safety and security. In the old days, people could hoard gold. This has been de-linked as the currency standard. Its place has been taken by the US dollar. At the same time, movement of capital from one country to another has become very quick and easy. The net effect is an ever-increasing transfer of wealth to the so-called 'safe havens' in the West.

Much is made of the riches of the oil producing countries. It is true, they have generated trillions of dollars in revenues but the countries themselves have profited very little from it. Most of the cash has filtered back into the western coffers, adding to their existing riches. (It was the same in Russia under Yeltsen when billions of dollars in World Bank loans to the country were siphoned off by his cronies and re-deposited in private accounts in New York). The end result is that the combined wealth of all the Arab countries today does not exceed that of Spain alone ----- a relatively minor economic power.

In the years before 2002, the transfers of funds to the United States alone from other parts of the world averaged at over one billion dollars a day. The rate of this flow increases every time there is political or economic instability in any country or region of the world. Turmoil in any other part of the world becomes a boon to the capital markets in the West. The same is true for the proceeds of ill gotten gains from corruption, etc. by the power elites in the more mismanaged countries. Given the size of her debt, the United States should be declared a bankrupt country by the normal standards but, in her case, huge budgetary deficits get financed by cash inflows from the rest of the world.

The cumulative outcome of all this has been that whereas before World War II the average income of a worker in the United States was sixteen times higher than that of the average worker in India by 1970 it was forty times higher. Today, it is 78 times as high. There is another significant statistic that is worth bearing in mind. The combined wealth of the world's 587 billionaires exceeds the combined GDP of the world's 135 poorest countries and more than forty percent of the entire wealth in the world is concentrated in the hands of only 350 people ----- almost all of them, barring perhaps King Fahad and Prince Walid of Saudi Arabia and the Sultan of Brunei, are westerners and a substantial number of them Jewish. Close to half the American billionaires are Jews. This phenomenon is by no means limited to the United States. Six of the seven Russian oligarchs, are Jews. It has great political implications since wealth and political power go hand in hand.

GDP per person in USA is now 54 per cent more than that in Europe. With less than five per cent of the world's population, the United States consumes more than fifty percent of its resources and generates twenty-six per cent of its pollution. In the last ten years of unbridled corporate globalisation, the world's total income has increased by an average of 2.5 percent a year. And yet the numbers of the poor in the world has increased by 100 million. The top one percent of the world population has the same combined income as the bottom fifty seven percent and the disparity is growing.

There is also growing disparity in the types of expenditures incurred in countries within the West itself that closely follows the emerging realities of power. The United States spends $28,000 for every member of its armed forces on military research and development compared with Europe's $7,000. Looking at these figures US economic and military supremacy is secure for at least a generation if not more. To get an idea of the US economic might, given the present rates of GDP growth in the two countries, it would take China 200 years to catch up with USA.

To put the corporate world in perspective, of the top one hundred biggest economies, fifty one are corporations, not countries. Only two companies dominate half the world's bananas trade and three control eighty-five per cent of the tea sold in the world. Walmart alone controls forty per cent of Mexico's retail food business. Monsanto dominates ninety-one per cent of the global genetically modified seeds market. The Swiss firm Nestle's profits are greater than Ghana's GDP and those of Unilever's a third more than the national income of Mozambique. Walmart earns more profit each year than the combined incomes of both these countries. It is the largest corporation in the world, employing one and half million people and constitutes two per cent of America's GDP.

Markets, and the profits accruing from them, are influenced in large measure by government policies. It helps greatly if government policies are sympathetic to the market and corporate interest because, at least in theory, it leads to job creation and prosperity. This is what determines national interest, more than any other factor, and this is where politics and corporate interest come together.

In the end it all boils down to money. Any politician wishing to get elected to the US Congress, for example, needs a kitty of at least fifty million dollars. The expenses for the presidential race may run upwards of two or three billion dollars. It is hard to find too many talented and honest individuals, committed to the public good, who can spare this kind of cash. The political parties have little choice but to turn to large corporations and other interest groups that have money to spare.

The donations come at a price, which is negotiated beforehand. As mentioned earlier, during the 1992 presidential campaign in the US some reporters tapped a phone conversation between Mr. Clinton's campaign manager and the president of Anti-Defamation League in which Jewish support for Clinton was promised in return for giving Israel the right to nominate the next US Secretary of State. The number of Jewish voters is about the same as the Muslim voters in America. The deal was not for votes so much as for Jewish influence and money which are disproportionately greater. It is the same with George W. Bush and his connections to the oil industry and Vice President Cheney and Halliburton Corporation.

As another example of the close links between politics and corporate interest, former Secretary of Defence, Caspar Weinberger was a Bechtel general counsel. Former Deputy Secretary of Energy, W. Kenneth Davis was Bechtel's vice president. Riley Bechtel, the company chairman, is on the President's Export Council. Jack Sheehan, a retired marine corps general, is a senior vice president at Bechtel and a member of the US Defence Policy Board. Former Secretary of State George Shultz, who is on the Board of Directors of the Bechtel Group, was the chairman of the advisory board of the Committee for the Liberation of Iraq.

Between 2001 and 2002, nine out of thirty members of the US Defence Policy Group were connected to companies that were awarded Defence contracts worth 76 billion dollars. Between 1990 and 2002 the Bechtel group has contributed $3.3 million to campaign funds, both Republican and

Democrat. Not surprisingly, since 1990 it has won more than 2000 government contracts worth more than 11 billion dollars.

The pharmaceutical industry in the United States is another big player in the political game. According to the National Women's Health Network, 1,274 people were registered in Washington to lobby for the drug makers in 2003. Some 476 of these are former federal officials, including 40 former members of Congress. The campaign contributions made by this industry alone run into hundreds of millions of dollars. The power and influence it provided were such that it was able to stop the medical reforms that had formed a key component of President Clinton's election manifesto, from being put into effect.

With typical American efficiency, the entire electoral process has been streamlined at every step of the way. For example, realising the tremendous impact of television on the lives of people, election campaigns are primarily based on this medium. Highly paid professionals select and decide the issues for the elections and drum these into the public mind through the media. They also select the likely candidates, primarily on the basis of how well they will sell on television. Then they set to work writing speeches, organizing photo-ops, handling public relations and running the campaigns for them.

Since half the voters are women for whom good-looking male figures hold an intrinsic attraction, sex appeal has become a significant requirement for any candidate. There is no future for roly-poly Patrick Moynihans or balding old Eisenhowers in the US politics any more. The same is true for any budding Churchill or Attlee look-alikes in Britain. It may sound a bit too cynical but this is the essence of the electoral process in the United States, and the rest of the western world is not far behind. It did not start out this way but this is what has become of democracy.

USA remains a free and democratic society generally but this may not be strictly true in all of its aspects. In many ways, it resembles an oligarchy or even an empire. Its structures of power, especially, the military and the intelligence agencies, are only nominally under the control of the legislature. There are intricate links within the very powerful military–intelligence–industrial complex and they remain a source of great wealth for various groups such as defence contractors, financial houses and some other behind-the-scenes organizations. Any political aspirant who does not kow-tow to these interest groups, realistically speaking, can have little hope of getting any where.

The total budget for the intelligence agencies in the United States exceeds one hundred billion dollars. Most of it is allocated to CIA, Defence and Communications intelligence agencies that are directly involved in manipulation and control of foreign governments and their policies, on their own or in collaboration with similar organizations in other western countries. It is mostly, but not always, through these channels that the western corporate interests manage events in other parts of the world. The use of military force is only an act of last resort.

There can be little doubt that the greatest long-term threat to global prosperity is climate change, which threatens to wreck many of America's key markets in the developing world. Coastal cities in the US, including New York, are threatened by rising sea levels. Florida could be hit by stronger and more frequent hurricanes. Both farms and cities are likely to be affected by droughts. Globally, it carries the potential of igniting all-out wars over food, water and energy supplies. Yet, United States has refused to sign the Kyoto protocol for the reduction of greenhouse gases mainly because it is not in the corporate interest to do so. It is the same when it comes to banning tobacco and alcohol, two of the most dangerous substances consumed by human beings (nicotine in tobacco is the most addictive substance known and alcohol is a factor in over fifty percent of all the cases involving homicide, assault and accidents in the West).

The history of corporate profits taking precedence over US interests goes back some way. After the rise of Hitler and Mussolini to power, US companies flocked to help them re-arm their countries. Among them, General Motors that set up a subsidiary in Germany to manufacture military trucks and supplied parts and engines for the Junker bombers and IBM that provided tabulation machines ---- fore-runners of modern computers ('*IBM and the Holocaust: The Strategic Alliance Between Nazi Germany and America's Most Powerful Corporation*', by Edwin Black, Crown Publishers, New York, 2001). Such shady dealings are by no means exclusive to the US. Investigations into the collapsed Banco Ambrosiano of Italy indicate involvement of Mafia, the Vatican and the very secretive Masonic (P-2) society in its affairs, that included money laundering and channeling funds for political purposes. The last named outfit, composed of about 2,000 of Italy's mostly financial, political and military elite, had been formed with the specific purpose of keeping the far left and communists from forming a government. There is widespread speculation that the bank acted as a conduit for CIA funds into Pope John Paul II's Poland to support the trade union *Solidarity* during the uprising against the communist rule in the country.

When, shortly after becoming president, Franklin D. Roosevelt introduced a set of laws and agencies to exercise some restraint on banks and big corporations, a plot was even hatched to overthrow and replace him with a fascist dictatorship (*'The Plot to Seize the White House'*, by Jules Archer, Hawthorn Books, 1973). It fizzled out when its central character, much decorated former marine general Smedley Darlington Butler, had a change of heart and decided to disclose the plot to the US Congress. Parts of his remarkably outspoken speech delivered at an American Legion convention may be worth quoting here:

'I spent 33 years ------- being a high-class muscle man for Big Business, for Wall Street and the bankers. I was a racketeer for capitalism -------

'I helped purify Nicaragua for the international banking house of Brown Brothers in 1909-1912. I helped make Mexico and especially Tampico safe for American oil interests in 1916. I brought light to the Dominican Republic for American sugar interests in 1916. I helped make Haiti and Cuba a decent place for the National City (Bank) boys to collect revenue in. I helped in the rape of half a dozen Central American republics for the benefit of Wall Street --------

'In China in 1927 I helped see to it that Standard Oil went its way unmolested ------- I was rewarded with honours, medals, promotions ------- I might have given Al Capone a few hints. The best he could do was to operate a racket in three cities. The marines operated on three continents (*'The Plot to Seize the White House'*, pp.118-119).

Corporate interests abroad are generally short-term. These are cheaper and easier to achieve by manipulating local autocratic set-ups. All it takes is to find and install a suitably sympathetic candidate and make sure he or she remains securely in place. CIA's role and expertise in such undertakings has been legendary from Indonesia, through the Middle East to almost every country in Latin

America. Since these regimes are required to sacrifice their national interest, invariably, the individuals involved are unscrupulous, avaricious, corrupt and unsavoury characters that are despised by the local masses. Because of the association, this resentment and hostility gets transferred to the West. It is this, more than anything else, that makes USA so unpopular and not her freedoms, as George W. Bush would have us believe.

It is also the main reason for democracy not taking root and flourishing in the less developed countries. It has simply not been given a fair chance. The surrogate rulers installed and supported to serve western corporate interests are intrinsically insecure and forever fearful of political dissent. They become increasingly intolerant and oppressive, driving any opposition underground and into desperate hands. In most cases, it leaves the people with only a choice between two evils.

In the Muslim countries the rise of religious extremism in recent years is directly linked to western intervention and exploitation. It provides the only credible opposition to despotic rule and when the latter ends this is all that the people are left with, as we saw in Iran. In Pakistan, traditionally, the religious parties seldom had more than a few seats in the National Assembly. When the present military dictator tried to suppress the main political party opposed to his rule, the right wing voters elected sixty religious candidates to the National Assembly instead and enabled the religious parties to form governments in two of the country's four provinces.

It is only in private conversations or moments of stress that we discover the circumspection, cynicism and dual standards of the western politicians about democracy in Muslim lands. When the Turkish Parliament voted against the use of Turkish soil by the US for staging the planned attack on Iraq, the US Deputy Secretary of Defence, Paul Wolfowitz, scolded the Turkish leaders for not being more supportive and admonished the Turkish Army for failing to intervene in the political process in support of the US. Imagine the uproar if a foreign leader had called upon the US armed forces to interfere with the Congress on his country's behalf?

The remarks by Wolfowitz also reveal the extent of involvement between the US and the armed forces of these countries, by-passing the national governments. In the book, *'Battle Ready'*, by Tom Clancy (Putnam, N.Y, p. 336) General Zinni, the commander of the US Central Command, relates how Pakistan's chiefs of army staff, General Jahangir Karamat and General Musharraf, had confided their dissatisfaction with the country's leaders to him on separate occasions. The level of intimacy and trust was such that Zinni felt comfortable enough to discuss with them if, indeed, the army would be contemplating a coup against the democratically elected governments.

Political rhetoric in the West is full of pious desire for the spread of democracy in the Muslim countries, particularly the Middle East. What is never mentioned is that such democratization would be totally unacceptable if it were to interfere with the western control of oil, co-operation and assistance on counter-terrorism, fostering a state of peace with Israel, stemming the proliferation of weapons of mass destruction and preventing Islamic radicals from gaining power. Viewed in this context, democracy does not involve freedom of choice for the Muslims but is reduced to little more than a euphemism for western subjugation and control. Since no self-respecting elected government could survive for long under such an imperial regime, the chances of any free democratic institutions taking root in the Middle

East must be regarded as slim, at least, as long as western interests in the region remain predominant.

For all the endless chatter about democracy, today the world is run by three of the most secretive institutions in the world: the International Monetary Fund, the World Bank, and the World Trade Organisation, all three of which, are in turn dominated by the US. Their decisions are made in secret. The people who head them are appointed behind closed doors. Nobody really knows anything about them, their politics, their beliefs or their intentions. Nobody elected them and nobody said they could make decisions on behalf of the world. It is a frightening thought indeed ------ a world run by a handful of greedy bankers and CEOs who are not elected nor do they represent any one except a small circle of moneyed interests.

To quote Harvard Professor, Alvin Toffler, '------ *the new global economy is dominated by the great transnational corporations. It is serviced by a ramified banking and financial industry ------. It breeds money and credit no nation can regulate ------. It is torn by a world-scale conflict between resource suppliers and users. It is riddled with shaky debt on a hitherto unimaginable scale- ------. And its ideology is not laissez faire or Marxism but globalism ---- the idea that nationalism is obsolete* ('The Third Wave', Bantam Books, New York, p. 324 - 5). Indeed, the transnationals have grown so large that they have taken on some of the features of nation states, including having their own corps of quasi-diplomats and their own highly effective intelligence agencies.

At the risk of getting branded a conspiracy theorist, one cannot ignore the existence of some other, more illusive and highly secretive organizations, like the Bilderberg Group and the Trilateral Commission, composed of eminent politicians and financiers from the US, Europe and Japan that meet regularly, it is said, to chart a political and financial course for the entire world. Nothing about these deliberations is made public and even their existence is assiduously denied. However, there is evidence to substantiate the presence of such a set-up in publications like '*The CIA and the Cult of Intelligence*', by Victor Marchetti, reportedly the first book the US Government ever went to court to censor before publication. Even prominent modern thinkers like Alvin Toffler testify to their influence in the shaping of our world ('*The Third Wave*', p. 325).

It is the domestic policy of a nation that determines its foreign policy. Since domestic policy in the West is based on corporate interest, this is what decides its attitude towards the rest of the world as well. There are a number of options available for imposing the will of the West on the other nations. These vary from country to country and from situation to situation. At any given time any combination of the available factors may be put into effect. These may include such simple measures as the removal of a recalcitrant head of government, as happened to Patrice Lumumba in the Congo or an all out military campaign as witnessed against Iraq and Afghanistan or a war by proxy as we see in Sudan. Economic and political sanctions, with and without the backing of the United Nations, are a more common option. From time to time, leaked documents have revealed that financial inducements have been used to influence the decisions of foreign leaders such as King Hussein of Jordan, Dalai Lama of Tibet and some members of the BJP government in India.

The West also exercises an insidious control over the minds of not only their own people but also on the people of the other nations. It does so through highly professional and imaginative manipulation of the news and information systems. If any one is naïve enough to believe that BBC, CNN and other similar outfits are there for the benefit of the natives they need to think again.

The same applies to the press in the West. The UN imposed economic sanctions against Iraq constituted the most comprehensive state of siege ever imposed in modern history. Millions of children suffered gruesomely in the process. Their suffering and death amounted to child sacrifice, certainly the most egregious instance of child abuse in modern times. They were brutally and lethally punished for political reasons. It provoked no outrage or serious comment in any of the, so called, quality newspapers in the West - ---- not even after the US Secretary of State disdainfully declared the suffering of the Iraqi people to be 'a price worth paying' for the achievement of US objectives.

Many UN officials campaigned to end the economic sanctions. Hans von Sponeck and Denis Halliday resigned their posts and traveled extensively to educate people about the effects of the economic sanctions, which Halliday termed 'genocidal.' UNICEF's Executive Director, Carol Bellamy, held a press conference in 1999 to release a *'Situation Analysis of Women and Children in Iraq'* which carefully explained that the economic sanctions contributed to the 'excess deaths' of over 500,000 Iraqi children. Not one US television network aired coverage of the press conference. Only two of the fifty leading US papers reported the actual number of half a million 'excess deaths' of children. The Wall Street Journal asserted that it was all Saddam's fault. The New York Times echoed this and quoted James Rubin of the State Department who questioned the study's methodology. If any one believes that suppression of such news was all a coincidence and not the work of a central media control policy, he or she must also believe that Santa

Claus and his Rudolph the red-nosed flying reindeer are real too.

Apart from hiding the truth from its own people the western media plays an insidious role in spreading disinformation to destroy individual reputations and destabilizing governments in targeted countries. There is nothing more devastating, short of war, than a sustained media campaign to create alarm, despondency and despair among the people aimed at destroying their morale and faith in the leadership and institutions of the country. It is a highly developed and sophisticated science and Pakistan, in particular, has been at its receiving end for a considerable time. Any one interested in getting more details on the subject may like to refer to a booklet entitled, '*Soft War on Pakistan.*'

There is a natural historic tendency among the people everywhere to try and emulate the norms and culture of the dominant economic power in the world. This is just as true today as it was in the days of the Roman Empire. The social and moral values, customs and norms of the ruling imperial power come to be accepted as the standard. The youth, in particular, are more susceptible and begin to view the world and the issues from a different and foreign perspective.

Since the indoctrination is more or less subliminal and hardly perceptible, the effects are deep-rooted, long-lasting and profound. Media such as films, television, radio, the Internet, books, newspapers and magazines all play a role. Hollywood and now also 'Bollywood' are highly significant in this context since film is an emotive medium, uniquely able to manipulate through lighting and music as well as words. The same is true to an even greater extent for television. The mere fact that the ruling elite in most of the developing countries use English as the language for communication it has in itself become a significant tool in the game of mind control.

As an indication of the effectiveness of this insidious process, some Iranian revolutionaries had taken a hundred or so members of the US embassy as hostages in Tehran after the overthrow of the Shah. It was an issue between Iran and the United States. Pakistan was not involved in any way, yet, ladies of Sind Club in Karachi held regular vigils and prayer meetings for the release of the American hostages. A few years later the Americans killed hundreds of thousands of Iraqis in the Gulf War and over half a million Iraqi children died as a result of the subsequent unending UN sanctions. There was no show of sympathy or support at the Sind Club or at any other such institution for the hapless Iraqis or for the suffering of the innocent people of Afghanistan when the Americans bombed them mercilessly. As the Persian couplet goes, *'Ber mazarey ma gharibaan nay chiraghey nay gulay.'* Conditioned by the media, members of Sind Club like so many other westernized institutions, only look at the world through the western eyes. They have been turned into what are popularly known as 'coconuts' ---- brown on the outside but white inside.

For it to be effective, it is important that the reputation of the media must be maintained as pristine in the eyes of the subjects, hence, the need for so much stress on slogans such as the 'freedom of expression' and 'freedom of the press,' etc. In reality there is no such thing. In the United Kingdom, for instance, the Prime Minister's office monitors the media and press directly through an outfit euphemistically called ' *The Whitehall 'D' Notices Committee*' to ensure that it complies with the requirements of national interest. As to the communications and news media in the United States, this is what John Swinton, former Chief of Staff at the New

York Times and the unofficial dean of his profession, said during a toast before the prestigious New York Press Club:

'*There is no such thing, at this date of the world's history, as an independent press. You know it and I know it. There is not one of you who dares to write your honest opinions, and if you did, you know beforehand that it would never appear in print. I am paid weekly for keeping my honest opinions out of the paper I am connected with. Others of you are paid similar salaries for similar things, and any of you who would be so foolish as to write honest opinions would be out on the streets looking for another job.*

'*If I allowed my honest opinions to appear in one issue of my paper, before twenty-four hours my occupation would be gone. The business of the journalist is to destroy the truth; to lie outright; to pervert; to vilify; to fawn at the feet of mammon, and to sell the country for his daily bread. You know it and I know it and what folly is this toasting an independent press. We are the tools and vassals of the rich men behind the scenes. We are the jumping jacks, they pull the strings and we dance. Our talents, our possibilities and our lives are all the property of other men. We are intellectual prostitutes.*'

No more need be said on the subject after this except that those of us who are used to treating every thing presented by the western media as Gospel truth need to re-examine their attitudes and take such things with a large grain of salt. If this is the state of the media in the West, where journalists receive generous benefits by comparison, it does not take much imagination to figure out what transpires in the news media in countries like Pakistan.

The totally inadequate coverage of the injustices, atrocities and brutalities committed in Afghanistan, Iraq, Chechniya, Bosnia, Kashmir and other places by the media in the

Muslim countries has been little short of a cover-up. It is understandable if the West hides what has gone on there but what motive could there be for the press in Pakistan to keep the news from its readers? All it requires to get the true picture at virtually any place in the world today is an Internet connection and a simple phone call. It is the same with the Press Pundits, posing as opinion makers, who indulge in endless inanities about subjects they understand very little while ignoring manifest realities that stare in their faces.

Western governments make extensive use of the malleable nature of the media to bring public opinion in line to support their planned objectives not only abroad but at home as well. Howard Zinn author of *'A People's History of the United States'* recently wrote in the *'Progressive'* '-------- *Don't make me point out how this fear of weapons of mass destruction does not extend to the United States. Bush officials think if they use that phrase "weapons of mass destruction" again and again and again that people will cower, cower, cower. Never mind that Iraq is a fifth-rate military power and not even the strongest military in the region. Israel, with 200 nuclear weapons, has that distinction. Bush is not demanding that Ariel Sharon rid himself of his weapons of mass destruction or face "regime change."*

'The media are a pitiful lot. They don't give us any history, they don't give us any analysis, they don't tell us anything. They don't raise the most basic questions: Who has the most weapons of mass destruction in the world by far? Who has used weapons of mass destruction more than any other nation? Who has killed more people in this world with weapons of mass destruction than any other nation? The answer: the United States.

'Please, I don't want to hear anything more about Saddam Hussein's possibly making a nuclear bomb in two years, in five years, nobody knows. We have 10,000 nuclear weapons.'

The United States department of defence runs a school at Fort Bragg that is exclusively devoted to the study of news management and the development of strategies for media manipulation to help achieve national objectives. It is beyond the scope of the present discussion to delve more deeply into this issue. Professor Noam Chomsky has carried out an excellent analysis of the subject in his book *'Manufacturing Consent'*. In addition, the booklet *'Soft War on Pakistan'* provides some insight that relates specifically to the country and Islam in general. For an interesting description of how the Bush Administration is selling its planned war on Iraq to the American people please see, *'Weapons of Mass Deception'*, by Sheldon Rampton and John Stauber, Robinson Books, London.

The demonisation of Islam and the Muslims in the western media in the more recent past has been very much deliberate and purposeful. It has been done mostly by playing upon the cultural differences between Islam and the West. Any culture essentially constitutes a man-made environment that has evolved over the millennia from instinctive to learned behaviour. It happened under the influence of a whole host of geographic, political and economic factors to develop language, beliefs, tools, social and moral values, codes of behaviour, etc. that naturally differ from one another. Society preceded culture ----- animals have societies but no culture as such which is unique to man. A child is born 'cultureless'. Its subsequent behaviour, attitudes, values, ideals, beliefs and actions are influenced by the environment surrounding it. Culture provides the basis for social organisation, economic systems, education, religion and belief, custom and law.

Since the environment differs from culture to culture, there is no objective yardstick for comparing differing cultures as such. Any culture, broadly speaking, has three main aspects ----- technological, sociological and ideological. It may be possible to make comparisons in terms of technological achievements but, as to the rest, it is impossible. The West, for example, may look upon the burka-clad women of Afghanistan as 'oppressed', 'persecuted' and 'backward' because of the restrictions placed on them. This is not how the vast majority of Afghan women view themselves. Their values are different that require men to protect and provide for them. If asked, they are apt to retort that it is the women in the West that need to be pitied for the men there are 'shameless' who allow their women to paint themselves like tarts and walk the streets with bared arms and legs to be ogled at by other men.

The fact that the point of view of the more rich and powerful society is seen to prevail does not make it more 'correct' or 'superior'. Military strength, affluence, or poverty and weakness in themselves do not constitute the criteria for culture. Certainly, there is no case or justification for imposing the norms, values and social practices of one culture upon members of the other societies. Any such attempt can only result in devastating consequences, as can be seen among the surviving native populations of North America and Australia.

The influence of culture is powerful for it overcomes basic instincts and urges such as survival, hunger and the need for sex. It is stronger than life and even death ----- people frequently risk certain death for their beliefs. Its primary purpose is to make life more secure and enduring, hence, the animosity and fear of other cultures. It is an extension of the survival instinct. This is what makes Berlusconis of this world so defensive as to make highly illogical assertions to re-assure themselves about the superiority of their culture over the others.

However, the deliberate and persistent demonisation of Islam that we have witnessed in the western media is quite another matter. It is a conscious act of policy for the achievement of certain political objectives. Had the issues been purely cultural, the discussion and criticism would have included and extended to other cultures as well and not dwelt exclusively on Islam.

Take the issue of women again, for example. Their treatment is different from the West not only among the Muslims but in almost every other culture in the world, yet, none of these are put under the microscope in the same way as the women in Islam. In Judaism, for instance, women are not allowed to study the Torah or to pray in the synagogue. Their role in religion is limited to 'maintaining the ritual purity of the home'. Even though the Rabbis teach that women were blessed by God, men are commanded to thank God during the Morning Prayer for not making them Gentiles, slaves or women (*'A History of God'* by Karen Armstrong, Alfred A. Knopf, New York, 1993, p.77). One Rabbi even declared, 'A hundred women are equal to only one witness' (*'Talmud, Yebamoth'*, 88b). Polygamy is certainly permissible in Judaism. A man may divorce his wife at any time for any number of reasons. According to Rabbi Akiba, who first recorded Hebrew oral laws (*Mishna*), it is enough grounds for divorce if a man finds another woman more beautiful or if the wife did not cover her hair or had a loud voice, etc. (*'Talmud, Gittin, LX, 10, Ketuboth VII, 6'* as quoted by Will Durant in *'The Age of Faith'*, p. 362). However, if the wife wishes to get a divorce, she has to obtain her husband's permission before she is allowed to do so and he can withhold this without any cause. This is still the law in the state of Israel.

The treatment of women in Hinduism is far worse. In the Indian state of Behar alone more than 160,000 unwanted female infants are killed at birth each year. By extrapolating this figure for the rest of India the number of such murders would exceed one million. They are killed because '*girls are considered a burden as they are not breadwinners. Parents have to pay to find them husbands and the poor people can't afford it.*' ('*Death By Fire. Sati, Dowry Death and Female Infanticide in Modern India,*' by Mala Sen, Weidenfeld & Nicolson, London, 2001). According to Hindu religious law, the Code of Manu, '*The source of dishonour is woman; the source of strife is woman; the source of earthly existence is woman; therefore avoid woman ------.*' In Hinduism, reading and writing were also ordained as inappropriate for women. ('*The Story of Civilisation, Part 1, Our Oriental Heritage*', by Will Durant, Simon and Schuster, New York in 1954, p.493).

The fate of a widow in Hindu culture is most unenviable. '*The widow becomes the menial of every other person in the house of her late husband. All the hardest and ugliest tasks are hers, no comforts, no ease. She may take but one meal a day and that of the meanest. She must perform strict fasts. Her hair must be shaven off. She must take care to absent herself from any scene of ceremony or rejoicing, from a marriage, from a religious celebration, from the sight of an expectant mother or of any person whom the curse of her glance might harm. Those who speak to her may speak in terms of contempt and reproach; and she herself is the priestess of her own misery, for its due continuance is her one remaining merit'* (*'Mother India'*, by Katherine Mayo, Jonathan Cape, London, p. 82). To ignore such cruelty and discrimination towards women in other cultures, while singling out the wearing of hijab and burka by Muslim women for criticism, smacks of not simply bias but complicity in a conspiracy against Islam that extends far beyond cultural considerations. Nuns, priests, Jewish settlers, Rabbis, Catholics and Orthodox Christians may cover their heads but not Muslim women, who are deemed 'oppressed' for doing the same. It reeks of nothing but prejudice and hypocrisy.

The same kind of tendentious coverage of Islam and the Muslim countries extends into other fields as well. Any report about the proliferation of so-called weapons of mass destruction no matter how spurious, if related to Muslim Pakistan, is bound to make headlines in the *'New York Times'*. However, when the United Nations inspectors find evidence that Indian companies have been supplying chemical ingredients and machinery for making poisonous gases and missile warheads to Iraq, in blatant disregard of the sanctions, it is glossed over and hardly merits a mention even in some obscure corner of the paper. Similarly, when referring to any possibility of nuclear and missile technology leaking into the hands of undesirable elements, western media invariably mention Pakistan as a likely source, while carefully avoiding any mention of India, Germany or any other country that was known or suspected of having been involved in the trade. The fact that the nuclear research facilities in Libya and Iran were chiefly staffed by Indian scientists is altogether ignored, dwelling exclusively on their connections to Pakistan.

Some of the worst human rights violations in the world have been committed in India in recent times. In a letter addressed to President Clinton, Congressmen Edolphus Towns, Cynthia McKinney, Dan Burton, Donald Payne, William J. Jefferson and others called for declaring India a terrorist state because her security forces had killed more than 250,000 Sikhs, over a ten year period, in a campaign to silence their demand for independence. They also stated, *'According to the State Department between 1991 and 1993 India paid out more than 41,000 cash bounties to police officers for killing Sikhs. India has killed more than 70,000 Kashmiri Muslims and destroyed a most revered mosque in Kashmir. Tens of thousands of Sikhs, Kashmiris, Christians, and others are being held as political prisoners'* (*'The Dawn,'* 13th June 2000).

During President Clinton's visit to India in March 2000 the Indian secret agencies massacred 35 Sikh villagers in Kashmir and then blamed the Kashmiri freedom fighters for this barbaric act. Movement Against State Repression (MASR) co-sponsored with the Punjab Human Rights Organization an investigation of the massacre of Sikhs in Chithisinghpora. It concluded that Indian security forces had carried out the killings. A separate investigation conducted by the International Human Rights Organization came to the same conclusion. An estimated two hundred thousand Christian Nagas tribesmen have been killed by the Indian security forces in Assam province since 1947 to put down their struggle for independence.

No government or media in the West, including the United States, took notice let aside made an issue out of it. As compared to this, the episode at Tiananmen Square is ritually resurrected year after year to discredit China.

Human rights issues have become a tool in the game of international politics. Their violations are noteworthy only when they occur in China, Sudan, Iraq or Taliban ruled Afghanistan but completely ignored when committed by America's friends like Israel, Egypt, Russia, Armenia and India. It is hypocrisy of this kind that has destroyed the credibility of the western politicians and media in the eyes of all but the most gullible in the world.

PAX AMERICANA

So far we have looked at some of the tools used by the West to pursue its interests short of war. We have also seen that western objectives abroad are primarily governed by economic factors. Religion is not an issue; it never has been one. Its significance is seldom more than that of an emotive tool for influencing public opinion, in this case, to demonise the Muslims and Islam in the public mind to justify subsequent actions against them. Bush did not attack Afghanistan nor is he preparing to attack Iraq simply because these are Muslim countries but because the United States needs to take possession of these countries in pursuance of its long-term economic objectives. Iraq is a secular nation and has never had any connection with al-Quaida or any other known terrorist group nor is it in any position to pose a serious threat to any one but this is a minor detail that can be easily altered in the minds of the people thanks to the power of the media.

Since the demise of the Soviet Union the United States has been trying to find a role for itself in the radically altered world that lay wide open begging for opportunity. In 1992, following the Gulf War, the US Department of Defence gave shape to its ambitions in a draft report that envisioned the United States as a colossus astride the world, imposing its will and keeping world peace through military and economic power. When leaked in final draft form, however, the proposal drew so much criticism that it was hastily withdrawn and repudiated by the first President Bush. The defence secretary in 1992 was Richard Cheney, now vice president, and the document was drafted by deputy secretary for defence, Paul Wolfowitz, who at the time was defence undersecretary for policy.

Clinton Democrats remained skeptical, more about the scope and practical problems associated with it than perhaps about the nature of such ambitions. The issue was revived under the name of 'Project for New American Century' under the leadership of Conservative hardliners like Richard Perle (also advisor to extremist Israeli Prime Minister Netanyahu) and Professor Donald Kagan of Yale, whose ideas sound eerily similar to those of the nineteenth century British imperialists. Included among the authors who completed the project report in September 2000 were Paul Wolfowitz, John Bolton, present undersecretary of state, Stephen Cambone, head of the Pentagon's Office of Program, Analysis and Evaluation, Eliot Cohen and Devon Cross, members of the Defense Policy Board which advises Rumsfeld, Lewis Libby, the chief of staff to Vice President Dick Cheney and Don Zakheim, comptroller for the Defense Department.

The basic theme as spelt out in the document is that '*At no time in history has the international security order been as conducive to American interests and ideals. The challenge of this coming century is to preserve and enhance this "American peace."* Overall, the 2000 report reads like a blueprint for current Bush defense policy. The close tracking of its recommendations with current policy is hardly surprising, given the presently held positions of the people who contributed to the 2000 report. Most of what it advocates, the Bush administration has tried to accomplish. For example, the project report urged the repudiation of the anti-ballistic missile treaty and a commitment to a global missile defense system. Bush has taken that course.

It recommended that to project sufficient power worldwide to enforce Pax Americana, the United States would have to increase defense spending from 3 percent of gross domestic product to as much as 3.8 percent. For next year, the Bush administration has requested a defense budget of $379 billion, almost exactly 3.8 percent of GDP.

It urges the development of small nuclear warheads 'required in targeting the very deep, underground hardened bunkers that are being built by many of our potential adversaries.' This year the GOP-led US House of Representatives gave the Pentagon the green light to develop such a weapon, called the Robust Nuclear Earth Penetrator, while the Senate has so far balked.

Back in 2000, they clearly identified Iran, Iraq and North Korea as primary short-term targets, well before President Bush tagged them as the Axis of Evil. In their report, they criticize the fact that in war planning against North Korea and Iraq, 'past Pentagon war games have given little or no consideration to the force requirements necessary not only to defeat an attack but to remove these regimes from power.'

To preserve the Pax Americana, the report says US forces will be required to perform 'constabulary duties' ---- the United States acting as policeman of the world ---- and says that such actions 'demand American political leadership rather than that of the United Nations.'

To meet those responsibilities, and to ensure that no country dares to challenge the United States, the report advocates a much larger military presence spread over more of the globe, in addition to the roughly 130 nations in which U.S. troops are already deployed. More specifically, USA needs permanent military bases in the Middle East, in Southeast Europe, in Latin America and in Southeast Asia, where no such bases now exist. That helps to explain another of the mysteries of post-11th September 2001 US reaction, in which the Bush administration rushed to install U.S. troops in Georgia and the Philippines, as well as its eagerness to send military advisers to assist in the civil war in Colombia.

Authors of the 2000 project willingly acknowledge the idea that the United States would establish permanent military bases in a post-war Iraq. Kagan has since stated, '*We will probably need a major concentration of forces in the Middle East over a long period of time. That will come at a price, but think of the price of not having it. When we have economic problems, it's been caused by disruptions in our oil supply. If we have a force in Iraq, there will be no disruption in oil supplies.*' ('*The Atlanta Journal,*' 29th September 2002).

The fact that all the talk today is about attacking Iraq and very little is said about what will happen after Saddam has been removed from power is a clear indication that the US intends to maintain a permanent presence in that country just as it does in Afghanistan, Central Asia and even in Pakistan.

It is doubtful if the American people have fully appreciated the true extent of Bush's ambitions that envision the creation and enforcement of 'Pax Americana' worldwide. Some of these were spelt out in the National Security Strategy, a document in which each administration outlines its approach to defending the country. The Bush administration plan, released on 20th September 2002, marks a significant departure from previous approaches, a change that it attributes largely to the attacks of a year earlier.

To address the terrorism threat, the president's report lays out a new aggressive military and foreign policy, embracing pre-emptive attack against perceived enemies. It speaks in blunt terms of what it calls 'American internationalism,' of ignoring international opinion if that suits U.S. interests. 'The best defense is a good offense,' the document asserts. It dismisses deterrence as a Cold War relic and instead talks of 'convincing or compelling states to accept their sovereign responsibilities'. As early as March 2002, it was revealed that the US has contingency plans for a nuclear attack on seven countries ----- Russia, China, Iraq, North Korea, Iran, Libya and Syria.

In essence, it lays out a plan for permanent U.S. military and economic domination of every region on the globe, unfettered by international treaty or concern. And to make that plan a reality, it envisions a stark expansion of the United States' global military presence. 'The United States will require bases and stations within and beyond Western Europe and Northeast Asia, as well as temporary access arrangements for the long-distance deployment of U.S. troops.'

Past history has shown that it is easy to get the military in but much more problematic to get it out once things start to get uncomfortable. The planners, no doubt, must have taken this into account even though no exit strategy has been made evident. One possibility could be the revival of Henry Kissinger's scheme of having 'regional influentials' ----- designated countries minding US interests in their respective areas. It hadn't worked then and there appears no reason to believe that it will work now. Much depends upon the time scales they have in mind.

The report's repeated references to terrorism are misleading, however, because the approach of the new National Security Strategy was clearly not inspired by the events of 11th September. They can be found in much the same language in the report issued a year before the attack, in September 2000, by the Project for the New American Century mentioned earlier. Whosoever was responsible for the attacks on the World Trade Centre and the Pentagon provided an invaluable excuse for justifying a policy to the American people that had been planned far in advance. The policy basically aims at world domination and empire building ----something about which the people of America would never feel comfortable and would never have approved of under any other circumstances.

The rest of the world is finding it hard to come to terms with this American aggressiveness. As Madeleine Bunting put in '*The Guardian*' of 11ᵗʰ March 2002, '------ *America has become a problem, and every commentator is visibly wriggling around it, wrestling with how to accommodate George Bush's America with a lifetime of respect for American creativity, meritocracy and cultural vibrancy.*

'----------- *this anti-Americanism debate principally concerns globalisation: first, the questions about how and whether this process can be managed and the multilateral institutions to do that; and second, how to respond to the violent and powerless political identities globalisation triggers, whether they be Hindu mobs in Gujrat or the Taliban. On both, the response of the world's only superpower is a combination of indifference and aggression, and it fails to acknowledge any responsibilities other than to its own electorate.*'

This US attitude was succinctly summed up by the leading Republican Newt Gingrich, '*There are only two teams on the planet in this war ----- there are no neutrals.*'

This is what Eric Margolis had to say in the Toronto Sunday Sun, '*As part of the growing merging of policy between Washington and Jerusalem, the Bush Administration's super-hawks have adopted two longstanding Israeli arguments to justify aggressive actions. First, "We have suffered enormously. This gives us the absolute right to attack anyone we deem a threat, including assassinating potentially dangerous individuals." Second, "We are faced by a mortal threat from terrorists. To hell with world, we'll do precisely as we see fit. The UN, the EU, the Geneva Convention, international law ----- all of them be damned."*

'Fifty years of painful efforts to build a framework of international law are being swept away by the Bush crusaders, who seem to have convinced themselves that they are re-fighting World War II rather than dealing with a dangerous criminal conspiracy made up of a few thousand individuals.

'Listening to the Bush people preach about the need to liberate Iranians and Iraqis from oppression is Olympic-class hypocrisy. If Bush really wanted to promote justice and human rights abroad, he should begin with those nations that are American protectorates: Morocco, a medieval police state with a frightful record of poverty, torture, and abuse; Tunisia and Egypt, both military dictatorships with odious human rights records; Turkey, another military state disguised as a democracy, where torture and murder of political opponents are the norm; Arabia's oil monarchies, which are propped up by US troops. And last, but certainly not least, Palestine, where an entire people are being crushed by a brutal army using US-made tanks, and US-made helicopter gunships, financed by US taxpayer's dollars, and sheltered from worldwide condemnation by America's oft-used UN veto.'

Most worrying of all the aspects of the Bush doctrine is the arrogation of the right to itself to carry out pre-emptive strikes against any nation suspected of developing a capability that might conceivably threaten US interests. '*We cannot launch an all-out war against an all-but-powerless nation based on what we imagine. In fact, if we look out on the world and try to imagine what each individual country or group could do to us, there is no end to the monsters we might find.------ A world in which people launch wars based on such far-fetched fears of each other would soon be little more than a smoking ruin*' (Jay Bookman in the Atlanta Journal of 30th January 2003).

Had any other country put forward such a proposition the politicians and media every where would be up in arms accusing her of being mad and delusional but such is the fear created by the current aggressive mood in the US that while disagreeing vehemently in private, few are willing to express themselves in the open. In the absence of any opposition there is nothing to stop them from going ahead with their plan to reshape the world according to their wishes.

The United States likes to think of itself as a nation of civilized peace lovers that has ostensibly been at peace since the end of the Second World War. While still at this peace it engaged in attacks on China (1945-46); Korea (1950-53); Guatemala (1954, 1967-69); Cuba (1959-60); Belgian Congo (1964); Vietnam (1961-73); Cambodia (1969-70); Grenada (1983); Libya (1986); El Salvador (1980-92); Nicaragua (1981-90); Panama (1989); Iraq (1991); Sudan (1998); Yugoslavia (1999); Afghanistan (2001-02); plus a grudge match soon to come in Iraq. Plus 'police actions' in Lebanon, Columbia (ongoing about drugs) and Somalia, an insurrection in Chile (1973), and numerous other covert bombings conducted by, or under the direction of, the CIA. From 1945 to the end of the 20th century, the U.S. attempted to overthrow more than forty foreign governments and to crush more than thirty populist movements fighting against insufferable regimes. In the process, they bombed about twenty five countries, killed several million people, and condemned many millions more to lives of agony, poverty and despair. If this is a nation of peace lovers, then God help us all.

The US massacred more than three million unarmed civilians in Vietnam in prosecuting a war that made no sense whatsoever. The carnage during the two great wars of 1914–18 and 1939–45 was unprecedented and perhaps more than in all the rest of the wars in human history put together, including the atrocities committed by such savages as Chengez Khan, Helaku and the Huns, etc. What the western historians choose to call 'World Wars', consumed the lives of an estimated eighty million people, mostly civilians. It would be more accurate to describe these as 'Wars of Western Civilization' since the protagonists on both the sides happened to be modern western nations. There is no crime in human history that comes even remotely close to the wanton and deliberate butchery of innocent civilians in the bombing of cities in England, Germany, Russia and Japan during World War II and it was not carried out by the Muslims. In the face of this, for historians like Samuel Huntington to speak of Islam having bloody borders in his *'The Clash of Civilizations'* is misleading, hypocritical as well as fatuous, to say the least.

The worst part of it is that the Americans have not only killed but plan on killing more innocent people around the world to achieve their political objectives. This is dangerous to the point of being mindless. In pursuing such policies they are making the world more insecure not only for themselves but for the others as well.

For more than fifty years Israel has tried to bludgeon the Palestinians into submission but it has not brought any security to her citizens. The Indians too have killed nearly eighty thousand Kashmiris in the past twelve years without persuading them to abandon their struggle for independence and are now at their wits end not knowing what to do next. It was the same with the Russians in Afghanistan and now in Chechniya. The French fared no better following the killings in Tunisia, Algeria and Viet Nam nor were the Americans any more successful after them. The use of indiscriminate and unjustified force has always produced contrary and unsavoury results for its perpetrators. There is no reason to believe that history will be any kinder to Bush and his coterie of policy planners.

On 11th December 2002 Harold Pinter, veteran British journalist, wrote in the '*Daily Telegraph*' under the heading, '*The American Administration is a Blood Thirsty Wild Animal,*' '--------- *However, I found that to emerge from a personal nightmare was to enter an infinitely more pervasive public nightmare ----- the nightmare of American hysteria, ignorance, arrogance, stupidity and belligerence; the most powerful nation the world has ever known effectively waging war against the rest of the world.*

"If you are not with us, you are against us," President George W. Bush has said. He has also said: "We will not allow the world's worst weapons to remain in the hands of the world's worst leaders." Quite right. Look in the mirror, chum. That's you.

'*America is at this moment developing advanced systems of "weapons of mass destruction" and is prepared to use them where it sees fit. It has more of them than the rest of the world put together. It has walked away from international agreements on biological and chemical weapons, refusing to allow inspection of its own factories. The hypocrisy* behind its public declarations and its own actions is almost a joke.

'America believes that the 3,000 deaths in New York are the only deaths that count, the only deaths that matter. They are American deaths. Other deaths are unreal, abstract, of no consequence.

'But what a misjudgment of the present and what a misreading of history this is. People do not forget. They do not forget the death of their fellows, they do not forget torture and mutilation, they do not forget injustice, they do not forget oppression, they do not forget the terrorism of mighty powers. They not only don't forget: they also strike back.'

IN DEFENCE OF ISLAM

Since the September 2001 tragedy, countless pages in western books, magazines and newspapers have been blackened by mostly negative writings about Islam. These invariably assume that Islam is a monolith and its more than one billion adherents act as a single body. Almost anything unacceptable done by any Muslim anywhere automatically becomes attributable in some way to his religion. It is like equating the West with Christianity and blaming all the evil acts committed by western individuals and governments, be they in Afghanistan, Algeria, Bosnia, Chechniya, Iraq, Kosovo, Lebanon, Palestine, the Philippines or within the western countries themselves, on the Christian faith. Castigation and targeting of Muslims and branding them as terrorists every where is no different to holding all the Christians in the world responsible for the genocide in Bosnia that took the lives of three hundred thousand innocent Muslims.

The portrayal of Muslims as a homogenous political and religious monolith by the likes of Lewis, Huntington and others is patently false. Equally false and misleading is the assumption that any dispute between a Muslim country and the West has its roots in the allegedly flawed doctrines of Islam. The routinely expressed sanctimonious hope that any difficulties between the two worlds would somehow be miraculously resolved if only the Muslims started to think and act like the westerners, is delusional and fatuous. It is an escape from reality. Nothing will change even if every Muslim in the world were to convert to Christianity for the very simple reason that the issues are not religious or cultural.

The problem is one of political and economic rights that have been violated and hijacked. Unless and until these are restored, any hope for peace will remain chimerical. The use of excessive force against the Muslims, as advocated by Bernard Lewis among others, will only further exacerbate the situation. It is a misreading of history. In the long run, it is impossible to have peace without justice that is manifest and tangible.

The West generally prides itself in its ability to reason with logic. Yet, when it comes to the opinions, rights and needs of other nations and peoples these attributes seem to take flight into the unknown. There will never be any understanding with the Muslims, or any one else for that matter, until the western powers learn to look at the point of view of the other side honestly with a clear and open mind and examine each issue on its own merit.

The political and economic problems that exist between the Muslim and the western nations need to be dealt with at that level, on a case-by-case basis and in a fair and equitable manner, without bringing religious considerations to bear on them ----- just as it happens when there is a dispute between two or more western nations. The entire Muslim community cannot be held accountable for the alleged actions of Osama bin Laden or al-Quaida in the same way as the entire Christendom is not responsible for the massacres in Bosnia and Chechniya or the activities of Ku Klux Klan or IRA. A criminal act by a few individuals, no matter how distressful, does not justify dispensing with due processes of law and letting massive war machines loose on totally innocent and hapless civilian populations.

If there are religious issues in Islam these are for the Muslims to resolve within themselves. The West has neither any business meddling in them nor any gratuitous right to tell the Muslims what to do. If some Muslim country or community appears to have a problem with democracy, liberalism and so-called modernity it is a problem for her and not for all of Islam and certainly not for any one in the West. For western writers to bring religion into issues that are essentially political or economic in nature smacks of obfuscation and side-tracking of the real problem and reluctance on their part to face the truth and reality.

There is no law that requires the Muslims to follow the path beaten by the West nor can they be denied their political and economic rights if they choose to follow their own creed in the best way they understand it. The human race can only hope to survive peacefully on the basis of a live and let live policy. There can be no peace as long as some people, including the Muslims, are continually denied their due rights. It is a lesson that should have been clear since the Dark Age in Europe.

To give peace and harmony in the world a chance, as a first step, the demonisation of other people, in particular Islam and the Muslims, must stop. It is not enough, in fact hypocritical, for George Bush or Prince Charles to visit some mosque, accompanied by a phalanx of whirring TV cameras, while US and British bombs continue to fall on innocent civilians in Afghanistan and Iraq. Napoleon too had declared himself as a true friend of the Muslims when he invaded and occupied Egypt in 1799. If anything, such public relations exercises have the opposite effect to that intended in the increasingly vitiated environment that has been created since the demise of the Soviet Union.

To some extent the Muslims themselves are in part to blame for the situation. Many of them who write about Islam do so on the basis of knowledge that they have acquired in the West. Consequently, they look at it from a western perspective and present it as such. There is a sense of apology and guilt in their writings arising out of western accusations of historical mistreatment of non-Muslim communities by the Muslims and their inability to modernize themselves. They also tend to accept too readily that somehow Islam is to be blamed for the present technologically backward state of the Muslim community. This, in turn, is taken as re-enforcement and confirmation of the views already held in the West. It has become a vicious circle which prevents the reality about Islam from becoming known.

It is not possible to explain all that needs to be explained about Islam in these pages. Only some of the more basic misconceptions that exist in the West can be dealt with at this time. The most significant of these relates to the Koran itself. It is not a book in the conventional sense of the word. There is no beginning, no subject-wise divisions and no conclusion as such. It is a collection of divine revelations received by the Prophet over a period of about twenty-three years. Unlike the Bible, there is no human endeavour involved and the Koran is the same for all the different Muslim sects that have evolved over the years.

Each revelation generally relates to a particular occasion or problem and any one subject may be covered by more than one revelation. Therefore, in order to properly understand Koranic injunctions, there is a need not only to know the context to which these relate but also to refer to all the rest of them that might have a bearing on the issue.

Since there is no clergy authorized in Islam, it is up to each individual to understand and interpret what is in the Koran, as best as he can. What Osama bin Laden believes is just as right or wrong as what Ayatullah Khomeini or some shopkeeper in Sumatra may think and there is no compulsion for the rest to follow any of them. It is strictly a personal choice.

At first sight, it may seem complicated and confusing but it is not so in reality. The Koran holds each individual responsible for his or her actions in this world which obviates the need for any intermediaries in religious matters. The issue is strictly and directly between man and his Creator. Confusion only sets in when self-appointed individuals start to arrogate to themselves the authority to interpret what is in the Koran and try to impose their views and will on the others.

What is manifestly wrong, as is being done in the western media, is to present people like Osama bin Laden as representative of Islam. It is like equating Meir Kahan with Judaism and Radovan Karadzic or Adolph Hitler with all of Christianity. While institutionalized torture of Muslim prisoners by the US military is attributed to 'a few rogue elements', all the Muslims en-bloc are somehow held responsible for the acts of terrorism by a few individuals. Earlier, when bin Laden and al-Quaida had formed a relationship with USA, they obviously did not consider the latter as evil. Any differences that developed between them subsequently, therefore, could not have been because of the religion itself. It was the same with Islamic religious organizations like the Muslim Brotherhood in Egypt and Jamaat-e-Islami that had worked hand in hand with CIA to counter communism.

Much has been written about intolerance in Islam towards members of the other faiths. Saudi Arabia has often been quoted as an example where propagation of Christianity is not permitted. All the rest of the Muslim world which lays no such restrictions is conveniently ignored as is the fact that Israel bans the carrying of the Cross and Christmas trees in the streets of Jerusalem. Saudi Arabia and Islam are not interchangeable.

This is what Karen Armstrong, an eminent scholar of Islam, Christianity and Judaism, professor of religious law at Jerusalem University and author of a number of excellent books on related subjects, has written about the attitudes of the three faiths towards each other: *'The Koran has a pluralistic vision and respects other faiths. Constantly, it insists that Muhammad has not come to cancel out the revelations of such earlier prophets as Abraham, Moses and Jesus. God commands Muslims to "speak courteously" to Jews and Christians, "the People of the Book," and to tell them: "We believe what you believe; your God and our God is one" (Koran 29:46). ----- Christianity and Judaism, on the other hand, do not accept any other faith as true and assume that it is the same with Islam ----- but that is not the issue ----- it is all a matter of using whatever is convenient to further political aims.'*

Western writers have often taken passages from the Koran out of context and quoted these as proof of intolerance and belligerence in Islam, while ignoring a host of similar writings in the Old and New Testaments. If only they had known their Bible and read passages such as Deutronomy 2:34, 3:6-7, 13:5,15,18-21; II Chronicles 15:13; I Samuel 15:2-3; Numbers 25:3-4, 31:16-18; Luke 19:27; Mathew 10:34-37; Exodus 11:4-5, 15:3, 21:7, 22:18-20, 35:2; Leviticus 19:19, 21:9, 24:10-16; 25:44-46; I Corinthians 11:3,8-9, 14:34-35; Isaiah 13:15-16; II Samuel 12:31 or Judges 8:10.

As Armstrong explains, *'There are passages in the Koran that seemingly give license to unfettered violence, and we have all heard bin Laden quoting these. But in the Koran, these verses are in almost every case followed by exhortations to peace and mercy. The Koran teaches that the only valid war is one of self-defense. War is always abhorrent and evil, but it is sometimes necessary to fight in order to preserve decent values or to defend oneself against persecution.'*

There is much confusion in the West about the prospects of democracy in Islam. It is quite erroneously assumed that the two may not be compatible. On this particular issue Karen Armstrong elaborates, *'It is often claimed that Muslims are incapable of separating religion and politics. For much of their history Muslims effected a de facto separation of church and state. During the Abbasid caliphate (750-1258) when Baghdad was the capital of the Islamic world the court was ruled by an aristocratic ethos, which had little to do with Islam. Indeed the shari'a, the system of Islamic law, initially developed as a countercultural revolt against this ethos. The clerics and the ruling class thus operated according to entirely different norms. Though secularism as practiced in the West has since acquired sinister connotations, Islam is a realistic faith; it understands that politics is a messy business that can corrupt religion. In Shiite Islam, religion and politics were separated as a matter of sacred principle.*

'Islam is by no means inherently opposed to the democratic ideal. It is true that fundamentalists, be they Jewish, Christian or Muslim, have little time for democracy, since their militant beliefs are not typical of any of these faiths' traditions. It is also true that Muslims would have difficulty with the classic definition of democracy, as "government of the people, by the people and for the people." In Islam, God, not the people, gives a government legitimacy, and this elevation of humanity could seem a usurpation of God's sovereignty. But Muslim countries could well introduce representative governments without relying on this Western slogan. This is what is beginning to happen in Iran, which

had never been permitted to have a fully functioning parliament before the Islamic Revolution. In fact, Muslim thinkers have pointed out that Islamic laws have principles that are eminently compatible with democracy. The notion of shura, for example, which decrees that there must be some form of "consultation" with the people before new legislation can be passed, is clearly congenial to the democratic ideal, as is ijma, the "consensus" of the people, which gives legitimacy to a legal decision.'

Then there are the epithets of fundamentalism and terrorism with which Muslims are frequently labelled. Fundamentalism is a term that is specific to the West and has no basis in Islam as such. It started to be applied to the Muslims only as recently as the revolution in Iran. Since there are no real doctrinal differences among the Muslims, it is hard to classify any individual as fundamentalist or otherwise. In the West, where it is used most frequently, the term is generally applied to any practising Muslim ----- that is any one who is not a 'coconut' or a WOG (western oriented gentleman).

Karen Armstrong, who has made a study of fundamentalism in Judaism, Christianity as well as among the Muslims, holds the view that fundamentalism always begins as an internal struggle. *'It is an intrareligious conflict, in that fundamentalists start by attacking their own coreligionists and fellow countrymen ----- the people who to them represent an ethos that is cruel, tyrannical and corrupt. ----- They are trying to bring God from the sidelines, to which he has been relegated in secular culture, and back to center stage. They create counter-cultures, enclaves of pure faith, such as the ultra-orthodox Jewish communities in New York City or Bob Jones University in Indiana.'*

The vast majority of fundamentalists, however, do not take part in acts of violence. They are simply struggling to keep the faith alive in what they see as an inimical world. She quotes the examples of Kutab in Egypt and Osama bin Laden whose original targets were the so-called Muslim regimes of Egypt, Saudi Arabia, Jordan and Iran which they regarded as defecting from the Islamic norm. It was only at a later stage that bin Laden turned his attention to the United States, which supports many of these regimes and which he has now designated as the root of the problem. '*So Muslim fundamentalism was not originally inspired by a hatred of America per se, but it has become increasingly disturbed by the role of the United States in Islamic countries.*'

There has been a concerted campaign in the western media to present the attack on the World Trade Centre and the Pentagon as if it had been motivated by Islam and was carried out by fundamentalist zealots. Karen Armstrong has certain reservations about this, '*It appears that Muhammad Atta* (the alleged leader of the attackers) *was drinking vodka before boarding the airplane. Alcohol is, of course, forbidden by the Koran, and it seems incredible that an avowed martyr of Islam would attempt to enter paradise with vodka on his breath*'.

'*Again, Ziad Jarrahi, the alleged Lebanese hijacker of the plane that crashed in Pennsylvania, seems to have frequented nightclubs in Hamburg.*

'*Muslim fundamentalists lead highly disciplined, orthodox lives, and would regard drinking and clubbing as elements of the jahili, Godless society that they are fighting to overcome.*

'*I have no theory to offer, but would just like to note that these seem to be very unusual fundamentalists indeed.*'

While so much has been written and talked about the dangers emanating from Islamic fundamentalism, the media in the West has maintained stupefying silence about its Christian counterpart. Potentially, the damage that can be inflicted by the Islamic fundamentalists is nothing as compared to what is possible at the hands of a Christian fundamentalist US President, the most powerful man on earth, who has control over 10,000 nuclear weapons and who claims to 'talk to God' and take directions from Him directly on all important issues, as he told the Israeli newspaper, *Ha'aretz*, recently. He is not alone in this by any means. His administration is full of them, including the most fundamentalist of them all, Attorney General John Ashcroft. If any thing should give the West and the rest of the world sleepless nights it is this and not some, so called, Islamic fundamentalists who have little power or resources and are almost exclusively preoccupied with maintaining the purity of their own faith and its values.

Hardly a day has passed since 11th September 2001 when President Bush has not talked about the 'war on terrorism.' In the past, countries have waged wars against other countries, nations, tribes and peoples but never against an abstraction like 'terrorism'. What is worse, it has been more than a year since he declared this war without actually defining what precisely he means by terrorism. There are others, like Britain's Tony Blair, who have enthusiastically joined Bush's crusade but remain equally vague. During a visit to Pakistan in 2002 Blair declared, *'The international community will not tolerate terrorism in support of political causes ----- even political causes whose strength and logic cannot be disputed and which must be settled.'* On the face of it, this constitutes a fine policy precept but what does he exactly mean by terrorism?

The former German defense minister and constitutional-law expert Rupert Scholz feels that the concept of terrorism is in need of internationally binding definition which does not exist at present. The U.S. Federal Bureau of Investigation (FBI) as per the Code of Federal Regulations (28 CFR Section 0.85), defines terrorism as '*the unlawful use of force and violence against persons or property to intimidate or coerce a government, the civilian population, or any segment thereof, in furtherance of political or social objectives.*' The wording used by the United States Department of Defense describes it as '*the calculated use of violence or threat of violence to inculcate fear; intended to coerce or to intimidate governments or societies in the pursuit of goals that are generally political, religious, or ideological.*' As per both these definitions even states could commit terrorist acts which the US State Department, anxious not to see certain US allies or the US itself labeled as terrorist states, finds unacceptable. In the end what it amounts to is that the US and her allies are waging war against some abstraction that they are unable or unwilling to define.

What is indisputable, however, is that definitions of what constitute terrorism and terrorists change with the times. In British-occupied Palestine in 1946, Menachim Begin, then a leader of the underground Irgun organization which blew up the King David Hotel, killing ninety one innocent people, was treated as a terrorist. A few decades later, Begin was prime minister of Israel and accorded the greatest respect by his former enemies as well as treated like royalty at the White House in Washington.

It was the same with another Israeli prime minister, Yitzhak Shamir. In the 1940s, he also was a terrorist, a leader of the Stern Gang that took responsibility for selective assassinations of British and UN officials.

So, too, Yasser Arafat ----- once a hated terrorist now the recipient of the Nobel Peace Prize. Israeli and US governments may not like the Palestinian leader these days, but they have been dealing with him and with the Palestinian Liberation Organization they once denounced as a gang of terrorists.

In the 1950s, Jomo Kenyatta spent time in jail for his role as a leader of the terrorist Mau Mau movement fighting the British occupation of Kenya. A few years later, Britain left Kenya and Kenyatta became the new country's first prime minister.

In South Africa, Nelson Mandela was branded a terrorist until 1990, when the white-supremacist government realized it had no choice but to deal with him. Now, at home and abroad, Mandela is treated as the embodiment of free South Africa.

The list goes on. The U.S. State Department branded the Kosovo Liberation Army as a terrorist organization until 1999. That's when it enlisted the ethnic Albanian Muslim organization's help in NATO's brief war against Yugoslavia.

Ironically, Osama bin Laden who has been marked as the main suspect in the attack on the U.S. was, just a few years ago, feted as a freedom fighter by the U.S ally, Saudi Arabia, for his role in driving the Soviet Union from Afghanistan. It is a disturbing fact that many of the individuals accused or convicted of terrorism in the United States recently, like Ramzi Yusuf and Amil Kansi, etc. have been intimately associated with CIA in the past. Only the Soviets referred to the Afghan Mujahideen as terrorists that included bin Laden as well as Taliban. In those days, the West treated such claims as Soviet propaganda.

In the end, it is the situation and circumstances at any given time that determine who is a terrorist and who is not. Depending upon the point of view, one man's terrorist can also be another man's freedom fighter. It is also true that the same individual can be a terrorist one day and a freedom fighter the next in the eyes of the same people.

Writing under the title, '*Some Dirty Little Secrets About Terrorism*' in the '*Toronto Star*' of 16th September 2001, Thomas Walkom, who has made a study of terrorism, states, '------- *history demonstrates two dirty little secrets about terrorism, neither of which governments are anxious to admit. The first is that terrorism is almost impossible to prevent unless its root causes are seriously and systematically addressed. The second is that, quite often, terrorists get what they want. ------- Israel was born in terror, it knows what terror is; it was active in creating it. I don't mean this as an insult. It is simply what happened.*

'------- *We can do things that will help lessen the possibility of a terrorist attack, but eliminate it we can't ------- To talk of a war against terrorism is not helpful.------- George W. Bush's and many Americans' absolutism and unquestioning righteousness are as terrifying and as potentially dangerous as much of what they now call terrorism without further ado.*

'------- *what is the lesson from all of this? ------- The circumstances which give rise to their appeal can be addressed, like the refugee camps outside Afghanistan. They produce the environment in which these things breed. But once that's done, the grievances that inspire such hatred of the U.S. and the West have to be addressed. Terrorism is bred when you have people in despair, people with nothing to lose, people with no other way to fight back ------ Sure, plenty may be bonkers. But plenty are not. Plenty are brutalized by living in these* (refugee) *camps and watching their mothers die in a bombing raid and by watching hopelessness. What they feel is abject injustice. ------- the international economic system must be reformed to remove the fundamentally inequitable structural impediments to development. ------- We must get it right. ------- We must cut off the desperation at the root. If we don't, we are ferociously vulnerable.'*

The word 'terrorism' in western media, since the start of the Palestinian struggle against Israeli occupation, has been increasingly associated with Muslims fighting for their rights anywhere in the world. This is by no means confined to Palestine. Of late, the US Government has labeled various Kashmiri groups, fighting for their rights that were promised in the United Nations but denied to them by India, as terrorists. Kashmiris are not the only people fighting for rights in India. Included among the others are Nagas, seeking independence in the northeast of the country, whose claims have not been recognized by the United Nations as such. Yet, it is the Muslim Kashmiris who are terrorists in the eyes of the US, international recognition of their rights notwithstanding, and not the Nagas, ULFA, NDFB and other groups in India that happen to profess the Christian faith, even though they have no claim to legitimacy in the eyes of the world.

Contrary to the impression that has been created, the majority of terrorists are not Muslims. The world leaders in suicide terrorism are the Tamil Tigers in Sri Lanka who are Hindus. University of Chicago Professor Robert Pape, who has made an exhaustive study of suicide terrorism in his book, *'Dying to Win: The Logic of Suicide Terrorism,'* concludes that over 95 per cent of the suicide-terrorist attacks are driven not by religion as much as they are by a clear strategic objective:

to vacate foreign military occupation from the territory that the terrorists view as their homeland.

USA is not alone in arrogating to itself the right to decide as to who is a terrorist and who is not. Recently, Altaf Hussain, a convicted terrorist, fled to the United Kingdom from Pakistan and was not only granted asylum by the Blair government but also made an honoured citizen of the country that prides itself in being in the fore-front of the war against terrorism. As Ardsher Cowasjee wrote in '*The Dawn*' of 11th November 2001, ' ------- *according to police records, there are 260 criminal cases, many involving acts of terrorism, pending / decided here in Pakistan against* (MQM) *party chief Altaf Hussain, who fled the country and is now in residence in London with a British passport in his pocket. In one case, FIR 211/91 of 24/6/91, filed by Major Kalimuddin in Landhi police station, Altaf Bhai and six others were awarded 27 years rigorous imprisonment by the special terrorist court. Tony Blair has given him asylum and by making him a British citizen has afforded him protection.*' Such double standards and hypocrisy have done irreparable harm to the credibility of the West and its leaders among the Muslims and cast serious doubts about their real intentions and objectives.

Similarly, when the United States and Britain support autocratic and tyrannical rulers, while professing and preaching democratic values, there is a particularly hollow ring to them. According to Karen Armstrong, '*Increasingly Muslims have felt helpless ----- some have said that they feel that they are prisoners in their own countries. Their rights and protests have too frequently been ignored. What America seemed to be saying to them was: "Yes, we have freedom and democracy, but you have to live under tyrannical governments."*

Most likely, it was Robert Fisk who wrote in '*The Independent*' at the start of the US bombing campaign in Afghanistan, ' *I have to admit ----- having been weaned on Israel's promiscuous use of the word "terror" every time a Palestinian throws a stone at his occupiers ----- that I find the very word "terrorism" increasingly mendacious as well as racist. Of course, despite the slavish use of the phrase "war on terrorism" on the BBC and CNN, it is nothing of the kind. We are not planning to attack Tamil Tiger suicide bombers or Eta killers or Real IRA murderers or Kurdish KDP guerrillas. Indeed, the US has spent a lot of time supporting terrorists in Latin America - the Contras spring to mind ----- not to mention the rabble we are now bombing in Afghanistan.*' To the Muslims the West's war on terrorism, in reality, is a thinly veiled euphemism for war specifically directed against Islam and Muslim aspirations.

A widespread impression has been created in the West that Islam is a militant creed. There could be nothing further from the truth. The Koran is very specific when it comes to waging war, '*Fight for the sake of God those who fight against you, but do not attack them first. God does not love the aggressors*' (2:190). It also holds all life as sacred, '*Whoever killed a human being, except as punishment for murder or other villainy in the land, shall be deemed as if he had killed all mankind; and that whoever saved a human life shall be deemed as though he had saved all mankind*' (5:32). It has been often suggested that Islam is intolerant towards other people and their beliefs. This is also not borne out by the Koran, '*There is to be no coercion in* (matters of) *religion* (2:256) and '*Believers, Jews, Christians and Shabaeans ----- whoever believes in God and the Day of Judgement and does what is right ----- shall be rewarded by their God; they have nothing to fear or to regret*' (2:62).

It is not only legitimate but the Muslims are specifically enjoined to struggle for their just rights '*Why should you not fight in the cause of God and those who being weak are ill treated, men, women and children who cry out, "Our Lord rescue us----"* (4:75). The process is known as *jihad*. The term does not specifically imply a holy war directed against non-believers, as is erroneously portrayed in the western media. The struggle could be against military aggression, illegal occupation, usurpation of rights of any kind or even against an abstraction like poverty or illiteracy. Jihad could take any number of forms and does not necessarily involve the use of arms. The concept was profoundly admired, eulogised and encouraged by the West at the time when the Afghans were fighting to oust the Soviets from their country but is now feared and vilified because Muslims in many parts of the world are struggling against excesses by the West.

There is a long-standing tradition throughout history under which volunteers from other lands have gone to the help of people fighting for common ideals. Thousands of devout Christians from England joined the Spaniards in ousting the Muslims from the Iberian Peninsula at the end of the fifteenth century. Others from western Europe volunteered their services to fight alongside the Russians in the Caucuses in the eighteenth century. We had the International Brigade of western volunteers in 1936 fighting the Fascists in the Spanish Civil War. These included such names as George Orwell who wrote *'Homage to Catalonia'* based on the experience and Ernest Hemingway of the *'For Whom the Bell Tolls'* fame.

At the beginning of World War II, before USA had joined in, President Roosevelt induced American pilots to volunteer their services for Britain by offering them three times their normal salaries. The United States military routinely gives leave to its Jewish servicemen to fight for Israel. Anthony Rogers in his book, *'Someone Else's War,'* (Harper Collins, 1998) lists scores of military operations, in more than a dozen different countries, in which volunteers from the United States, Russia and other European nations have been fighting in recent times. Some of these include Congo, Rhodesia, Angola, Namibia, Mozambique, Biafra, Sudan, Surinam, Columbia, Yugoslavia and Israel.

If there has been any condemnation of these it must have been highly muted because very few of us ever heard it. On the other hand, the western media and their 'coconut' counterparts in Muslims lands vituperate viciously against any Muslim volunteers who decide to join the liberation struggles of the enslaved and oppressed fellow human beings in Kashmir, Chechniya and other troubled Muslim lands. Why is an Arab volunteer lauded when he fights to save Afghanistan from the Soviet Union but condemned to be exterminated without mercy, like an animal, when he tries to defend the same country against an invasion by the West? What is the moral or ethical difference between a Jewish American volunteering to fight for Israel and a Muslim Pakistani going to the aid of Kashmiris?

Fighting and dying for a cause one believes in is a noble act regardless of who undertakes it. When it is undertaken to help others who are weak and oppressed, the selflessness involved can only be admired as supreme to the point of being sublime. This will always be so as long as the actions remain directed against the aggressor and not against any innocent people. Looking at it in any other way would be both subjective as well as narrow-minded. The criterion rests in the nature of the motive and the spirit involved in the sacrifice and not on whose behalf it is undertaken.

We can understand if the western media indulge in double standards when it comes to Muslim causes. They may find some way to salve their consciences in feeling outraged when innocent civilians are killed at the World Trade Centre but not having any such qualms at US bombers blowing to pieces equally innocent Afghani women and children or at half a million Iraqi children being condemned to die slow and painful deaths as a result of the never-ending UN sanctions. When a Palestinian, unable to stop Israeli excesses against his people in any other way, blows himself up in a bus out of desperation his action is despised as aggression against innocent people but when Israeli tanks and helicopter gun ships blow up Palestinian homes and kill indiscriminately they are acting in self-defence. What is totally incomprehensible, however, is when media in the Muslim countries echo the same flawed logic.

There are other Arabic terms that are frequently misrepresented in the western media. One of these is '*fatwa*' that gained widespread notoriety in the case of Salman Rushdie. It is equated with a religious edict or decree, which is untrue. '*Fatwa*' simply means an opinion; that is all. Islam does not sanction any institutionalized religious hierarchy or priesthood nor does it allow any separate religious courts of the kind common at one time in Christian Europe. Consequently, no individual has the right to pass any sentence in the name of religion except in a court of law and that too only after due process.

It would be patently illegal to execute any one or administer any other punishment on the basis of a '*fatwa*'. Death sentence is only permissible in two instances ---- as punishment for pre-meditated murder and for incitement of grave disorder and insurrection. Killing for any other reason amounts to exceeding the limits laid down in the Koran.

The opinion expressed by any individual is just that ---- an opinion. To present it as any thing more is misleading and mal-intended. The fact that media in the West prefer to use the Arabic expression that appears menacing and which hardly any one understands, and not its harmless-sounding

English translation, tends to confirm the underlying intention to convey a more sinister meaning.

A frequently asked question in the West these days is, 'Why do the Muslims hate us so much?' The short answer is that the vast majority of them do not hate the West nor every thing connected with it. They most certainly do not hate its freedoms or its achievements, as presumed by George W Bush. If they feel concerned and unhappy with the genocide of Muslims in Bosnia, Iraq and Afghanistan it does not mean that they hate all of Christendom. Similarly, if they object to and resent being deprived of their land and freedom in Palestine it is not the same thing as hating all Jews.

What is true is that they have serious reservations about the cultural and moral drift in the western world. They fear the sexual permissiveness and moral decadence that seem to have become endemic in the West. The breakdown of the family (two out of every three marriages end in divorce); fading morality (more than one third of the children born to British women are not fathered by their husbands); widespread promiscuity (U.S radio talk show host, Dr. Dave Mirkin, estimates that half the girls in U.S colleges are infected with venereal diseases); unwed teen age mothers (two out of three children in the US are born to them); legalisation of homosexuality and same-sex marriages; spreading paedophelia; sexual depravity (according to talk show host, Dr. Laura Schlessinger, Professor Singer who holds the chair of Human Ethics at Princeton University, condones sex with animals) are all seen as freedom gone too far and awry and threatening the fabric of society.

These are not criticism of the West as such but an indication that Islam has a different value system that it wishes to preserve, without trying to impose or assert its superiority in any way. It is unacceptable, for example, as happened in Italy in September 2000, where the Supreme Court ruled in a case that adultery was legal for a wife as long it was committed in day time so as 'not to wound the husband's honour' ('*The Times*', London, 8th September 2000, reported by John Phillips).

Then there is the mindless violence (more than six thousand students were expelled from US schools for carrying guns in 1998 alone and, according to President Clinton, thirteen children are killed in US schools every day). Oprah Winfrey has claimed on her TV show that one woman is reported raped every minute in US (not counting the many times more cases that go unreported). She also quoted that 25 per cent of all the children in USA have been molested, mostly by members of the immediate family or by the priests and 25 per cent of the wives are victims of violence by their husbands. With only four per cent of the world's population USA holds more than 25 per cent of its prisoners in its jails (over two million). Add to these the unbridled pursuit of pleasure; love of money; emphasis on consumerism; commercialisation; spread of AIDS and addiction to drugs, alcohol and gambling currently witnessed in the West. All of these are viewed as indications of a society on the decline.

The seedy sex scandals involving US Presidents Kennedy and Clinton, members of the British Royal family and child molestation by hundreds of church officials, in the United States, Canada, Ireland and other countries of Europe only help to confirm that moral turpitude and decadence have become endemic. Recent financial mal-practices on an unprecedented scale in the corporate world, by individuals closely connected to those in the corridors of power in the West, too leave the impression that greed and corruption are out of control. Granted that neither every thing nor every one in the West is corrupt but what one witnesses on popular TV shows like Jerry Springer, Ricki Lake and Jeraldo, to name a few, is enough to strain the faith of any God-fearing individual. Muslims constantly worry that increased contact with the West may result in similar corruption invading their societies as well.

They appreciate and admire the technological progress that has been made and would like to imitate it but not at the risk of importing some of the above mentioned frightening cultural viruses with it. Because of this fear, some of them mistakenly reject the entire package, like the proverbial throwing out of the baby with the bath water, including much that is good and admirable. Islam has no problem with Christianity or Judaism and their intrinsic religion-based value systems, but there is a world of difference between what is Christian and what is practiced in the West at the present time.

This does not imply in any way that societies in Muslim countries are perfect by any means. They fall short of the Islamic ideal in other equally disturbing ways. In some of the tribal cultures in Africa, Pakistan, Iran and Afghanistan, women are treated abominably. Often sold into marriage, they are kept in seclusion inside houses and have very little say in personal, social or tribal affairs. Most of the time, they are regarded as little more than chattels.

The attitude is born out of archaic pre-Islamic customs and traditions that are reinforced through ignorance and illiteracy. It has nothing to do with Islam and, in fact, largely stems from the inability to comprehend it properly. Great wealth is hoarded in a few hands while vast sections of populations live in abject poverty. There are dismaying tales of national wealth being squandered by a few privileged individuals in the flesh pots and gambling houses of Paris, London, Monte Carlo and Las Vegas. The players may call themselves Muslims but that should not make their actions any more Islamic than what the Nazis did could be labeled as Christian.

Much of what is wrong with the Muslims is their own fault and cannot be blamed on the West. In the absence of any ordained clergy they have allowed mostly ignorant and personally motivated agitators to hijack their religion. Not knowing the true ethos and spirit of dynamism inherent in Islam these people want to turn the clock back in search and promise of past glory. That is not where they will find it.

Even an orthodox thinker like Maulana Abul Ala Maodoodi admits in his book '*Sood*' (pp. 183-4) '*We accept, conditions in the world have changed. A great revolution has taken place in cultural and economic fields and it has completely altered the financial and commercial environment. Under these new conditions the evolutionary stipulations that were put into effect in the early days of Islam, based on the economic and cultural conditions in Hijaz, Iraq, Syria and Egypt, do not meet the present requirements of Muslims. The rules of Sharia formulated by the theologians in the past were relevant only to the conditions that existed around them at the time. Many of these conditions are no longer relevant and many new situations have arisen that did not exist in the past. Therefore, the provisions concerning commerce, finance and economics found in the old books of Fika are in need of considerable elaboration and broadening in scope. There is no disputing the fact that the Islamic laws governing economic and financial matters need to be revised. All that remain to be determined are the lines along which this should be done.*'

What is true for economic, financial and commercial matters applies equally to science and technology, law, medicine and all the other fields of human endeavour. If Kazi Hussain Ahmed of Pakistan's Jamaat-e-Islami can benefit from the advances made in medicine in the West, by having heart by-pass surgery done at one of the clinics in London's Harley Street, there is no logical reason to deny the rest of the Muslims similar opportunities that might exist in other disciplines.

Unlike in Judaism with its divine law, *Sharia* in Islam is the result of human endeavour, except for what is specifically stipulated in the Koran. Among its more than 6,200 verses, only 70 deal with personal law, another 70 with civil law, 30 or so with penal law, and about 20 with issues of testimony and justice. In other words, less than three per cent of the Koran is about laws and related legal matters. This in itself should be an indication of the relative emphasis to be laid on different issues.

Since it is impossible to cover the entire gamut of law in the few verses included in the Koran, it stands to reason that any law, provided it does not contravene the provisions of the Koran, is acceptable as such in Islam. There is no need for an entirely new code of untried law to be enacted by theologians who are not familiar and well-versed with the complexities and requirements of modern jurisprudence. Any such attempt will only cause massive confusion and disruption. There is a perfect example of this in Sudan where thoughtless imposition of archaic Sharia has led to the creation of a dysfunctional state. It has provided the West with an excuse to intervene. The end result, most likely, will be a breakdown and dismemberment of the country.

Only the principles are immutable, the rest can change with time and circumstances. This is how the first four caliphs interpreted Islam at the time of its greatest triumph and expansion. To get a true picture of the spirit of pragmatism and dynamism inherent in Islam it is preferable that one should turn to the source. One of the best references in this context, among many others, is the biography of the second Caliph Omer *'Al-Farook,'* by Maulana Shibli Naumani, (Azam Garh, 1898).

In a series of three articles published between January and March 1999 in the '*Dawn*', late Professor Eqbal Ahmad analyzed what he called the roots of the religious right, coming down very harshly on the mutilations of Islam by absolutists and fanatical tyrants whose obsession with regulating personal behaviour promotes '*an Islamic order reduced to a penal code, stripped of its humanism, aesthetics, intellectual quests, and spiritual devotion.*' (This) *entails an absolute assertion of one, generally de-contextualized, aspect of religion and a total disregard of another. The phenomenon distorts religion, debases tradition, and twists the political process wherever it unfolds.-----------*-------(they are) *concerned with power, not with the soul; with the mobilization of people for political purposes rather than with sharing and alleviating their sufferings and aspirations. Theirs is a very limited and time-bound political agenda.*' It will only create a retrogressive and dysfunctional theocratic police state and nothing more, just as it has happened in Sudan.

The modern state in the Muslim world is still a plaything of elites. Many of these are under dictatorial and autocratic rule where freedom of expression and respect for popular will are non-existent. The majority of their populations feel alienated, disenfranchised and resentful. It suits the West because the rulers depend on it to save them from their own people and keep them in place, which is very convenient for manipulating their policies. Apart from this, it helps to present the Muslim societies as corrupt, retrogressive, undemocratic and uncivilized. More than anything else, it is this perception of the Muslim world that drives its youth to try and emulate everything that they see in the West in the expectation that it will, somehow, help to transform them.

Wherever two cultures exist side by side, inevitably, they compete. In the past such clashes have mostly turned to violence and it is not any different today. It is worth noting what Huntington has to say on the subject, '*It is my hypothesis that the fundamental source of conflict in this new world will not be primarily ideological or primarily economic. The great divisions among humankind and the dominating source of conflict will be cultural. Nation states will remain the most powerful actors in world affairs, but the principal conflicts of global politics will occur between nations and groups of different civilizations. The clash of civilizations will dominate global politics. The fault lines between civilizations will be the battle lines of the future.*'

History does not support this hypothesis and we may not agree with his down playing of economics, for instance, as a source of conflict but his predictions of a clash, for whatever reasons, are basically well founded and cannot be ignored. The excuse for the clash is not important. Even if it is to secure oil supplies for the West or to eliminate potential threats to Israel, the end result remains the same. The bare basic truth is that weakness invites aggression and as long as Muslims remain weak and divided there will always be the temptation for one power or another to usurp what they possess.

If they are to save themselves from the excesses that are being committed against them they have to put their own house in order, acquire the knowledge and skills necessary to compete in the modern world and put the resources available with them to optimum use for their well being and survival. It would be a folly of immense proportions to look to the western powers for justice or fair play. There is no such thing in international politics and if they exist at all it is only for those who have some leverage and power. There is only one crime in the game of nations and that is to be weak.

EPILOGUE

The Russians invaded Afghanistan in 1979. In the guerrilla war that ensued more than a million Muslim men, women and children died and close to five million ----- a quarter of the country's population ----- were driven out to look for safety as refugees in camps in Iran and Pakistan. The West used the Afghan Mujahids to bleed the Soviet Union and ultimately bring about its demise. Apart from some monetary donations by wealthy Arab nations, very few Muslims went to their help and those that did are now being mercilessly hunted by the western troops.

During the time when the Soviets had occupied Afghanistan, a vast oil fortune was spent by the Arab states in supporting Iraq's utterly uncalled for war against fellow Muslim Iran, aided and abetted by Britain, the United States and other western countries, that took the lives of at least another one million Muslim young men.

In 1982, Israel attacked Lebanon and occupied the country killing tens of thousands of Muslims, most of them Palestinian refugees sheltering in camps run and protected by the UN. The occupation lasted more than fifteen years. Only Syria and to a lesser extent Iran, among all the Muslim countries, took some steps to save Lebanon. It is open to question if Israel could have ventured into Lebanon without first ensuring peace with Egypt at Camp David and dividing the Arabs.

In 1991, Iraq occupied the fellow Arab state of Kuwait. Instead of settling the issue between themselves, the rest of the oil rich Arab countries invited USA to destroy Iraq and more than paid for the expenses that she might have incurred in the process. Many years later Secretary of State, Lawrence Eagleburger, admitted on television that the primary US motive in the Gulf War had been the removal of potential Iraqi threat to Israel (CNN 13th Sept. 2001).

Twelve years have passed since then but the bombing of Iraq has not stopped nor sanctions against her lifted. An estimated one million Iraqis have been killed due to causes related to the war and subsequent UN sanctions. Another US Secretary of State, Madeline Albright, told CBS' *60 Minutes'* Leslie Stahl on television that the price paid by the Iraqis was worth it for achieving western objectives in the area (ITV's *'Paying the Price'* by John Pilger, March 2000). There is little visible evidence of any outrage or serious official protest against the continuing atrocity from rest of the Muslim nations till this date.

In early 1992, Serbia and Croatia embarked upon systematic genocide of Muslims in the fledgling country of Bosnia. Western powers tried their best to keep the news from leaking out to the rest of the world and under wraps for four long months. Such organisations as the Red Cross and Amnesty International became willing partners in the cover up and did not divulge the terrible events that were fully in their knowledge (*'The Guardian'* and other publications). Even after the news leaked out, the atrocity was not termed genocide but inventively described as *'ethnic cleansing'* to circumvent the obligatory action called for under the UN Charter.

As the UN and the world community waited and watched, more than three hundred thousand Muslim men, women and children were slaughtered. It took two and a half years before any outside intervention was permitted, probably, only because the Muslims were getting better at defending themselves. The sympathy in the West extended as far as Pope John Paul II advising the Muslim women, who had become pregnant after being gang raped by the Serbs, not to abort their pregnancies. There is little evidence of any significant stirring of conscience at the official level among the Muslim countries during that period except in Turkey and, to some extent, Iran.

At about the same time, elections were taking place in Algeria. When it became apparent that a party with Islamic leanings might win, the military staged a coup and the elections were aborted. The action received enthusiastic support from all the western nations, led by France. There was no protest from the Muslim countries. Algeria plunged into a horrendous civil war that has devastated the country and is still raging after ten years with over one hundred thousand killed, many more disabled and the economy destroyed. It may only be a coincidence that, after Iraq, Algeria happened to be economically and technologically the most advanced among the Arab countries.

Not long afterwards, it was the turn of first the Chechen and then the Azeri and Kosovar Muslims. They suffered the worst human rights violations at the hands of Russia, Armenia and Serbia. One fifth of Azerbaijan has been occupied by Christian Armenia and all of its Muslim population driven out. More than a million of them are living in abject misery in camps around Baku. In the case of Chechniya the atrocities continue unabated to this day. Yet we hear no voices of protest and no offers of support coming from any of the governments in the Islamic countries.

There is the on-going Israeli occupation of Palestinian territories that has lasted thirty-five years. An estimated three thousand Palestinians have been killed since they started to protest twenty years ago. Nearly four million of them have been living in sordid refugee camps for the past fifty years, unable to return to their homes in Israel. In their case, to be fair, there have been words of support but, sadly, the action to back these has been lacking.

The struggle of the Muslims of Kashmir for their rights is as old as that of the Palestinians. All their cries for justice and help have fallen on deaf ears in the UN and elsewhere. Twelve years ago, they decided to take matters into their own hands and have been waging a guerrilla war against the illegal occupation of their state by India. The Indian Security Forces have been carrying out a murderous campaign of repression, killing almost eighty thousand men, women and children, torturing many more and raping over twenty thousand women, with little effect. In desperation, she amassed a million troops on Pakistan's border accusing her of training and supporting the guerrillas. How this will endear India to the Kashmiri Muslims is unclear but the sad part is that neither the Kashmiris nor Pakistan received any visible support from brotherly Islamic nations in their hour of need.

After the blame was laid on Osama bin Laden, a Saudi national who had worked closely with CIA in Afghanistan, for the 11th September 2001 incident, President Bush rejected any public investigation either by FBI or the US Congress or any other agency. He then unleashed a murderous bombardment of Afghan towns and villages killing thousands of innocent men, women and children who, in all certainty, had never even heard of the World Trade Centre.

The Afghan Government was replaced by a motley crowd with a dubious past and little power or influence. Its writ does not extend beyond the capital. Its president cannot even find half a dozen Afghans that he can trust to guard him and has to be protected from his own people by American soldiers. The country is in the grip of chaos, anarchy and famine with no end in sight. All the Muslim nations watched the proceedings in silence, while some even collaborated with the US in the destruction of Afghanistan for reasons of their own.

In a grotesque orgy of rape and killing more than five thousand Muslims have been killed and countless women raped by Hindu mobs recently in the Indian state of Gujrat. The killings are still going on. Hundreds of thousands of Muslims have been rendered homeless and are languishing in refugee camps with no help from any quarter. The Indian Prime Minister casually dismissed the tragedy as 'unfortunate' and put the blame squarely on the Muslims every where for not wanting to live in peace. The United States' Government termed it an 'internal matter' for India. The reaction from the world Muslim community was not much different.

This is not all by any means. The open season on Muslims also extends to the Philippines where the Muslim Moros are being forcibly evicted from their lands by the government, with support from USA, to make room for Christian settlers. A similar situation reportedly exists in China's Sinkiang Province. Christian Armenia attacked and annexed a quarter of neighbouring Muslim Azerbaijan, killing scores of thousands of its inhabitants. The area has been cleansed of its Muslim population. Over a million of them have been forced out to live in sordid refugee camps around Baku. A proxy war, financed by the Christian West, is being waged in the south of Sudan in an effort to separate the oil-rich region from the rest of the country. The struggles and sufferings of the Muslims in these and so many other countries are not only lost on the governments but the media in the other Muslim nations also fail to take much notice of them.

264

It is a sad irony that if the battered Muslims received meaningful help from anywhere it was mostly from western sources, albeit due to self-interest more than for reasons of justice and altruism. The inaction on the part of the Islamic countries is incomprehensible since not all of them are helpless by any means. Iran and the Arab countries of Middle East and North Africa produce the life-blood that fuels the world economy. Even a hint of closing the tap is enough to send the stock markets reeling and governments scurrying for deliverance. In recent months the Arabs, fearful of new legislation in the US, have started to withdraw some of their fortunes from there. The effect on the stock market has been dramatic.

It is plausible that fears of coercion or retaliation by the West prevent the governments of these countries from contemplating such action. But this does not explain their inability to institute steps against India, for instance, to relieve the suffering of Muslims in Kashmir and ease the pressure on Pakistan. Oil is by no means the only leverage they have. More than forty per cent of the expatriates working in Saudi Arabia, by far the largest among all the nationalities, are Hindus from India. Their proportion is even greater in places like Dubai. A simple reminder of a possible end to this lucrative source of income will send a powerful message to India. Such selective measures, while greatly serving the cause of Muslim unity, will also help to put other would be aggressors on notice.

On a different note, it is estimated that private Saudi citizens alone have deposits of over eight hundred billion dollars hoarded in western financial institutions (see *'Foreign Affairs'* June 2000 issue). The Zakat on this amount alone comes to twenty billion dollars annually. The dues on the personal wealth of the ruling families and wealthy citizens in the oil-rich Muslim nations could, conceivably, double this amount. King Fahad of Saudi Arabia alone has a personal wealth estimated at $44 billion and the Zakat due on this fortune is sufficient to build and run at least a couple of new first-rate universities in the Muslim world every year.

The total amount of the so-called 'aid' doled out in the form of repayable loans to all of the world's poor nations by the West does not exceed ten billion dollars a year. This is less than one quarter of the amount that is due in charity from only the Arabs if they followed Islam in the true sense. Had these people lived up to the injunctions in the Koran the fate of Muslims throughout the world today would be very different indeed.

The time for them to act is now while the opportunity exists. If they failed to do so the words of the German Pastor Martin Neimoller will come to haunt them. He had been jailed by the Nazis and this is how he explained the circumstances of his arrest, '*First they came for the socialists, and I did not speak out because I was not a socialist. Then they came for the trade unionists, and I did not speak out because I was not a trade unionist. Then they came for the Jews, and I did not speak out because I was not a Jew. Then they came for me, and there was no one left to speak for me.*'

More than three and a half million Muslims have been killed, in one country after another, in the past twenty years. This is one thousand times more than the number of Americans that died on 11th September 2001. The vast majority of refugees today ---- more than eight million --- - happen to be Muslims living in squalid refugee camps all over the world. The world has been turned upside down and we will never hear the end of it because 3,000 Americans died. No one bothers in the least how many Muslims have been murdered in cold blood either before or since that day.

It is time there was a stirring of conscience and governments and institutions in the Islamic states took note of what is happening and acted for themselves. If they did not, sooner or later, their turn will come just as surely as it came for the Palestinians, the Libyans, the Algerians, the Lebanese, the Iraqis, the Kashmiris, the Bosnians, the Somalis, the Chechens, the Azerbaijanis, the Kosovars, the Afghans, the Gujratis and the Moros.

There have been five cases of genocide recorded since World War I ---- against the Jews in Germany, the Muslims in East Punjab (India) and again in Bosnia, against the Tutsis in Rwanda and by the Khmer Rouge in Cambodia. The Muslims were not the guilty party in any of these and in three of the cases the perpetrators of the crimes happened to profess the Christian faith. Yet, it is Islam that gets branded as bloody, dangerous and violent.

As far as Pakistan is concerned, everything in the new Bush doctrine that applies to Iraq applies equally to her as well. It would be naïve in the extreme to think that by being compliant, placating and subservient in the face of western demands there could be any reprieve. What matters to the West is not what Pakistan does but what she has. Their eventual goal extends far beyond the elimination of nuclear weapons in her possession. A capability once acquired can always be regained. Therefore, the West will aim to reduce Pakistan to a state which leaves her in no position to possess such weapons ever again.

This will always remain at the core of any western policy towards Pakistan. Regardless of any difference in views, there is little choice but to plan and act on this assumption. As a principle, where issues of critical national interest and survival are involved, all contingency planning must be based on the scenario that presents the most dangerous threat. This automatically takes care of all the other situations that fall short of it. This is not an issue that is open to argument.

If there is one consistent theme in the litany above it is that no Muslim government will act in time to help another fellow Muslim state in peril. On the contrary, there is no shortage of examples where they have joined in the destruction of other Muslim countries, sometimes, to the detriment of their own long-term interests. Pakistan cannot expect nor does she need any outside help.

Once a nation has demonstrated credible nuclear capability it becomes as safe as can be from external military aggression provided the likely aggressor is not left in any doubt about her resolve to use that capability to maximum effect when pressed. It is only when doubt is created, indicating a lack of resolve or clarity of mind, that peace is threatened and situations like Kargil and the recent massing of troops on Pakistan's border by India become evident.

Earlier public statements by Generals Musharraf and Moinuddin Haider, as reported in the '*Dawn*,' asserting that it is possible for nuclear powers to limit their conflict to conventional weapons and assuring foreign correspondents that Pakistan will not resort to the use of nuclear weapons in the event of war, had a direct bearing on precipitating these two crises. For obvious reasons, the Indian generals have endorsed and encouraged such unprofessional notions. Any war, once started, has a will and momentum of its own. It is a fallacy and misreading of military history to think that the duration or extent of a war can even be predicted, let aside, controlled. One only has to reflect on some of statements by political and military leaders promising the conclusion of WWI within months, if not weeks, for instance. The Indians themselves had grandly announced to complete the

Kargil operation 'within 48 hours'. Five months later, they were still where they had started. There are literally dozens of other such examples.

When a capability as devastating as the nuclear weapons exists it is extremely dangerous to be ambiguous, ambivalent or apologetic about it because these can induce a country like India into making fatal miscalculations. It also keeps the western hopes of divesting Pakistan of the capability, without having to resort to extreme measures, needlessly alive. This is why it continues to persist in its policy of maintaining relentless pressures of all kinds against Pakistan instead of coming to terms and adjusting to the reality that is here to stay. Such measures have, in any case, proved to be counter-productive in the past and are unlikely to achieve results that are any different in the future.

Pakistan is faced with a nuclear threat and has every right to make appropriate preparations for her defence. It is not for the West to decide what these should be. Her actions are perfectly compatible with the UN Charter, just as these are for Britain, Israel or India and there is no need or reason for her to provide any justification to any one or feel apologetic about them.

It has been suggested that the West would destroy Pakistan's nuclear assets if she did not comply with its wishes and demands. This is easier said than done. Had it been at all possible the West would have taken the action a long time ago. The only reason they have desisted so far is because there are no fool-proof assurances or guarantees of success in any undertaking of this nature. The pressures, through the press and diplomatic sources, for Pakistan to sign CTBT were principally aimed at gaining access to nuclear and missile sites for placing devices, such as miniaturized dormant homing beacons for incoming missiles, to improve the probability of success. Even so, one nuclear tipped missile left in tact could do enough damage to western interests in the adjoining areas to make the attempt not worth their while.

Paradoxically, while it is the acquisition of nuclear capability that has placed Pakistan as the target in the centre of western cross-wires, her salvation also lies in her ability to preserve and maintain this very capability. Regardless of all the rhetoric, no one in their right mind would provoke or attempt to deliberately destabilize politically, economically or militarily a nuclear armed nation. The situation is fraught with unforeseen and unpredictable consequences. There may be threats and bluster galore to force the weak-kneed into cowering but it is a different matter when it comes to giving practical shape to any such notions. The best example of this is the difference in treatments meted out to Iraq on the one hand and North Korea on the other on the issue of weapons of mass destruction.

While talking to newsmen in the Governor's House in Lahore in early February 2003, General Musharraf mused that after the US has finished with Iraq her next target would be Pakistan. This has prompted questions from a number of quarters about how he plans to deal with the likely scenario. He has not responded to these questions nor elaborated in any other way.

Whatever his plans or the lack thereof, when faced with situations such as this, it is always best to review how other people have acted in the past under similar circumstances and with what results. One such situation was described by Professor Noam Chomsky in an interview with Michel Albert of ZNET on 29th August 2002. In answer to one of the questions he said:

270

' -------- *Suppose Israel reacts by threatening the US - --- not threatening to bomb it, but in other ways. For example, suppose Israel sends bombers over the Saudi oil fields (maybe nuclear armed, but that's unnecessary), just to indicate what it can do to the world if the US doesn't get on board again. It would be too late to react, because Israel could then carry out its warnings. That scenario has a certain plausibility because apparently it actually happened, twenty years ago, when the Saudi government floated a similar plan* (for Israeli withdrawal from the West Bank in exchange for security guarantees), *violently opposed by Israel.*

'*According to the Israeli press, Israel reacted by sending bombers over the oil fields, as a warning to the US, but one that was unnecessary because the Reagan administration joined Israel in rejecting that possibility for a political settlement, as it has consistently done* (the plan renewed by Saudi Arabia recently has been cold shouldered by George W. Bush). *True, Israel might have been facing destruction, but one might argue that Israel's strategy allows that possibility.*

'*As far back as the 1950s, leaders of the then-ruling Labour Party advised that Israel should "go crazy" if the US wouldn't go along with its demands, and the "Samson complex" has been an element of planning ---- how seriously, we don't know ---- ever since.*'

Pakistan's situation is not much different to that of Israel in terms of threats to its security. Factors such as geography and relative military strength make defence of the country against a determined attack by India, for instance, very difficult. To deter any prospective aggressor there is no choice but to raise the stakes as high as possible. If nuclear weapons are used, it will be during the starting phase of the confrontation before any of these are lost due to pre-emptive enemy action. It is dangerous to give the other side the opportunity to strike first, especially, when a second-strike capability is not there, as is the case with Pakistan. In any nuclear conflict, the side that strikes first will always enjoy a disproportionately large advantage.

It must be unequivocally clear to all concerned that if Pakistan is to go down it will not do so alone and the price to the aggressor will be made as unbearable as possible. The security of Pakistan is just as important and dear to the Pakistanis as that of America is to George W. Bush. If, in order to secure their perceived vital interests, the Israelis are prepared to 'go crazy' so will the Pakistanis to save their country. There can be little doubt that in the event of an imminent military threat against Pakistan from India or the West nuclear weapons must and will be used. What remains to be clarified is if Pakistan's security perimeter extends to include the western borders of Iran. From a logical military and strategic point of view it should.

POSTSCRIPT

The book was first published two years ago, in February 2003, to examine and explain the prevailing situation in the world from the perspective of the Muslims. At the time the US-led attack on Iraq seemed imminent. Since then, many issues have crystallized and new facts come to light. Much of what was predicted in the first edition has happened. Iraq was attacked and occupied without any difficulty and Saddam Hussein has been put in jail awaiting trial. No US Senator or member of the Administration would now wish to be reminded of the words of admiration and blandishment that were used in the West to eulogise the dictator not so long ago. Having served his purpose, he is now expendable and deserves what he will get for the treachery that has brought such havoc and calamity to the people of Iraq.

As in the past, none of the Arab or Muslim countries raised any meaningful protests or obstacles against the invasion, abandoning the poor Iraqis to their fate. As with Afghanistan, many of them secretly facilitated the invasion, once again, proving that their ruling elites are only concerned with their own survival, unmindful and uncaring of the true nature of the threat to their countries. There is every possibility that such apathy and opportunism will encourage and invite further aggression against other Muslim countries. The only hope now lies in the spirited resistance to the occupation being put up by the ordinary Afghans and Iraqis.

The cost in human lives and suffering thus far has been horrendous. Last September, UNICEF reported that malnutrition among Iraqi children had doubled under the US occupation. Infant mortality in Iraq is now at the level of Burundi. There is crippling poverty and a chronic shortage of medicines. Cases of cancer are rising rapidly, especially breast cancer; radioactive pollution is widespread. According to estimates published in the British Medical Association journal, more than one hundred thousand unarmed men, women and children have been killed by the invading troops in the past eighteen months. This is not the end by any means.

The unemployment in occupied Iraq exceeds seventy five per cent and women are having to prostitute themselves to put bread on the family table. The only avenue left open for earning a decent living is to join the security forces being raised by the occupying power. It carries the stigma and risk of becoming a collaborator and a target for the insurgents. This is of little concern to the US as long as it can get Iraqis to die for its cause. The state of law and order in the country is such that the US troops cannot even ensure safety on the road leading to the air port from Baghdad and have to transport visitors in and out by helicopter. In central parts of the country in particular there is utter chaos, misery and complete societal breakdown.

Iraq is rightly known as the cradle of civilisation ---- the land where, 7,000 years or so ago, most things we consider to be the hallmarks of civilisation had their origin ---- writing, mathematics, urban living, rule of law, arts, crafts and agriculture among others. The Iraq Museum in Baghdad was one of the most important repositories of culture, history and beauty on earth. Its priceless treasures were looted, with the involvement of international dealers and resident diplomats, when the US forces occupied the capital (*'The Looting of the Iraq Museum: The Lost Legacy of Ancient Mesopotamia'* by Milbry Polk and Angela Schuster). Ancient archaeological sites, like Babylon, have been vandalized and its rubble used as construction material for new US military bases. It has not bothered the conscience of either Mr. Bush or Blair and the western media do their best to keep such news out of sight of the American people.

There have been widespread protests by men of conscience throughout the world. An estimated thirty five million citizens took to the streets in scores of cities all over the world to demonstrate against the uncalled for invasion of an already devastated country. Important European nations like France and Germany refused to endorse the crime. Their stance was vindicated when the excuses put forward for the invasion were proven to have been spurious and dishonestly fabricated. Even if rather late in the day, the UN Secretary General, Kofi Anan, was moved to declare it an illegal war. In all probability, it will cost him his job just as it happened with his predecessor, Boutros Boutros Ghali when he tried to investigate the Israeli attack on UN troops in Lebanon.

Important though such actions may be, as witnessed in the case of Vietnam, these will not stop the aggression. It will only end when the cost of persisting with it becomes unacceptable to the US. Considering that the grounds for the attack on Iraq and the excuses put forward had been patently false and fabricated, it raises a host of new questions about the events, as told, concerning the World Trade Centre tragedy and the justification for the attack on Afghanistan and subsequent actions by the US.

It is significant that the decision for going to war was taken by small groups of people in private in the US, Britain, Australia, etc. against the wishes of the majority of their people. Electoral democracy and representative assemblies had little to do with that process. With the exception of two or three newspapers in Britain, by and large, the rest of western news media became willing participants in deceit and cover-up that accompanied the attack. It only proves, once again, that it is the influential groups and vested interests that wield real power in the system and not the people.

As to the real motive of the war, one only has to look at some of the very first actions taken by the occupiers in Iraq. According to the author Arundhati Roy, *'Iraq is the logical culmination of the process of corporate globalization in which neo-colonialism and neo-liberalism have fused. If we can find it in ourselves to peep behind the curtain of blood, we would glimpse the pitiless transactions taking place backstage.----------*

'The US government has privatized and sold entire sectors of Iraq's economy. Economic policies and tax laws have been re-written. Foreign companies can now buy 100% of Iraqi firms and expatriate the profits. This is an outright violation of international laws that govern an occupying force, and is among the main reasons for the stealthy, hurried charade in which power was "handed over" to an "interim Iraqi government" (its appointed head is widely believed to have been one of Saddam's hit men).

'Invaded and occupied Iraq has been made to pay out 200 million dollars in "reparations" for lost profits to corporations like Halliburton, Shell, Mobil, Nestle, Pepsi, Kentucky Fried Chicken and Toys R Us. That's apart from its 125 billion dollar sovereign debt forcing it to turn to the IMF, waiting in the wings like the angel of death, with its Structural Adjustment program. ------------

'Bechtel has been awarded reconstruction contracts in Iraq worth over a billion dollars, which include contracts to re-build power generation plants, electrical grids, water supply, sewage systems, and airport facilities. Never mind

revolving doors, this --- if it weren't so drenched in blood --- would be a bedroom farce. ----------- Time was when weapons were manufactured in order to fight wars. Now wars are manufactured in order to sell weapons (speech at Dec. 2004 Peace Prize award in Sydney, Australia).

To confirm what Arundhati Roy had to say, a part of op-ed columnist Mureen Dowd's article *'Swindler on a Gusher'* in the *New York Times* on 30th April 2005 is reproduced below:

'Ahmad Chalabi - convicted embezzler in Jordan, suspected Iranian spy, double-crosser of America, purveyor of phony war-instigating intelligence ---- is the new acting Iraqi oil minister.

'Is that why we went to war, to put the oily in charge of the oil, to set the swindler who pretended to be Spartacus atop the ultimate gusher?

'Does anybody still think the path to war wasn't greased by oil?

'The neocons' con man had been paid millions by the U.S. to tell the Bushies what they wanted to hear on Iraqi W.M.D. A year ago, the State Department and factions in the Pentagon turned on him after he began bashing America and using Saddam's secret files to discredit his enemies.

'Right after the invasion, the charlatan was escorted into Iraq by U.S. troops and cultivated an axis of Americans, Iraqis and Iranians. He got a fancy house with layers of armed guards and pulled-down shades, and began helping himself to Iraqi assets. ------------ '.

The original reason put forward by Bush and Blair for the war was the elimination of weapons of mass destruction. When none were found in Iraq, it became a crusade for bringing democracy to the Middle East. As with Afghanistan, the characters entrusted with this noble task happen to be despicable renegades with horrendous criminal pasts ---- the likes of Rashid Dostam and Iyad Allawi or ex-hirelings of western multi-national companies, like Hamid Karzai and Ahmed Chalabi. Since that charade too has been less than convincing, it has now become part of the war against terrorism even though the Iraqis had never been involved and had never committed any acts of terrorism. One may be forgiven for thinking that there is an uncanny Orwellian ring to all this. A line in Orwell's *1984* reads, *'War is peace'*. In April 2003, George W. Bush declared, *'War in Iraq is really about peace'*.

The confusion gets further confounded when the Pentagon's anti-terrorism chief, General William Boykin, adds religion to the constantly evolving list of reasons and excuses and lectures church groups, in a style only too reminiscent of the Crusades, about America's 'Christian Army', waging a holy war against the 'idol' of Islam's false God. He styles himself as a 'warrior for the kingdom of God' and claims, *'We in the army of God, in the house of God, in the kingdom of God, have been raised for such a time as this'*. He also believes *'George W. Bush was not elected by a majority of voters in the United States'* but that *'He was appointed by God. ----- He is in the White House because God put him there'* (*'God's Politics'* by Jim Wallis, Harper Collins, San Francisco, p. 156).

It seems any excuse is good enough for occupying the lands of Muslims and violating their lives. Recently, US Marine General, James Mattis, declared, *'You go into Afghanistan, you got guys who slap women around for five years because they don't wear a veil. You know guys like that ain't got no manhood left any way. So, it's hell of a lot of fun to shoot 'em'* (*'The News'*, 15th February 2005). This from a man in whose own country one woman is reported raped every minute (not counting the many times more cases that go unreported) and where a quarter of all the children have been molested, mostly by members of the immediate family or by the priests and 25 per cent of the wives are victims of violence by their husbands (see p.237). There has to be a limit to self-righteousness based on such ignorance. When homicidal maniacs like Mattis are let loose, with little accountability and terrifying modern weapons at their disposal, against mostly unarmed civilian populations, the results are predictably horrifying.

The new twist by Bush, Blair and their ilk to label the Iraqi resistance to foreign occupation as 'terrorism' is hypocritical as well as untenable. When you refuse to define the expression, any thing and every thing can be conveniently included or excluded from its ambit. It enables them, for instance, to declare the killing of civilians in the World Trade Centre as an act of terrorism but not the massacres of hundreds of thousands of equally innocent civilians in Afghanistan and Iraq by the western troops. Why is the killing of one set of civilians terrorism and other set not?

Mark Thatcher, the son of former British prime minister, walks free in Britain after making a botched attempt to stage a coup in the oil-rich African state of Congo with the help of some white mercenaries. He is not labelled as a terrorist, or Tim Spicer, another British soldier of fortune who was involved in the recapture of the island of Bougainville for the government of Papua New Guinea in 1997 and in shipping arms to the rebels in Sierra Leone in 1998. He is regarded as a respected businessman who has been awarded $300 million dollar contract for security work, a euphemism for privatization of war, in Iraq by the US and gives lectures at the Royal United Services Institute and at the School of Oriental and African Studies in London.

The persistent claim on the part of NATO and the US that terrorism poses the greatest threat to the world, since the demise of the Soviet Union, has also become exceedingly questionable in the light of recently revealed facts. Last December (2004) George Monbiot wrote in the *Guardian*:

'*In February* (2004), *a leaked report from the Pentagon revealed that it sees global warming as far more dangerous to US interests than terrorism. --------- As a result of abrupt climate change, it claimed, "warfare may again come to define human life... As the planet's carrying capacity shrinks, an ancient pattern re-emerges: the eruption of desperate, all-out wars over food, water, and energy supplies." The nuclear powers are likely to invade each other's territories as they scramble for diminishing resources.*

"No one can say with any certainty", Bush asserts, "what constitutes a dangerous level of warming, and therefore what level must be avoided." As we don't know how bad it is going to be, he suggests, we shouldn't take costly steps to prevent it. Now read that statement again and substitute "terrorism" for "warming".

'*When anticipating possible terrorist attacks, the US administration, or so it claims, prepares for the worst. When anticipating the impacts of climate change, it prepares for the best. The "precautionary principle" is applied so enthusiastically to matters of national security that it now threatens American civil liberties. But it is rejected altogether when discussing the environment.*'

It is becoming more and more clear that the US aims are far more ambitious and extend much beyond countering any terrorism. There is a desire to redraw the map of the world, to start with, in the Middle East. In 1996, now under secretary of defence for policy, Douglas Feith, ex-head of Defence Policy Board at the Pentagon, Richard Perle and assistant to the under secretary for arms control, David Wurmser were among the authors of a policy paper issued by an Israeli think tank and written for newly elected Israeli Prime Minister Netanyahu that urged Israel to make a 'clean break' from pursuit of the peace process. It required the Arabs to unconditionally accept Israel's rights, including its territorial rights in the occupied territories. Referring to Saddam Hussein's ouster as 'an important Israeli strategic objective,' the paper observed that 'Iraq's future could affect the strategic balance in the Middle East profoundly'. The authors urged Israel to support the Hashemites in their 'efforts to redefine Iraq'. Perle gave further impetus to this thrust when, in September 2002, he gave a briefing for Pentagon officials that included a slide depicting a recommended strategic goal for the U.S. in the Middle East. It showed all of Palestine as Israel, Jordan as Palestine, and Iraq as the Hashemite kingdom ('*A Rose By Any Other Name ---- The Bush Administration's Dual Loyalties*', by former CIA political analysts, Kathleen and Bill Christison).

As the events are unfolding, Iraq will be probably broken up into three states. A recent study, '*US Strategy in the Muslim World After 9/11*' carried out by the Rand Corporation for the US Air Force, recommended ways to '*identify the key cleavages and faultlines among sectarian, ethnic, regional and national lines* (among the Muslims) *and to assess how these cleavages generate challenges and opportunities for the United States*'. After this, can the vast majority of Muslims be blamed for believing that the West's so called war on terror is little more than a thinly veiled cover for what in reality is a war against all the Muslims for the benefit of Israel and exploitation of their resources? There is nothing new about the proposed tactic. During their rule in India and Egypt, the British routinely bribed the imams in mosques to undermine and manipulate Muslim causes. It is just another manifestation of the age old policy of 'divide and rule'.

The Israelis are already busy laying down the infrastructure and wherewithal needed for independent Kurdistan ('*Plan B*', by Seymour Hersh in the '*New Yorker*' of 26th June 2004). In the south, Mulla Seestani is cooperating with the invaders in expectation of support for a Shia dominated state. Sunni Arabs in the middle have been isolated and are being bludgeoned into submission, so far, without much success. More than one hundred thousand of their men, women and children have been massacred in merciless bombardment, armour and infantry assaults on cities like Falluja. If this was not a crime against humanity then what else is? It is a sign of increasing loss of hope and desperation that the US forces are resorting to destroying entire cities in order to get at a few scores of insurgents in Iraq.

Thousands of innocent Iraqis have been tortured and humiliated in most inhuman and perverted manner, in utter and contemptuous disregard of all international conventions and norms of decency, in US detention centres like the air base at Bagram, Abu Ghraib and Guantanamo Bay with the knowledge and approval of the highest US officials in Washington, including the Bush counsel and nominee for Attorney General, Alberto Gonzales and Secretary Defence, Donald Rumsfeld. The US also routinely sends prisoners for torture in camps set up outside the jurisdiction of its courts in countries like Syria, Jordan, Egypt and Pakistan where human rights violations are common.

According to Amnesty International, the total number of Muslims held by the US for purposes of 'rendition' (interrogation under torture) in these and other countries is 70,000 (Professor Huck Gutman in the *Dawn,* 6th July 2005).

For over three and a half years since the cessation of hostilities, the United States has detained more than 600 prisoners of the Afghan war in Camps Delta, X-ray, etc. at Guantanamo Bay ---- some of these as old as ninety and others less than twelve. These include the Afghan ambassador in Pakistan at the time of the US invasion. No charges have been laid against them and they have been denied the right to any legal recourse. Such contemptuous disregard of international conventions and the norms of diplomacy and justice does little to enhance the image of the US but such is the corruption of power that it hardly cares.

There are persistent reports from various human rights organisations and other sources that these men are held in isolated cages, like animals, and subjected to systematic physical and psychological torture. This includes such demeaning acts as smearing Muslim prisoners with excrement and menstrual blood by women interrogators to render them 'unclean' and leaving them without water to wash before offering prayers. The prison officials routinely desecrate the Koran, insult Islam and obstruct prayer meetings (*'N.Y Times,'* 1st May 2005). The prisoners are often severely beaten and their broken bones and teeth are left untreated (*'Inside the Wire'*, by Erik Saar, as narrated on *'60 Minutes'*, and other publications).

This from the New Yorker's 30th May 2005 issue, *'The worst of these horrors are typified by some that came to light just last Friday, in an extraordinary report by Tim Golden, in the Times, about the routine use of torture at the Bagram Collection Point in Afghanistan, in 2002. The most heartrending passages of Golden's story, which was drawn from a two-thousand-page confidential Army file provided by an anonymous source, describe the death by torture of a slight, shy, illiterate young Afghan villager who was shackled by the wrists to the wire ceiling of his cell for days, struck more than a hundred times in one day for the amusement of captors who found his agonized screams of "Allah!" funny, and beaten on the legs until the tissue, in a coroner's words, "had basically been pulpified." By the time he died, most of his interrogators had concluded that he was guiltless ----------'.*

A few British citizens who have been recently released without charge from Camp X-ray have reported that they were *'repeatedly struck with rifle butts, punched, kicked and slapped. They were short shackled in painful stress positions for many hours ------ causing deep flesh wounds and permanent scarring. They were also threatened with unmuzzled dogs, forced to strip naked, subjected to repeated forced body cavity searches, intentionally subjected to extremes of heat and cold for the purpose of causing suffering'* (*'The Independent'*, 12th January 2005). Apart from the horrifying psychological effects on the detainees themselves that will take years to heal, if at all, it has taken a terrible toll on their families as well. Thousands of lives have been shattered as a result. What is being done in Camp X-ray is also being repeated in many other centres, including Abu Ghraib prison near Baghdad, as shown in lurid detail in recently published photographs (see 'minprod. com/abughraibpix.html', 'mindprod.com/iraqwarpix.html', 'mindprod.com/iraqwarextrapix.html#FALLUJAPIX')

There is no indication of how long this nightmare will last. It will not bring peace to Iraq or stability to the Middle East but that is unimportant as long as the potential threat to Israel and western oil interests is eliminated. We may not like it, but in a uni-polar world with no balance of power, it is the will of the West that will be the law. The downfall of the Soviet Union, brought about in large part by Muslim sacrifices, has boomeranged. They are suffering the most as a result of its demise since it has left the West free to act as it pleases in the Muslim lands. We can expect the US occupation troops to remain in the Middle East, on one pretext or another, for as long as western interests demand it. No amount of internal or external pressure is going to change this policy.

The realization that the oil under their sands has been more of a bane than a boon for the Arabs is eventually beginning to dawn upon them. Oil installations and pipelines are being regularly attacked and destroyed by the insurgents, most notably, in Iraq. It is forcing the western oil companies to look for more secure sources of supply away from the currently volatile Persian Gulf region. Hence, we notice a Machiavellian twist in western attitude towards Libya, for instance. British, French, German and Canadian heads of state and government, among others, have been queuing up to pay homage to Moammer Kaddafi, the man they had been condemning for the past twenty years as Looney Toon, 'mad dog' and terrorist pariah. There is also intensified activity afoot to corral Sudan's oil producing regions in the country's south and west. A propaganda barrage has been unleashed by the western media for months to harass and pressurize the Sudanese government into making appropriate concessions.

The course of western actions in the Muslim world has been determined more by oil than any thing else. This is confirmed by Mr. Michael Meacher, British Member of Parliament and Environment Minister in the cabinet of Tony Blair for six years, from May 1997 to June 2003, in an article in the *Guardian* on 8th September 2003, '*Sept. 11 - A Tragedy or an Opportunity?* It is highly significant considering the position occupied by Mr. Meacher and his access to information in that critical period.

'Massive attention has now been given — and rightly so — to the reasons why Britain went to war against Iraq. But far too little attention has focused on why the US went to war, and that throws light on British motives too. The conventional explanation is that after the Twin Towers were hit, retaliation against Al-Qaeda bases in Afghanistan was a natural first step in launching a global war against terrorism. Then, because Saddam Hussein was alleged by the US and UK governments to retain weapons of mass destruction, the war could be extended to Iraq as well. However this theory does not fit all the facts. The truth may be a great deal murkier.

'We now know that a blueprint for the creation of a global Pax Americana was drawn up for Dick Cheney (now vice president), Donald Rumsfeld (defense secretary), Paul Wolfowitz (Rumsfeld's deputy), Jeb Bush (George Bush's younger brother) and Lewis Libby (Cheney's chief of staff). The document, entitled Rebuilding America's Defenses, was written in September 2000 by the neoconservative think tank, Project for the New American Century (PNAC).------------

'It refers to key allies such as the UK as "the most effective and efficient means of exercising American global leadership". It describes peacekeeping missions as "demanding American political leadership rather than that of the UN". It says that "even should Saddam pass from the scene", US bases in Saudi Arabia and Kuwait will remain permanently..... as "Iran may well prove as large a threat to US interests as Iraq has". It spotlights China for "regime change", saying, "it is time to increase the presence of American forces in SE Asia".

'The document also calls for the creation of "US space forces" to dominate space, and the total control of cyberspace to prevent "enemies" using the Internet against the US. It also hints that the US may consider developing biological weapons "that can target specific genotypes (and) may transform biological warfare from the realm of terror to a politically useful tool". Finally — written a year before Sept. 11 — it pinpoints North Korea, Syria and Iran as dangerous regimes, and says their existence justifies the creation of a "worldwide command and control system". This is a blueprint for US world domination. But before it is dismissed as an agenda for right-wing fantasists, it is clear it provides a much better explanation of what actually happened before, during and after Sept. 11 than the global war on terrorism thesis.

'This can be seen in several ways. First, it is clear the US authorities did little or nothing to pre-empt the events of Sept. 11. It is known that at least 11 countries provided advance warning to the US of the 9/11 attacks. Two senior Mossad experts were sent to Washington in August 2001 to alert the CIA and FBI to a cell of 200 terrorists said to be preparing a big operation (Daily Telegraph, Sept. 16, 2001). The list they provided included the names of four of the Sept. 11 hijackers, none of whom was arrested. It had been known as early as 1996 that there were plans to hit Washington targets with aeroplanes. Then in 1999 a US national intelligence council report noted that "Al-Qaeda suicide bombers could crash-land an aircraft packed with high explosives into the Pentagon, the headquarters of the CIA, or the White House."

'Michael Springman, the former head of the American visa bureau in Jeddah, has stated that since 1987 the CIA had been illicitly issuing visas to unqualified applicants from the Middle East and bringing them to the US for training *in terrorism for the Afghan war in collaboration with Bin Laden (BBC, Nov. 6, 2001). It seems this operation continued after the Afghan war for other purposes. It is also reported that five of the hijackers received training at secure US military installations in the 1990s (Newsweek, Sept. 15, 2001). Instructive leads prior to Sept. 11 were not followed up.* ------------------

'All of this makes it all the more astonishing — on the war on terrorism perspective — that there was such slow reaction on Sept. 11 itself. The first hijacking was suspected at not later than 8.20 a.m., and the last hijacked aircraft crashed in Pennsylvania at 10.06 a.m. Not a single fighter plane was scrambled to investigate from the US Andrews Air Force Base, just 10 miles from Washington DC, until after the third plane had hit the Pentagon at 9.38 a.m. Why not? There was standard FAA intercept procedures for hijacked aircraft before Sept. 11. Between September 2000 and June 2001, the US military launched fighter aircraft on 67 occasions to chase suspicious aircraft (AP, Aug. 13, 2002). It is a US legal requirement that once an aircraft has moved significantly off its flight plan, fighter planes are sent up to investigate. Was this inaction simply the result of key people disregarding, or being ignorant of, the evidence? Or could US air security operations have been deliberately stood down on Sept. 11? If so, why, and on whose authority?

'The former US federal crimes prosecutor, John Loftus, has said: "The information provided by European intelligence services prior to 9/11 was so extensive that it is no longer possible for either the CIA or FBI to assert a defense of incompetence." Nor is the US response after 9/11 any better. No serious attempt has ever been made to catch Bin Laden. ---------------

'None of this assembled evidence, all of which comes from sources already in the public domain, is compatible with the idea of a real, determined war on terrorism. The catalogue of evidence does, however, fall into place when set against the PNAC blueprint. From this it seems that the so-called "war on terrorism" is being used largely as bogus cover for achieving wider US strategic geopolitical objectives. Indeed British Prime Minister Tony Blair himself hinted at this when he said to the Commons liaison committee: "To be truthful about it, there was no way we could have got the public consent to have suddenly launched a campaign on Afghanistan but for what happened on Sept. 11" (Times, July 17 2002). Similarly Rumsfeld was so determined to obtain a rationale for an attack on Iraq that on 10 separate occasions he asked the CIA to find evidence linking Iraq to 9/11; the CIA repeatedly came back empty-handed (Time Magazine, May 13, 2002).

'In fact, Sept. 11 offered an extremely convenient pretext to put the PNAC plan into action. The evidence again is quite clear that plans for military action against Afghanistan and Iraq were in hand well before 9/11. A report prepared for the US government from the Baker Institute of Public Policy stated in April 2001 that "the US remains a prisoner of its energy dilemma. Iraq remains a destabilizing influence to .... the flow of oil to international markets from the Middle East". Submitted to Vice President Cheney's energy task group, the report recommended that because this was an unacceptable risk to the US, "military intervention" was necessary (Sunday Herald, Oct. 6, 2002).

'Similar evidence exists in regard to Afghanistan. The BBC reported (Sept. 18 2001) that Niaz Naik, a former Pakistan foreign secretary, was told by senior American officials at a meeting in Berlin in mid-July 2001 that "military action against Afghanistan would go ahead by the middle *of October". Until July 2001 the US government saw the Taleban regime as a source of stability in Central Asia that would enable the construction of hydrocarbon pipelines from the oil and gas fields in Turkmenistan, Uzbekistan, Kazakhstan, through Afghanistan and Pakistan, to the Indian Ocean. But, confronted with the Taleban's refusal to accept US conditions, the US representatives told them "either you accept our offer of a carpet of gold, or we bury you under a carpet of bombs" (Inter Press Service, Nov. 15, 2001).*

Given this background, it is not surprising that some have seen the US failure to avert the 9/11 attacks as creating an invaluable pretext for attacking Afghanistan in a war that had clearly already been well planned in advance. ------------

'The Sept. 11 attacks allowed the US to press the "go" button for a strategy in accordance with the PNAC agenda, which it would otherwise have been politically impossible to implement. The overriding motivation for this political smokescreen is that the US and the UK are beginning to run out of secure hydrocarbon energy supplies. By 2010 the Muslim world will control as much as 60 percent of the world's oil production and, even more importantly, 95 percent of remaining global oil export capacity. As demand is increasing, so supply is decreasing, continually since the 1960s. This is leading to increasing dependence on foreign oil supplies for both the US and the UK. The US, which in 1990 produced domestically 57 percent of its total energy demand, is predicted to produce only 39 percent of its needs by 2010. A DTI minister has admitted that the UK could be facing "severe" gas shortages by 2005. The UK government has confirmed that 70 percent of our electricity will come from gas by 2020, and 90 percent of that will be imported. In that context it should be noted that Iraq

has 110 trillion cubic feet of gas reserves in addition to its oil. A report from the Commission on America's National Interests in July 2000 noted that the most promising new source of world supplies was the Caspian region, and this would relieve US dependence on Saudi Arabia. To diversify supply routes from the Caspian, one pipeline would run westward via Azerbaijan and Georgia to the Turkish port of Ceyhan. Another would extend eastwards through Afghanistan and Pakistan and terminate near the Indian border. This would rescue Enron's beleaguered power plant at Dabhol on India's west coast, in which Enron had sunk $3 billion investment and whose economic survival was dependent on access to cheap gas.

'Nor has the UK been disinterested in this scramble for the remaining world supplies of hydrocarbons, and this may partly explain British participation in US military actions. Lord Browne, chief executive of BP, warned Washington not to carve up Iraq for its own oil companies in the aftermath of war (Guardian, Oct. 30, 2002). And when a British foreign minister met Qaddaffi in his desert tent in August 2002, it was said that "the UK does not want to lose out to other European nations already jostling for advantage when it comes to potentially lucrative oil contracts" with Libya (BBC Online, Aug. 10, 2002). The conclusion of all this analysis must surely be that the "global war on terrorism" has the hallmarks of a political myth propagated to pave the way for a wholly different agenda — the US goal of world hegemony, built around securing by force command over the oil supplies required to drive the whole project.--- ---------------'.

Earlier on in Bush presidency, his neo-con policy makers claimed that 'the road to peace in the Middle East lay through Baghdad.' When the misadventure in Iraq became an unmitigated disaster, Bush decided that it was democracy that lies at the heart of the Palestinian issue. These are really extraneous and irrelevant considerations. The real obstacle to peace is the continued illegal Israeli occupation of Palestinian lands that Bush is unwilling to face. On the contrary, he has gone so far as to endorse the usurpation by Israel by stating, 'Existing major Israeli population centres (on the West Bank) will have to be recognized in any peace deal'. Regardless of how Bush or any one else might feel, peace will only come to the Middle East if there is a fair and equitable resolution of the problem that is acceptable to the Palestinians.

There may be a realization eventually in Washington that without a solution to the Palestine and similar other issues there is little hope of pacifying the Muslim world. However, it is doubtful if there is enough resolve to strive for equitable settlements. Given the entanglements of the US legislature and the Bush Administration with Israel and her supporters, it is highly doubtful if a solution acceptable to the Arabs will be found. According to former US National Security Advisor, Brent Snowcroft, Israeli Prime Minister Ariel Sharon has 'wrapped George Bush around his little finger.'

Bush can only offer what the Israelis are willing to part with and it cannot be much. Although the US has considerable leverage over Israel, for reasons stated elsewhere, it has not been in a position to exercise it. Chances are Arafat's successor, Mahmood Abbas, will be subjected to extreme pressure to relent and compromise. If he has learnt any thing from Arafat's sorry fate, he might resist and remain firm. If not, the imposed solution will be rejected by the Palestinians and along with it Mahmood Abbas himself as just another name in the long list of Arab collaborators in the tradition of Husain Sharif and Amir Faisal.

The resulting situation, if any thing, will be more chaotic than what it is today. This may be exactly what the Israelis want but it will not be conducive to western interests in the area. It is naïve to think that with the removal of Yasser Arafat from the scene, the Palestinians will accept any thing that they regard as less than a fair deal nor is there a way to impose a solution upon them. Given the dismal track record of miscalculation and misdirection on the part of the Bush Administration, there is a considerable probability that it will remain true to its past and end up backing some unfair and unworkable proposition with predictable results.

There has been little change in the situation in Afghanistan in the past two years except that in a farcical election ex-UNOCAL employee, Hamid Karzai, has been confirmed as the president. He still has to be guarded by US marines and his writ still does not extend beyond Kabul. In reality, the government in Kabul is controlled by the Panjsheeri junta known for its deep antipathy towards Pakistan and intimate links with the US and India. The rest of the country remains in the hands of lawless warlords who continue to commit the worst human rights violations. According to UN figures, Afghanistan now exports more than ninety percent of the world's heroin ---- something that had been eradicated by Taliban altogether. But for the presence of some 20,000 US and NATO troops, backed by a much larger deployment of the Pakistan army just over the border, people would have happily brought Taliban back to power, if for no other reason than the security and stability they had provided.

The much anticipated construction of oil and gas pipelines from Central Asia, through Afghanistan and Pakistan, to the Arabian Sea remains a dream more than three years after the puppet Karzai and Pakistan's Musharraf signed the deal in such indecent haste. This is only partly due the unsettled situation in Afghanistan. It appears, the Russians have taken an exception to the unwarranted intrusion into their backyard. They want the pipelines to run through Russia for her to reap the benefits from the revenues as well as to gain some measure of control over future oil supplies to the West. The situation is not one that can be easily resolved and it could well mean that Afghanistan and Pakistan will be the greatest losers in the end.

Pakistan's economy suffered heavy losses as a consequence of the decision to join the US led coalition against Afghanistan. The information provided on US CENTCOM website reads in part: '*Operation Enduring Freedom adversely affected the already fragile economy of Pakistan. Major losses were caused to the civil aviation, tourism, investment and shipping due to rise in the rates of insurance. Besides this, Pakistani exports also suffered adversely and foreign investments experienced a visible decline. According to a rough estimate, Pakistan's economy suffered a loss of over US$ 10 billion since October 2001*' (see Annex for details).

This is just for one year and it does not include the large-scale ongoing expenditure on extensive military operations along the Afghan frontier that help to prop up the puppet regime in Kabul. Strangely, or perhaps not so strangely, it is not this huge sacrifice that makes the news but the one billion dollars worth of loans the US has agreed to write off as a reward for joining her coalition. The media also conveniently omitted to mention, that while promising a billion dollars in aid to Pakistan, President Bush granted a large agricultural subsidy to cotton growers in the United States. It caused cotton prices in the international market to collapse, resulting in a much greater loss to Pakistan's export earnings. Looking at these figures, one is left wondering why a country whose economy can withstand the loss of over ten billion dollars in one year need a few hundred million dollars worth of foreign 'aid' any way?

The situation in Afghanistan can never be stabilized without the willing participation of its majority Pashtoon population. So far, they have been excluded and persecuted not only in Afghanistan but in Pakistan as well. The Pakistan army has killed hundreds of mostly Mahsud men, women and children in South Waziristan who had done no harm and committed no crime against Pakistan or its people. At the same time, it has ignored the deteriorating law and order situation in neighbouring Baluchistan province where there have been over one thousand incidents of rocket attacks and bomb blasts against oil and gas pipelines, railway bridges, electricity and communications towers, etc. in the past one year alone. It cannot do so indefinitely and soon it will be forced to deploy troops to deal with Baluchi insurgents as well. Such operations will cast a long shadow and do incalculable harm to the country's delicate relationship with tribesmen on both sides of the Durand Line. It has all the makings of an unholy mess arising out of criminally short-sighted policies. There is no recent known instance of a country undertaking military operations, at its own expense and against its own people, to further the aims of an alien power for virtually nothing in return.

One cannot help but admire the commitment, tenacity and sense of purpose of the Pathans. Though destitute and desperately poor, not one of them has denounced or betrayed Osama bin Laden to claim the $25 million award set for him 'dead or alive'. Western propaganda notwithstanding, it has been an object lesson in fealty, honour, dignity and integrity that will long be remembered by those who cherish such values. It is but inevitable that such indomitable spirit will prevail in the end. Perhaps, sooner than later, the US will be seen to be negotiating with Taliban, only they may not call them by that name. There is no other choice. When that happens, Pakistan will be once again faced with the consequences of its ill-advised involvement, at the behest of outside interests, in Afghanistan.

Peace and stability are crucial for the West not only in Afghanistan but also in Pakistan before there can be any hope of getting access to the resources in Central Asia. The grossly miscalculated Anglo-American adventure in the area has thrown every thing up in the air. It has destabilized Afghanistan, at the same time, put life in the inept moribund military dictatorship in Pakistan. The internal situation in the two countries remains full of perilous uncertainties. People are restive as surrogate regimes, lacking popular base, do the bidding of external interests. Since dissent can be contagious, force is being increasingly used to silence it. Issues are piling up and pressure continues to build until one day every thing will explode, as it did in Iran. When that happens, it will not be the grossly unwise western policies that will get the blame but, most likely, the Muslims and their flawed creed for 'rejecting civilization and modernisation'.

The five Central Asian Republics to the north are more or less in a similar bind. All of these are crushed under the heels of ruthless dictators, totally mismanaged and seething with resentment. Take Turkmenistan; its president, Saparmurad Niyazov, has been giving himself extensions in office though rigged referenda, the latest due to expire in 2020. He has installed a twelve meter high gold statue of himself on a platform in Ashkabad that rotates so that the dictator is always facing the sun. His pictures are on every thing imaginable. No person is allowed to enter or leave the country without his permission. Any political opposition is ruthlessly put down.

It is more or less the same with the rest of them. Kyrgyzstan and Tajikistan have suffered heavily as a result of revolts against autocratic rule and civil wars that still simmer. The former has permitted the US to establish a military base in Manas. Alarmed by this development, the Russians have now set-up a similar base nearby. Former warlords who now support ex-Communist Party boss, President Askar Akayev, get to control the lucrative drug traffic (Akayev was deposed in a coup and fled to Russia in April 2005). The situation is much the same in Tajikistan, under President Emomali Rahmonov.

Kazakistan has a land mass three times the size of Pakistan with only one-tenths its population. The country is endowed with huge reserves of oil, natural gas and other minerals. President Nursultan A. Nazarbayev has ruled the country with an iron hand since its independence. All of these countries have serious economic problems, with unemployment rates running close to fifty per cent. Nearly all of their difficulties are self-created and the result of political instability, mismanagement and exclusion of public participation.

Islam Karimov, president of Uzbekistan, also keeps prolonging his term in office through the familiar referenda; the latest having extended his rule until 2009. Uzbekistan has one of the worst human rights record in the world. Among other things, it provides funds, bodyguards and logistical support to the criminal and sadist Afghan warlord, Rashid Dostum, an ethnic Uzbek. To cover himself, Karimov has passed a law granting him immunity against prosecution in perpetuity. In an interview on UK's Channel Four TV the British ambassador, Craig Murray, described in graphic detail what political dissidents have to endure under his rule, '*People come to me very often after being tortured. Normally this includes homosexual and heterosexual rape of close relatives in front of the victim; rape with objects such as broken bottles; asphyxiation; pulling out of fingernails; smashing of limbs with blunt objects; and use of boiling liquids including complete immersion of the body. Victims are known to be boiled to death. This is not uncommon. Thousands of people a year suffer from this torture at the hands of the authorities.'*

The *Guardian* reported that in October 2002, Murray made a speech to his then fellow diplomats and Uzbekistani officials at a human rights conference in Tashkent in which he described the Uzbekistan regime as 'kleptocratic' and accused that 'all economic activity, from the cotton picked by child labour to the gold mines, lines the presidential elite's pockets'. In an e-mail to the foreign office he pointed out that the very things for which the United States and the UK had invaded Iraq ---- 'dismantling the apparatus of terror and removing the torture and rape rooms' ---- were commonplace in Uzbekistan. *'When it comes to the Karimov regime, systematic torture and rape appear to be treated as peccadilloes, not to effect the relationship and to be downplayed in the international fora ---- I hope that once the present crisis is over we will make plain to the United States, at senior level, our serious concern over their policy in Uzbekistan.'*

But Uzbekistan has great strategic significance and has provided a military base at Karshi for the United States. The latter leaned heavily on Tony Blair to put a muzzle on Murray. Anxious not to cause any discomfiture to the administration of President Bush, the British government ordered the ambassador not to mention the subject again and to resign within a week or face prosecution and possible imprisonment under the Official Secrets Act. So much for freedom of speech and expression in the West. Ambassador Murray paid the price for being truthful in a world run by people who claim to be guided by God in every thing they do.

In a recently published book '*Imperial Hubris: Why the West is Losing the War on Terrorism*', senior CIA terrorism analyst, Michael Scheuer, writes, '*The Muslim world believes it is under total attack led by President Bush and ally, Israel's Ariel Sharon: a massive effort to crush all who oppose US domination, destroy Islam's inherent political role, eliminate Muslim charities, impose western values on the Islamic world, and maintain compliant puppet rulers ---- what is known as "spreading democracy" in Bush's lexicon.---- America stands by governments determined to exterminate Islamic fighters struggling not just for independence but against institutionalized barbarism.*'

The US is repeating the same mistakes it made earlier in countries like Iran when it blindly supported the despotic Shah. It will only help to sow fertile ground for a future resurgence of violence in the region. Whether the revolution comes peacefully or violently, whether it comes in a secular form or in the guise of radical Islam, it will certainly bear the imprimatur of anti-Americanism. Once more, the US commitment to democracy abroad is being tested as the US befriends the wrong powers for the wrong reasons. Just as it was in Zaire, Iran and elsewhere it will be the hapless people of these countries who will pay the price for western hubris, avarice and cynical expediency.

The US is not alone in ignoring the lessons of history and acting against her own long-term interests. Pakistan's military ruler, General Musharraf, too has been following a logic that transcends comprehension. One can understand the US concerns about terrorism and her need to counter it. If Britain, Australia and Italy want to join this bandwagon it is their business. What is utterly incomprehensible is the general's total pre-occupation and commitment to some one else's war at Pakistan's expense. All his efforts have brought little reward or appreciation for the country itself. When Pakistan apprehended the high ranking al-Quaida operative, Abu Farraj al-Libby in May 2005, the *Washington Times* succinctly summed up the situation in a cartoon that showed a dog marked 'Pakistan' being patted on the head by a US soldier with the words, *'Good boy ---- now let's go find bin Laden'*.

Each country has its own set of priorities. For Pakistan, these must be the very worrying growth of population, a deteriorating law and order situation, crumbling education, health and transport services, declining state of agriculture, water and power supplies, administrative incompetence and mismanagement, to name a few. What concerns the man in the street is if he has a job, a roof over his head, food for his family, some basic services and a system that protects his rights. Fighting another country's war is not on his list of top-most priorities, nor should it be for the people who rule in his name and at his cost.

The money, and effort expended on maintaining 665 army check posts along the 600-kilometer stretch of Durand Line indefinitely (as against only 69 posts by the US and Afghans on their side --- *the 'Dawn', 17th Dec. 2004*), to protect a regime that few Afghans want and that serves no useful purpose for Pakistan, could make so much difference if used to build and equip some more technical schools in the country, for instance. The fact that it does not happen is proof of the disconnect that exists between the rulers and the ruled. It manifests itself in scores of other ways as well, for instance, when the government spends two billion dollars to purchase Boeing airliners while the rail and road transport systems used by the masses remain wholly inadequate and lie in tatters due to lack of investment. This amount of money could have built at least four first-rate universities that would have made a world of difference to the country's future but that is another issue.

Pakistan has unresolved issues with neighbouring India. The dispute over Kashmir is one of them. It is centred on the Kashmiri's right to self-determination. In a fit of sudden generosity, General Musharraf proclaimed to forego this right which was not his to give away in the first place. At the same time, he gratuitously conceded almost every demand made by India, without entering into negotiations first and without asking or getting any thing in return. What was even more pathetic and difficult to understand was when, having thrown away all the leverage, he complained to the press that the Indians had not responded to his generosity. If they got all that they wanted, what interest is left for them to humour him? In similar vein a few years earlier, Benazir Bhutto too had gone out of her way to please the Indians only to lament in an interview with David Frost later that her gratuitous largesse never received appropriate response. If only these people had known their history and remembered the fate of Bhutto-Swaran Singh dialogue in 1962 or the earlier agreement on Beru Bari Union negotiated with Mr. Nehru himself.

These are not the only issues that have not been fully explained or shared with the people of Pakistan. In 2002, the Indians massed troops on the border in full knowledge of Pakistan's nuclear capability. The nature of their troop deployment and concentration suggested that they had precluded the involvement of nuclear weapons. It remained a mystery how they managed to take such a huge risk? That was until their chief of army staff, General S. Padmanabhan, held a press conference in Delhi to launch his book. A part of what he said, as printed in the *'Dawn'* of 2nd February 2004, reads:

'Retired General S. Padmanabhan, a former chief of army staff, on Monday disclosed that India was ready to strike against Pakistan around January 26, 2002 but "favourable circumstances and tides" were allowed to "pass" during the year-long deployment of troops at the border under Operation Parkaram ------------." Pakistan's response had been adequately studied and factored in. No, they had nothing. We had them by the tail." he said, adding that "nange thhe woh (they were exposed)." The general said any nuclear conflict between India and Pakistan would not last beyond one strike each.------------'

The reference to one nuclear strike each is meaningful. Evidently, they had planned the whole operation on the basis of this pivotal assumption. Did it mean that there was a limitation on the availability of these weapons to Pakistan and the Indians had been aware of it? If this was not the case, what made them so certain that Pakistan was so woefully exposed? If indeed it was so, how and why did Pakistan 'expose' herself so dangerously?

Earlier, there had been reports in the British press (denied by the Pakistan Army spokesman) that Pakistan had placed her nuclear weapons under the US control. At her Congressional confirmation hearings recently the new US Secretary of State, Condoleezza Rice, confirmed the existence of an arrangement of some kind on the nuclear weapons issue with Pakistan, but declined to disclose any details on grounds of security. Added to all this are the repeated assertions by General Musharraf that the Indians were eventually deterred and obliged to back down not because of Pakistan's nuclear but conventional military capability ---- a curiously unprofessional analysis given the relative military positions of the two countries in conventional terms.

This is not the way the Indians saw it. According to *General Padmanabhan*, US Secretary of State, Colin Powell, persuaded Bajpai to abort the planned invasion. It cannot be that Bajpai backed down without receiving assurances of some kind from the US. Obviously, whatever their nature, these had something to do with Pakistan that offered sufficient inducement to India to make calling off the attack worth their while. The nature of the undertaking and commitments made to the US and India at the time, if any, still remains unexplained.

To add to what has already been stated about the attitudes and workings of the western media; the Tsunami that hit Indonesia and neighbouring coastal areas has left terrible devastation in its wake. There has been an immense outpouring of compassion and generosity towards the victims, especially in the western countries. However, in terms of human suffering, the losses in South-east Asia pale in comparison with what the people of Iraq have gone through since the US first invaded the country in 1991. As against an estimated two hundred thousand that died in the Tsunami disaster, more than seven times that number were killed in the first Gulf War and its aftermath. Since the second invasion in 2003, one hundred thousand more have been killed so far and there is no end in sight. What is infinitely worse is that the tragedy in Iraq has not been caused by any unanticipated wrath of nature but deliberately inflicted by fellow human beings and was totally avoidable.

The reactions to the two tragic events have been very different in the West. In case of the Tsunami disaster, western media remained in over-drive for weeks on end, to the exclusion of almost all the other news. In total contrast, the plight and suffering of the Iraqis hardly gets a mention as if they are the children of some lesser God. It makes an important point. As Mike Whitney put it on ZNet on 31st

December 2004 under the heading, '*Iraq vs. Tsunami: The Duplicity of the Media*':

'*Where was this "free press" in Iraq when the death toll was skyrocketing towards 100,000? So far, we've seen nothing of the devastation in Falluja where more than 6,000 were killed and where corpses were lined along the city's streets for weeks on end. Is death less photogenic in Iraq? Or, are there political motives behind the coverage?*

'*Wasn't Ted Koppel commenting just days ago, that the media was restricting its coverage of Iraq to show sensitivity for the squeamishness of its audience? He reiterated the mantra that filming dead Iraqis was "in bad taste" and that his American audience would be repelled by such images? How many times have we heard the same rubbish from Brokaw, Jennings and the rest of their ilk?*

'*Well, it looks like Koppel and the others have quickly switched directions. The tsunami has turned into a 24 hour-a-day media frenzy of carnage and ruin, exploring every facet of human misery in agonizing detail. ----------*

'*When it comes to Iraq, however, the whole paradigm shifts to the right. The dead and maimed are faithfully hidden from view. No station would dare show a dead Marine or even an Iraqi national mutilated by an errant American bomb. That might undermine the patriotic objectives of our mission: to democratize the natives and enter them into the global economic system. Besides, if Iraq was covered like the tsunami, public support would erode extremely quickly, and Americans would have to buy their oil rather than extracting it at gunpoint. What good would that do?*

'*Looks like the media's got it right: carnage IS different in Iraq than Thailand, Indonesia or India. The Iraqi butchery is part of a much grander scheme: a plan for conquest, subjugation and the theft of vital resources, the foundation blocks for maintaining white privilege into the next century.*

'*The Iraq conflict is an illustration of how the media is governed by the political agenda of ownership. The media cherry-picks the news according to the requirements of the investor class, dumping footage (like dead American soldiers) that doesn't support their policies. That way, information can be fit into the appropriate doctrinal package, one that serves corporate interests. It's a matter of selectively excluding anything that compromises the broader, imperial objectives. Alternatively, the coverage of the Asian tsunami allows the media to whet the public's appetite for tragedy and feed the macabre preoccupation with misfortune. Both tendencies are an affront to honest journalism and to any reasonable commitment to an informed citizenry. -----------------*'

The western media also adopt less obvious and more subtle means to convey their message and influence the minds. Shortly after the World Trade Centre bombing, on 21st October 2001, BBC TV aired 'Clash of Cultures' on its prestigious *Panorama* programme. Two panels of participants, one in Islamabad and the other in New York, discussed various sides of the issue. Among others, the panels included two women. From Pakistan it was Amina Sajjad, a school teacher and from the United States it was Lisa Pinto, identified as an 'average housewife'. It turned out that Lisa Pinto was anything but an average American housewife. She happens to be a lawyer and a Republican Party strategist, a fact that was not disclosed at the time. It cannot be that BBC was unaware of this information that is freely available on the Internet. The question is why would BBC TV mislead its viewers into believing that the views expressed by a Republican Party strategist were those of an average American housewife?

The story does not end here. Amina Sajjad claims that she was misled as to the nature of the programme and felt manipulated (*'Lisa Pinto, the BBC and I '*, in *The News*, 6th February 2005). BBC again approached Amina Sajjad to do a follow-up on *'Panorama'* under the title 'A Tale of Two Women'. It was during the preparations for this programme she noticed that, apart from political figures such as Lisa Pinto, representatives of the US government were involved and a deliberate effort was being made to portray the Muslims and their way of life in a negative way. The involvement of US government officials as well as political party strategists in the production of BBC programmes is indeed a shocking revelation. To her credit, Amina Sajjad declined to go along with what she felt was a deception and the programme had to be cancelled.

The continued and persistent portrayal of Muslims and Islam in negative light by the media must have a purpose. It can only be to condition the minds of the people to accept western aggression against Muslim countries as necessary and justified. The effort is paying dividends and Muslims in all the western lands are already feeling alienated and sensing palpable hostility towards them. It has increased their sense of insecurity and vulnerability ---- not unlike that of the Jews in pre-World War II Europe. The world is once more beginning to divide, this time on the basis of religion. There is no choice ---- you are either with us or against us. The great fear is that the people who have decreed this know not what they have done. Political differences and divisions can be mended easily after the need has passed but religious fires, once ignited, burn for a very long time.

The confusion created after 9 / 11 had clouded the picture that is only now beginning to clear to reveal a discernable pattern. It indicates a desire and plan to establish a new world order. Since this order will be managed and controlled by the United States, it will operate largely for its benefit, much like the empires of yore.

It goes beyond the limits of economic exploitation and manipulation hitherto exercised through the World Bank, the International Monetary Fund and the World Trade Organization. The US increasingly envisages and anticipates military occupation of foreign countries. It has established scores of military bases around the world and, after the lessons learnt in Afghanistan and Iraq, it is now training its troops to not simply occupy but also administer territories it conquers on a long-term basis. It seems to be based on the rather naïve and mistaken assumption that the resentment and hostility experienced in both the countries is due to the mismanagement of the occupation and not ire against the uncalled for brutal aggression and unacceptable usurpation of freedom. In the ultimate analysis it matters little for they are only interested in some semblance of apparent peace and resignation to placate the qualms of conscience of their own people. New weapons systems are being developed with the imperial objective in mind, including the earth penetrating nuclear bombs and the so called missile defence shield. The latter is a misnomer intended to enable the US to position nuclear weapons and interceptors in space.

Just as the writings of Bernard Lewis and Samuel Huntington heralded the designation of Islam and the Muslims as the new enemy of the West, fresh literature has started to appear suggesting that the concept of an American empire was both natural and necessary. Notable among this are books by the economic historian, Niall Ferguson (*'Empire'* and *'Colossus'*), described in the *Times* of London as 'the most brilliant British historian of his time'. He proffers the hypothesis that since the governments in the erstwhile colonies have failed to deliver on the promises of independence, a new world-wide empire under the tutelage of (Anglo-Saxon) USA may not be such a bad idea.

Viewed in this context, Tony Blair's speech at the Labour Party's annual conference in Brighton too falls into place. In words so reminiscent of Rudyard Kipling, he declared 'the need for re-ordering the world around us' in the context of the 'politics of globalization'. He also emphasized the need to have 'true democracy, no more excuses for dictatorship, abuses of human rights; no tolerance for bad government ------ ending the endemic corruption ------ justice to bring those same values of democracy and freedom around the world ----------' (*'Empire'* pp. 374-7). The expression of such noble sentiments is eerily reminiscent, and rings just as hollow, as the pronouncements made by his nineteenth century European colonizing predecessors to justify the rape of Asian and African continents. Whatever form the new empire may take, one thing is certain, as with its predecessors the natives will not be its primary beneficiaries.

Both Bush and Blair have declared the right to interfere with regimes that are unacceptable to them. This is arbitrary as well as ominous in its implications and carries within it the potential for world-wide insecurity and instability. Using political instability or mismanagement in neighbouring countries as the excuse, any number of powers could choose to intervene in the affairs of weaker nations. For example, the prevailing situation in Baluchistan may tempt Indian leaders to find justification for once again meddling in Pakistan's internal situation. It is not beyond the realm of possibility that she might even engineer circumstances to justify such action.

In the past, empires have been profitable only when their burden and expense was passed on to the natives. This is a lesson that the Americans have yet to learn. If they had only followed the British example they might not have been in the mess they find themselves in Afghanistan and Iraq. The British had created the Indian Army and used it extensively not only to enforce their rule in India but also in expeditions from North Africa all the way to China. It is reasonable to expect that an attempt will be made to replicate this example in one form or another. Without an assured supply of colonial cannon fodder and proxy armies empires are liable to become unacceptably costly enterprises to maintain in the long run.

It is possible that the understanding reached by the US with India recently, for a 'strategic partnership', may be with just this purpose in mind. The objective of this alliance has not yet been publicly spelled out. It could be to facilitate US control over dwindling resources or to counter the weight of China. Chances are that the Indians are only in it for themselves, as became clear when they refused to commit troops for Iraq. There are other more promising options for the West in the Middle East like getting the Shias and Kurds to fight for the US in Iraq and exploiting the suspicion and animosity among the Arab states towards Iran.

There is a rather sinister effort already afoot to alter the character of Islam to make it more amenable and accommodating of western political and economic aims and objectives. It involves using fringe characters and interpretations to redefine the religion in the name of 'reform', 'enlightenment' and 'moderation'. So far, it has extended to only the more westernised Muslims ----- 'wogs' and 'coconuts' ----- with next to no credibility or appreciation of Islam and its history. However, it is an important segment because it constitutes the ruling elite in the majority of Muslim countries. It is far fetched to think that these efforts will succeed in effecting a fundamental change in the religion itself but whatever else might happen they will, most definitely, deepen the cleavage that already exists between the Muslim masses and the miniscule westernised minorities who rule over them. Ultimately, it will only translate into further instability and turmoil in Muslim lands, in the process, inviting even greater western intervention.

Whichever way one looks, it only points to instability, discord, betrayal, deprivation and generally troubled times for the Muslims in the foreseeable future. They can expect little sympathy and even less understanding in a world dominated by the West. It is a price they must pay for being weak and divided in a world in which there is no justice and where predatory West seldom misses any opportunity, fair or foul, to advance its own interests.

ANNEX

US CENTCOM published a page on their website listing details of the co-operation they had received from various countries, including Pakistan, since September 2001. This brief report about Pakistan's contribution had been available on the following link:

http://www.centcom.mil/Operations/Coalition/Coalition_pages/pakistan.html. It has now been removed, apparently, in response to a request by the Pakistan government. The actual report as it had appeared on the website is reproduced below. This should be read in the context of the telephone call made by the US Secretary of State, Colin Powell, to General Musharraf as reported by Woodward in '*Bush At War*'(p. 166 ante):

CENTCOM WEB PAGE ON PAKISTAN

"Immediately after 9/11, Pakistan was prompt in declaring unequivocal support to US in its war against terrorism. It expressed its complete solidarity with US in combating terrorism in all forms and, was willing to provide not only moral but also logistical support and its military bases. Details of the efforts and participation of Pakistan and the adverse effects of following this policy are given in the ensuing paragraphs:

A. Support Provided by Pakistan for OEF. Up till Oct 2002, some of the specific assistance provided by Pakistan for Operation Enduring Freedom is as follows:

1. Provision of Air Bases / Airfields. In order to meet the requirement of US/Coalition Forces, Pakistan provided five air bases / airfields. However in emergency planes could land anywhere in Pakistan. On the average 0.4 million litres of fuel per day has been provided to US forces as well as all other services on the bases used by them. A total of 57800 sorties have been generated from Pakistan's air space/soil.

2. Provision of Air Corridor. In order to facilitate launching of air ops into Afghanistan, Pakistan provided 2/3 of its air space as air corridor to the US/Coalition Forces. By so doing, Pakistan had to reschedule/ redirect many of the commercial flights.

3. Provision of Naval Facilities. Pakistan Navy provided landing facility to the US/Coalition ships at Pasni. At sea, Pakistan Navy operations/training were curtailed in order to accommodate and facilitate the operations of US/Coalition Naval Forces. According to the US Marine Corps Gazette of June 2002, the Coalition Naval Operations at Pasni were the largest amphibious operations in size, duration and depth that the Marine Corps had conducted since the Korean War. In all, 8000 Marines, 330 vehicles and over 1350 tons of equipment/logistic were off loaded at the beach and later flown to Kandahar from Pasni.

4. Summary of US Requests. Details of request since 11 September 2001 are as follows:

(a) Requests received 2160

(b) Action completed 2008

(c) Action in process 152

5. Foreign Nationals Apprehended. Two of the most wanted Al-Qaida terrorists, Abu-Zubaida and Ramzi Bin Al-Shaiba, were arrested by the Pakistan's law enforcing agencies during well planned and carefully conducted raids and handed over to US authorities. Abu Zubaida was considered Number 2 man in Al Qaida leadership thus his apprehension has given a boost to OEF. Ramzi Bin Al-Shaiba is suspected to be actually involved in the terrorist attacks of September 11. Overall details since 11 September 2001 are:

(a) Total Raids 99

(b) Foreign National Apprehended 420

(c) Handed Over to USA 332

(d) Extradited to countries other than USA 34

(e) Released 38

(f) Under Interrogation 16

6. ISAF. To facilitate the operations of ISAF in Afghanistan, the Karachi Airport (FMB) and Sea Port facilities along with logistic support have been extended. A MOU in this regard was signed between the Governments of UK and Pakistan. Now that the role of lead Nation has been taken over by Turkey, the same facilities / assistance are being provided to them.

B. Pakistan's Operations along Pak-Afghan Border

1. Measures Taken to Penetrate "Tribal Areas". Tora Bora operations provided a window of opportunity to penetrate these areas which was capitalized by quickly moving the Army in Tirah Valley which captured 250 Al Qaida/Taliban fleeing into Pakistan. Later the Pak Army along with FC extended its operations to Miran Shah and Wana. In return, tribals have been offered a sizeable development package. The region, being remote and under developed warrants bringing it at par with rest of the country in terms of provision of basic facilities like communication infrastructure, health, education and employment opportunities. Same analogy is being followed in North Waziristan Agency/South Waziristan Agency (NWA/SWA) to prevent slipping in of Al Qaida/Taliban into our territory. In spite of ominous threat on Eastern Border, Pakistan is maintaining a sizeable portion of her strategic forces on Western Border. This clearly speaks of our resolve to support coalition operations against Al Qaida/Taliban elements.

2. On 25 June 2002, an operation was launched against suspected Al Qaida/Taliban elements in area Azam Warsak (Wana). During this operation 2 x Al Qaida members were killed, one apprehended whereas 13 x security personnel were killed including 2 x officers. This shows Pakistan's resolve to not only "drain the swamp" but also nab the "alligators".

3. Our Compulsions

a. Shortage of manpower, technical equipment and funds.

b. Threats of war from India due to unresolved Kashmir dispute despite UN resolutions and Indian/international commitments even after 54 years.

c. Constitutional restraint of operations in the FATAs (Federally Administered Tribal Areas).

d. Domestic sensitivity to allow operations within Pak territory by foreign soldiers.

e. Cultural and religious sensitivities.

4. Deployment of Forces

a. Initial Deployment. Initially two Army corps along with large contingents of FC troops (para military) were deployed along Western border including some of the areas hitherto considered as no go tribal areas. A total of 60,000 regular troops and 55000 paramilitary personnel were employed on sealing of western border, internal security duties and protection of various bases being used by US / Coalition Forces. Later bulk of the regular formations was shifted towards the eastern border due to Indian Military build up. Because of very effective security arrangements ensured by Pakistan, not a single breach of security has occurred around the bases in use by Coalition Forces.

b. Current Deployment. In spite of imminent threat of war on our Eastern border and at peril to our security Army till today continues to retain 3 x brigades size regular force along with 40 x FC Wings totalling approximately 45000 troops along Pak-Afghan Border.

5. On Going Operations. A division (-) size force is operating along Pak-Afghan border with the purpose of eliminating suspected Al Qaida/Taliban elements and regular monitoring.

C. Effects of Operation Enduring Freedom on Economy of Pakistan.

Operation Enduring Freedom adversely affected the already fragile economy of Pakistan. Major losses were caused to the civil aviation, tourism, investment and shipping due to rise in the rates of insurance. Besides this, Pakistani exports also suffered adversely and foreign investments experienced a visible decline. According to a rough estimate, Pakistan's economy suffered a loss of over US$ 10 billion since October 2001."

NOTES:

Pakistan has established 665 check-posts (each comprising about 40-plus soldiers) along her side of the 600 kilometre

Durand Line. As against this, the coalition forces and Afghan National army between them have only 69 posts on the Afghan side.

The current strength of 75,000 troops deployed along the Durand Line by Pakistan includes 42 wings of different corps, three divisions, nine brigades from two regional headquarters, 27 infantry battalions, four engineering battalions plus a couple of FC corps. This is in sharp contrast to the strength of US and Afghan troops across the border which is less than 25,000 men all told (*'The Dawn'*).

Apart from deployment by the army, a Pakistan Navy frigate operates alongside the US Navy on patrol duties in the Persian Gulf. In view of the growing confrontation between Iran and the United States, potentially, it could lead to awkward and anxious moments in the country's relations with Iran.

According to the *'Dawn'*, during a visit to Islamabad by the First Sea Lord in 2003, it was agreed that NATO war ships may patrol inside Pakistan's territorial waters. Strictly speaking, this amounts to surrender of territorial sovereignty that can only be done through an act of the National Assembly and not through any old executive order.

Index

Symbols

60 Minutes 1, 7, 105, 260, 282

A

Abdul Rahim Bogadur 43
Abu-Zubaida 311
Abu Ali Sena 30
Abu Ghraib 281, 283
Afghanistan 8, 21, 45, 51, 52, 62, 111, 115, 127, 146, 149, 151,
        152, 153, 154, 156, 160, 168, 169, 170, 171, 172, 173,
        174, 176, 177, 179, 180, 181, 182, 187, 189, 190, 191,
        192, 209, 212, 213, 216, 221, 222, 225, 229, 231, 233,
        235, 244, 245, 248, 250, 252, 254, 259, 262, 263, 272,
        274, 277, 292, 293, 294, 295, 311, 312
Africa 26, 32, 58, 59, 68, 100, 244, 254, 264
Agra 124
Ahad Ha'am 82
AIDS 253
al-Ahram 93, 107, 108
Al-Beiruni 30
Al-Fatah 88
al-Quaida 111, 152, 153, 156, 159, 162, 166, 168, 170, 177, 179,
        186, 222, 234, 237
Al-Zulfikar 88
Albania 38, 131
Albert, Michel 269
Albright, Madeline 105, 260
Alcazar 29
Alexei Tolstoy 49
Algeria 95, 231, 233, 261
Alhambra 29
Alkhan-Kala 53
All Souls College 120
Almeria 29

318

Altaf Hussain 247
Alvaro, Paul 27
Al Capone 205
Al Gore 101
America Israel Public Affairs Committee (AIPAC) 91
Amherst, Jeffery 60
Amil Kansi 244
Amina Sajjad 304, 305
Amnesty International 136, 148, 179, 182, 186, 260
Amritsar 119
AMR Corp 159
Anan, Kofi 274
Anatolia 67
Anglo-Saxon 172, 173
Angola 250
Anna Politkovskaya 52
anthrax 99, 161
Anti-Christ 32
April Gillespie 101
Arafat, Yasser 88, 89, 124, 126, 244, 291, 292
Arbuthnot, Felicity 106
Archer, Jules 205
Ardebil 47
Argentine 154
Argun 53
Aristotle 30
Arizona 59, 91
Armageddon 40
Armenia 38, 42, 46, 66, 261, 263
Armitage 173, 174, 175
Armstrong, Karen 15, 23, 33, 72, 217, 238, 239, 240, 241, 247
Arundhati Roy 126, 167, 173, 275
ASEAN 69
Ashcroft, Attorney General, John 5, 77, 242
Ashkabad 295
Asin 39
Askar Akayev 296
Assad 110
Assam 119, 220

Atlanta Journal 225, 229
Atta 241
Australia 34, 58, 63, 66, 216, 274, 276, 298
Austria 75, 134
Avital, Colette 110
Axis of Evil 109, 224
Azerbaijan 46, 48, 261, 263
Azeri 261

B

Ba'athists 108
Babrak Karmal 149
Baghdad 7, 18, 99, 101, 105, 106, 109, 113, 116, 239, 273, 283, 290
Bahrain 103
Bajpai 302
Baker, James 101, 152
Baku 46, 47, 261, 263
Baldwin, Stanley 80
Balfour, Arthur 79
Balfour Declaration' 65, 80, 81
Balkans 32, 131, 133, 146, 147
Balkan states 130
Baltic 46, 49
Bangladesh 193, 197
Banja Luka 138
Basque 95
BBC 210, 248, 304, 305
Beaumont, Christopher 120
Bechtel 201, 275
Behar 218
Belarus 49
Bellamy 210
Benazir Bhutto 300
Bengal 119
Berlin 6, 114, 182
Berlusconi, Silvio, Prime Minister 6, 14
Beru Bari Union 300
Biafra 250

Bible 22, 32, 59, 76, 77, 81, 236, 238
Biden, Joseph 144
Biffi, Giacomo, Cardinal 6
Bilderberg Group 208
Billy Graham 22
bin Laden 51, 109, 110, 117, 146, 152, 153, 154, 155, 159, 165,
        166, 168, 171, 172, 173, 174, 185, 234, 236, 237, 238,
        241, 244, 262, 294
Bishop J. Delano Ellis 1
Bismarck, Chancellor 64
BJP 125, 127, 209
Black Sea 37, 46, 48, 49, 66
Blair, Tony 23, 171, 172, 176, 188, 242, 247, 274, 276, 278, 297
Blunt, W.S 65
Bodin, Jean 38
Bolsheviks 67
Bolton, John 223
Bookman, Jay 229
Bosnia 7, 38, 49, 69, 90, 121, 131, 133, 134, 135, 137, 138, 139,
        140, 141, 142, 143, 145, 147, 213, 233, 234, 252, 260,
        266
Bosnia-Herzgovina 7, 131
Boston Airport 166
Bougainville 278
Bouquet, Colonel Henry 60
Bradley, Ed 7
Brezovo Polje 135
Briquemont, General 141
Britain 60, 63, 65, 66, 67, 68, 69, 72, 73, 76, 79, 80, 81, 83, 87,
        102, 103, 104, 108, 109, 116, 119, 121, 123, 136, 139,
        141, 145, 148, 167, 172, 173, 190, 202, 242, 244, 247,
        249, 259, 268, 274, 278, 298
British Empire 83
Brokaw, Tom 303
Brown Brothers 205
Bryce, James 67
Buchanan, Pat 110
Bulgaria 131
Bunting, Madeleine 227

burka 216, 219
Burton, Dan 220
Burundi 273
Bush, George ix, 1, 5, 14, 21, 23, 40, 51, 61, 71, 90, 91, 92, 102,
        109, 110, 111, 112, 113, 114, 115, 118, 139, 150, 152,
        156, 157, 158, 160, 163, 165, 167, 168, 169, 172, 173,
        175, 184, 185, 187, 188, 190, 201, 206, 214, 222, 223,
        224, 225, 227, 228, 231, 235, 242, 245, 252, 262, 266,
        270, 271, 274, 276, 278, 279, 281, 290, 291, 292, 293,
        297, 298, 310
Bush Senior ix, 152
Butler, Smedley Darlington 205
Byzantine Empire 11, 16, 37

C

Cairo 58, 101, 107, 112
Calicut 56, 57
California 59, 68
Caliph Omer 11, 27, 256
Cambodia 229, 266
Cambone, Stephen 223
Cambon Letter' 79
Cameron, Carl 161
Camp David 87, 170, 259
Canada 59, 60, 69, 82, 93, 140, 141, 190, 253
Cannistraro, Vince 162
Caparde 135
Carlucci, Frank 152
Carlyle Group 152
Carl Conetta 184
Cartagena 29
Carter, Jimmy 74, 145
Caucasus 48, 50
Caucuses 37, 42, 46, 47, 48, 49, 249
CENTCOM 177, 293, 310
Central Asia 42, 43, 66, 68, 153, 191, 192, 193, 194, 196, 225,
        295
Central Asian Republics 68, 173, 295
Chankala 53

Chechen Aul 54

Chechen Yurt 53

Chechniya 8, 46, 48, 49, 50, 51, 52, 53, 95, 213, 231, 233, 234, 250, 261

Chemical and Biological Institute 100

Cheney, Dick 114, 157, 158, 169, 201, 222, 223

Chengez Khan 230

Chile 229

China 109, 123, 127, 191, 200, 205, 220, 226, 229, 263

Chipperfield, Mark 125

Chithisinghpora 220

Chomsky, Noam 156, 215, 269

Christ 13, 15, 19, 22, 31, 32, 33, 39, 76

Christianity 6, 12, 13, 22, 25, 31, 32, 35, 41, 47, 48, 58, 59, 63, 64, 76, 77, 78, 130, 233, 237, 238, 240, 254

Christians xi, 11, 12, 14, 17, 18, 22, 24, 25, 26, 27, 28, 30, 31, 33, 34, 37, 39, 42, 56, 58, 59, 69, 71, 78, 80, 139, 220, 233, 238, 248, 249

Christian Coalition 1, 77

Christian Identity 2

Christian Right 1, 5, 22, 78, 90

church 12, 19, 33, 41, 59, 146, 239, 253, 277

Churchill, Winston 60, 65, 66, 82, 83, 131, 202

Church of England 76

CIA 74, 97, 100, 111, 143, 152, 162, 174, 182, 183, 203, 205, 209, 229, 237, 244, 262, 298

Circassia 38, 42, 48

Clancy 207

Clinton 8, 50, 91, 92, 142, 143, 144, 153, 201, 220, 223, 253

cluster bombs 150, 180

CNN ix, 114, 157, 165, 181, 210, 248, 260

Coalition Forces 310, 311, 314

Code of Federal Regulations 243

Code of Manu 218

Cohen, Elliot 223

Cohen, Richard 1

Coja Mehmed Markar 58

Cold War 226

Columbia 158, 229, 250

Columbus 30, 59
Commonwealth Institute 184
Congo 209, 229, 250, 278, 298
Cordoba 29
Cossack 42
Cossacks 43, 44, 45
Coulter, Anne 6
Cowasjee 247
Croatia 131, 133, 134, 260
Cross 11, 78, 223, 237
Crusades 14, 17, 18, 19, 20, 22, 23
CTBT 107, 268
Cuba 88, 186, 205, 229
Cuny, Fred 138
Cyprus 76

D

'D' Notices Committee' 212
Daghestan 46, 48, 49
Daily Telegraph 125, 171, 231
Dalai Lama 209
Darwin, Charles 65
Daschle, Tom 157
Dashte Laili 182
David Rieff 138, 148
Davis, Kenneth 201
Dawn, The 124, 177, 220, 247, 257, 267, 299, 300, 315
Dayton 90, 105, 139, 145
Dayton Accord 90
Defense Policy Board 201, 223
Delawares 60
Delhi 20, 300
Der Judenstaat 75
Dioxin 103
Dole, Bob 144
Dominican 48, 205
Dostum, Rashid 184, 296
Dostum, Rashid, General 184
Dubai 152, 264

Ducros, Francine 112
Duke of Lerma 35
Dukmah Aka 48
Durand Line 294, 299, 315
Durant, Will 15, 16, 217, 218

E

Eagleburger, Lawrence ix, 137, 139, 145, 260
Earl of Shaftesbury 76
East Timur 121
Ed Vulliamy 137
Egypt 13, 16, 17, 19, 72, 73, 87, 95, 116, 151, 165, 221, 228,
        235, 237, 241, 255, 259, 281
Eisenhower, Dwight, Prisident 87
El-Al 100
Eliot, George 76
Emomali Rahmonov 296
Emperor Constantine 13
Eqbal Ahmad 257
Estonia 49
Eta 248
ethnic cleansing 135, 139, 147, 260
Europe x, 6, 7, 15, 18, 20, 22, 23, 24, 28, 29, 30, 35, 37, 38, 39,
        41, 66, 68, 69, 75, 76, 80, 87, 98, 109, 121, 130, 132, 134,
        139, 145, 147, 199, 200, 209, 224, 226, 235, 249, 251,
        253, 305
European Union 38, 69, 94, 133, 135, 146, 186

F

Faisal 84
Falwell, Jerry 1
Farland, Ambassador 178
fatwa 33, 251
FBI 159, 160, 163, 165, 166, 177, 179, 243, 262
Ferguson, Niall 306
Ferozepur 119
Findley, Congressman Paul 91
Fisk, Robert 63, 71, 181, 185, 248

Fleischer, Ari 71, 181
Flight 11 166
Flight 93 166
Food and Agricultural Organization 104
Foreign Affairs 96, 264
Fort Bragg 215
France x, 16, 17, 21, 28, 65, 73, 79, 87, 123, 139, 141, 148, 261, 274
Franklin, Benjamin 84
Friedrich von Bernhardi 64
Frost, David 102, 300
fundamentalism 94, 240, 241, 242

G

Gaza 6, 71, 86, 93
General Allenby 23
General Kaufmann 43
General Motors 204
Geneva Contravention 61
Geneva Convention 187, 228
Gentile, Louis 138
Georgia 38, 42, 225
Geraldo Rivera 168
Germany x, 7, 19, 23, 28, 33, 42, 61, 63, 64, 65, 69, 87, 133, 134, 159, 204, 266, 274
Ghali, Boutros Boutros 138, 148, 274
Ghana 200
Ghazali 30
Gingrich, Newt 227
Global Hawk 164
Goebbels 70, 169
Golan Heights 87
Golda Meir 87
Gonzales 281
Gordon, Thomas 40
Gore Vidal 160
Goths 26, 27
Goulding, Marrack 138
Graham, Billy 1

Graham, Franklin 1, 146, 188
Graham, Reverend Franklin, 1
Granada 29, 30, 31
Grass, Guenter 7
Greece 13, 38, 131
Grozny 50, 53
Guantanamo Bay 62, 186, 281, 282
Gujrat 72, 227, 263
Gulf of Tonkin 167
Gulf War ix, xi, 102, 106, 107, 115, 212, 222, 260, 302
Gulistan 47
Gumplowitcz 64
Gurdaspur 119
Gurion, David Ben 86
Gutman, Roy 134
Gwadar 192
Gypsies 70, 75

H

H. L. Mencken 96
Ha'aretz 164, 242
Habermas, Juergen 7
Hafizullah Amin 149
Haiti 106, 205
Haji Barzak 48
Halliburton 201, 275
Halliday, Denis 105, 107, 112, 210
Hamid Karzai 118, 190, 292
Handelsblad 100
Harley Street 255
Harris, Marshall 137
Heinrich von Treietschke 64
Helaku 230
Hemingway, Ernest 249
Hermann Goering 97
Herzl, Theodor 75
High Commissioner for Human Rights 184
hijab 14, 219
Hinduism 127, 218

Hindus 25, 120, 264
Hiroshima 61, 104
Hitler 1, 63, 102, 112, 169, 204, 237
Holbrooke, Richard 145
Hollywood 211
Holocaust 70, 91, 204
Holy Office 34
Hosni Mubarak 165
Houllebecq, Michel 7
House of Representatives 224
Hudson River 162
Human Rights Watch 53, 54, 104
Hungary 131, 134
Huntington, Samuel xi, 45, 95, 96, 97, 196, 230, 233, 258
Hurd, Douglas 145
Husain, Sharif 84

I

IBM 204
Ibne Khaldoon 30
Ibne Rushd 30
Imam Shamayl 48
IMF 275
Inderforth, Karl 154
India 5, 18, 29, 56, 68, 72, 76, 88, 119, 121, 122, 123, 124, 126,
        127, 128, 173, 177, 179, 189, 199, 209, 218, 219, 220,
        221, 246, 262, 263, 264, 267, 268, 270, 271, 281, 292,
        300, 301, 302, 303, 313
Indian Army 125
Indonesia 88, 121, 205, 302, 303
Infinite Justice 167
Ingushtia 48, 49
Inhofe, Senator James 77
Inquisition 34, 35
International Brigade 249
International Monetary Fund 208
International War Crimes Tribunal 146
Intifada 89
IRA 156, 173, 234, 248

328

Iran xi, 6, 47, 73, 74, 94, 95, 99, 100, 101, 108, 147, 149, 151,
    179, 206, 212, 224, 226, 239, 240, 241, 254, 259, 261,
    264, 271, 295, 298
Iraq ix, x, 6, 8, 17, 21, 46, 60, 74, 88, 96, 99, 100, 101, 102,
    103, 104, 105, 106, 107, 108, 111, 112, 113, 115, 116,
    117, 121, 138, 147, 166, 170, 201, 207, 209, 210, 213,
    214, 219, 221, 222, 224, 225, 226, 229, 233, 235, 252,
    255, 259, 260, 261, 266, 269, 272, 273, 274, 275, 276,
    278, 280, 281, 283, 284, 290, 297, 302, 303, 304
Ireland 95, 253
Irving, Professor David 70
Isaacson 181
ISI 174
Islam x, xi, xii, 1, 5, 6, 7, 8, 9, 10, 12, 13, 18, 20, 21, 22, 23, 24,
    25, 27, 28, 33, 35, 38, 39, 40, 45, 48, 59, 66, 69, 78, 94,
    95, 97, 130, 151, 152, 188, 195, 215, 217, 219, 222, 230,
    233, 234, 235, 236, 237, 238, 239, 240, 241, 248, 251,
    252, 254, 255, 256, 257, 265, 266, 298, 305
Islamabad 175, 304
Islam Karimov 296
Israel 5, 7, 16, 77, 78, 81, 85, 86, 87, 88, 89, 90, 91, 92, 93, 100,
    101, 108, 109, 110, 112, 123, 128, 163, 164, 201, 207,
    214, 218, 221, 230, 237, 243, 245, 248, 249, 250, 258,
    259, 260, 262, 268, 270, 283, 291, 298
Italy 6, 13, 38, 252, 298
ITN 179
Ivan IV 'the Terrible' 41

J

Jamaat-e-Islami 237, 255
Jamali, Prime Minister 177
Japan 61, 62, 102, 167, 192, 209
Jefferson, William J 220
Jenin 90, 108
Jennings, Peter 303
Jeraldo 253
Jerusalem 8, 11, 14, 15, 16, 17, 22, 23, 27, 40, 77, 78, 89, 163,
    164, 227, 238
Jews xi, 1, 11, 12, 15, 16, 18, 25, 28, 30, 31, 32, 33, 38, 65, 66,

68, 69, 70, 71, 75, 76, 77, 78, 79, 80, 81, 82, 83, 84, 85,
    87, 90, 91, 121, 132, 238, 248, 252, 265, 266, 305
jihad 249
John le Carre 109
Jordan 40, 83, 86, 116, 209, 241, 281
Judaism 5, 13, 217, 237, 238, 240, 254, 256
Judea and Samaria 77
Jullunder 119, 120, 121
Jutta Burghardt 105

K

Kabul 88, 149, 153, 179, 186, 189, 190, 292, 293
Kadri 48
Kagan 223, 225
Kaiser Wilhelm 23
Kamal Ata Turk 80
Kandahar 154
Kandhar 311
Kapurthala 120
Karachi 212, 312
Karadzic, Radovan 7, 133, 146, 237
Kargil 125, 267, 268
Karshi 297
Karzai 190, 192
Kashmir 88, 95, 115, 119, 120, 121, 122, 123, 124, 125, 126,
    128, 148, 220, 250, 262, 264, 300, 313
Kazakistan 296
Kazan 41
Kazi Hussain Ahmed 255
KDP 248
Kentucky Fried Chicken 275
Kenya 153, 244
Kenyatta 244
Khiva 42, 43
Khmer Rouge 266
Khomeini 9, 236
Khwarzimi 29
Kila Jangi 45, 182
Kindersley, Jemima 28

King David Hotel 243
King Fahad 199, 265
King Faisal xi
King Ferdinand 30
King Hussein 209
Kipling, Rudyard 65, 307
Kissinger, Henry ix, 92, 226
Knesset 78, 91, 110
Kofman, Daniel 140
Koppel, Ted 303
Koran 7, 10, 12, 24, 25, 166, 188, 236, 237, 238, 241, 248, 251,
        256, 265
Kosovo 121, 130, 131, 233, 244
Krasnostepnovskoye 53
Kremlin 41, 50, 51
Krystyna Kurczab-Redlich 52
Kunduz 182, 184
Kunta Haji Kishiev 48
Kurdistan 67, 281
Kurds 67, 100
Kutab 241
Kuwait xi, 46, 101, 102, 103, 106, 107, 108, 116, 138, 259
Ku Klux Klan 234
Kyoto protocol 204
Kyrgyzstan 296

L

Lake, Ricki 253
Lamb, Christina 180
Lantos, Tom 110
Las Vegas 254
Latin America 34, 206, 224, 248
Latvia 49
Law of Return 78, 86
Lebanon 65, 79, 86, 88, 141, 229, 233, 259, 274
Lewinsky, Monica 153
Lewis, Bernard xi, 12, 37, 94, 233, 234
Libby, Lewis 223
Libya 76, 117, 226, 229, 284

Lieberman, Joseph 101, 144
Lithuania 49
Lloyd George 76, 80
London 7, 17, 18, 27, 33, 37, 61, 68, 70, 77, 80, 81, 85, 91, 120,
        156, 158, 159, 172, 178, 179, 183, 188, 218, 219, 247,
        253, 254, 255, 279
Lowry, Rich 6
Lumumba, Patrice 209
Luther, Martin 32, 33, 39

M

Macedonia 131, 133
MacGahan 43, 44
Machiavelli 101
Mackenzie, Lewis 140, 141
Mahmood Abbas 291
Mahmood Ahmed 174
Mahsud 294
Major, John 145, 147, 152
Makka 6, 22, 56, 84
Manas 296
Mandela, Nelson 244
Manifest Destiny 59, 63
Mansur Ushurmah 48
Maodoodi, Maulana 255
Margolis, Eric 50, 99, 115, 227
Maria 162
Marshal Tito 131
Marxism 208
Massachusetts 184
Massacre at Mazar 182
Mattis 277
Maulana Shibli Naumani 256
Mau Mau 244
Mayo 219
Mazare Sharif 182
McCain, John 144
McCarthyism 109
McKinney, Cynthia 220

McKntee, Andrew 182
McWilliams, Brian 164
Medak 141
Mediterranean 66
Mehdi 95
Mein Kampf 66
Meir Kahan 237
Meskyer Yurt 53
Mexico 59, 200, 205
Meyssan, Thierry 159, 164
Milbank, Dana 111
Milosevic, Slobodan 89, 105, 131, 145, 146
Mingos 60
Miran Shah 312
Mirkin 252
MI 6 99
Mladic, Radko 133, 142, 143, 144, 146
Moammer Kaddafi 284
Mobil 275
Mohammad Sacirby 138
Mohammed, Prophet 1, 24, 25, 39
Mohammed Ali Jinnah 119
Mohiyuddin Ibne Arabi 30, 39
Moinuddin Haider 124, 267
Moldova 49
Monbiot, George 279
Monroe Doctrine 114
Monsanto 200
Montenegro 131
Monte Carlo 254
Moorish 30, 35
Moors 12, 17, 26, 30, 31, 35
Moral Majority 1
Morford, Mark 114
Moriscos 31, 35
Morocco 116, 228
Moros 263, 266
Morris dancing 30
Moscow 41, 50, 51, 52, 149

Mossad 163
Moynihans 202
Mozambique 200, 250
Muhammad Yukar Yarak 48
Mujahideen 244
Mullah Omar 154, 171, 174
mullas 47, 94
Murcia 29
Murray, Craig 296
Musharraf 124, 154, 169, 171, 174, 175, 176, 177, 192, 207,
        267, 269, 298, 300, 301, 310
Muslim Brotherthood 95
Mussolini 204

N

Nabha 120
NAFTA 69
Nagas 121, 220, 246
Najaf 47
Nakshbandi 48
Namibia 250
Napoleon 235
Natanyahu, Benyamin 223
National Security Strategy 225, 226
NATO 69, 112, 140, 142, 143, 144, 146, 244, 279, 292
Nazis 63, 66, 69, 70, 132, 133, 185, 204, 254, 265
NDFB 246
Nehru, Jawaharlal 120, 300
Neimoller, Martin 265
Nestle 200, 275
New American Century Project 223
New Delhi 68, 125
New Jersey 162
New Testament 78
New York 7, 15, 20, 28, 34, 38, 43, 54, 63, 77, 79, 81, 85, 111,
        114, 134, 138, 155, 157, 162, 163, 164, 169, 189, 197,
        203, 204, 208, 210, 213, 217, 218, 219, 232, 240, 304
New York Herald 43
Niaz Naik 154

Nicaragua 205, 229
Nick Burns 143
Nietzsche 64
Nobel Peace Prize 89, 105, 244
NORAD 161
Noriega, Manuel 102
North-West Frontier Province 119
Northern Alliance 176, 179, 183, 184
North America 28, 63, 216
North Korea 109, 224, 226, 269
Novaya Gazeta 52
Novo Selo 136
nuclear weapons 100, 110, 172, 214, 215, 242, 266, 267, 268,
        270, 271, 300, 301
Nuremberg 97, 185
Nuremberg Laws 63
Nursultan A. Nazarbayev 296

O

O'Keefe, Ken Nichols 112
O'Kane, Maggie 103
Oklahoma City 156
Omarska 136
OMON 54
Operation Enduring Freedom 293, 310, 314
opium 190
Orwell, George 122, 146, 150, 249
Osama bin Laden 152, 154, 171, 172, 185
Oslo Accord 89
Osmama bin Laden 97
Ottawas 60
Ottomans 32, 38
Ottoman Empire 18, 37, 42, 76
Owen, Lord David 145
Oxford 63, 112, 120, 140

P

Pacific Fleet 167

Padmanabhan, General 300, 301, 302

Pahlavi 73, 74

Pakhtoon-wali 152

Pakistan 88, 115, 119, 120, 121, 122, 123, 124, 125, 126, 127,
128, 140, 149, 151, 153, 154, 169, 171, 173, 174, 175,
176, 177, 178, 179, 186, 189, 190, 192, 193, 197, 206,
207, 211, 212, 213, 214, 215, 219, 225, 242, 247, 254,
255, 262, 264, 266, 267, 268, 269, 270, 271, 281, 292,
293, 294, 295, 296, 298, 299, 300, 301, 302, 304, 310,
311, 312, 313, 314, 315

Pale 133

Palestine 11, 14, 16, 19, 40, 65, 66, 75, 76, 77, 78, 79, 80, 81,
82, 83, 84, 85, 86, 87, 88, 89, 90, 93, 95, 148, 228, 233,
243, 246, 252, 291

Palestinian Authority' 89

Palmerston, Lord 76

Paris 33, 254

Parkinson, Professor Northcote 96

Parrish, Carolyn 93

Pashtoon 294

Pasni 311

Patel 120

Pathans 120, 121, 294

Patiala 120

Pax Americana 224, 225

Payne, Donald 220

Pearl Harbour 167

Pearson, Karl 64

Peloponnes 40

Pennsylvania 84, 100, 155, 161, 241

Pentagon 155, 160, 161, 163, 166, 180, 181, 184, 223, 224, 227,
241, 277, 279

Pepsi 275

Perle, Richard 223

Perry, William 141

Persian Gulf 148, 196, 284, 315

Peshawar 171

Philippines 225, 233, 263

Pilger, John 100, 105, 171, 260

Pinkas, Alon 163
Pinter, Harold 231
Pinto, Lisa 304, 305
Plato 30
Pope Benedict XIII 32, 33
Pope Clement V 33
Pope Gregory IX 33, 34
Pope John Paul II 6, 21, 69, 146, 261
Pope Pius XII 69
Pope Sylvester II 29
Pope Urban II 14
Portugal 17, 84
Port Qasim 192, 194
Powell, Colin 106, 108, 166, 170, 173, 174, 175, 302, 310
Power, Samantha 142
President Nixon 92
President Truman 61
Pressler, Larry 68
Princeton University 252
Prince Abdul Rahman 189
Prince Kochubey 42
Prince Turki 153
Prince Walid 189
Project for Defence Alternatives 184
Project for the New American Century 227
Prophet of Islam 1
Pulitzer Prize 134
Punjab 119, 120, 220, 266
Punjabi Establishment 193
Putin, Vladimir 51, 55

Q

Qatar 103
Queen Isabella 30
Qum 47

R

Rabbis 33, 217

Rabin, Issak 91
Racism 35
Radcliffe, Lord 119, 120
Ramazan 176
Ramzi Bin Al-Shaiba 311
Ramzi Yusuf 244
Rand Corporation 280
Reconstructionis 2
Red Crescent 147
Red Cross 104, 136, 147, 183, 260
Reformation 32
Renaissance 30
Rhodesia 250
Rice, Condoleeza 169, 170, 301
Ridley, Yvonne 187
Rio Guadalete 26
Ritter, Colonel Scott 113
Roberta Combs 77
Roberts, Andrew 120
Robertson, Pat 1, 5, 146
Robert Fisk 71, 181, 185, 248
Robinson, Mary 184
Robust Nuclear Earth Penetrator 224
Rodrigo, King 26, 27
Romania 131
Romans 11, 27, 37
Roman Catholic 10, 33, 58, 69, 133
Roman Catholic Church 10, 69
Roman Empire 211
Roosevelt, Theodore 65
Rose, Charlie 139
Rose, General Michael 141
Rothschild, Lord 80
Rothschilds 75
Rubin, James 210
Rumsfeld, Donald 101, 111, 152, 170, 172, 176, 190, 223, 281
Runcie, Dr. Robert 21, 102
Russia 42, 46, 47, 49, 50, 51, 53, 55, 65, 67, 69, 109, 130, 177,
        189, 193, 221, 226, 250, 261

Russian Revolution 49
Rwanda 266

S

Sabra 108
Saddam Hussein ix, xi, 9, 74, 92, 99, 100, 101, 103, 107, 108,
        109, 110, 113, 115, 170, 210, 215, 225, 272, 275
safe havens 141, 198
Said, Edward 71, 93, 108
Saint Basil 41
Salahuddin 17, 28
Salman Rushdie 94, 251
Samarkand 43
Samson complex 270
Santa Claus 211
San Francisco 114
San Stefano 130
Saparmurad Niyazov 295
Sarin gas 100
Saudi Arabia xi, 102, 103, 112, 152, 191, 199, 237, 241, 244,
        264, 265, 270
Saudi bin Laden Group 152
Scheuer 298
Schimmel, Annemarie 7
Schlessinger, Dr. Laura 252
Schmidig, John 162
Scholz, Rupert 243
Security Council 99, 142, 148, 175
Senate 77, 137, 144, 157, 224
Serbia 105, 131, 138, 146, 260, 261
Serbs 130, 131, 132, 133, 134, 136, 138, 139, 140, 141, 144,
        145, 147, 185, 261
Seville 29, 34
Shah, the xi, 74, 94, 212
Shaikh Mansur 48
Shakespeare 7, 39, 97
Shamir, Yitzhak 243
Sharia 255, 256
Sharon, Ariel 90, 214, 291, 298

Shatilla 108
Shattuck, John 143
Sheberghan 182
Sheehan, Jack 201
Shell 275
Shia 281
Shirin Mazari 177
Shultz 201
Sierra Leone 278
Sikhs 120, 220
Simons, Tom 155
Sinai 12, 76, 87
Sind Club 212
Singer, Professor 252
Sir StanleyLane-Poole 35
slaves 24, 27, 28, 59, 217
Slovenia 131, 133, 134
Snowcroft, Brent 291
Sodre 57, 58
Solkatronic Chemicals 100
Somalia 139, 229
South Africa 58, 244
South America 58
South Waziristan 294, 313
Soviet Union xi, 23, 45, 49, 50, 68, 85, 87, 94, 97, 98, 123, 149,
        150, 151, 167, 222, 235, 244, 250, 259, 279
Spain 12, 18, 26, 28, 29, 30, 31, 33, 34, 35, 37, 41, 84, 114, 189
Spetsnaz 54
Spicer, Tim 278
Springer, Jerry 253
Srebrenica 141, 142, 143, 144
Stahl, Leslie 260
Stalin, Josef 49, 131
Standard Oil 205
State Department 69, 100, 136, 174, 210, 220, 243, 244
Stauffer, Thomas 92
Stephanopoulos, George 1
Stern Gang 243
Students for Democratic Society (SDS) 117

340

Sudan 95, 152, 209, 229, 250, 256, 257, 263, 284
Sufism 48
Sultan M. Khan 178
Sultan of Brunei 199
Sultan Suleyman 37
Sumatra 236
Sunday Express 187
Sunday Telegraph 180
Sunni 281
Surinam 250
Swaggert, Reverend Jimmy 146
Swaran Singh 300
Swinton, John 212
Sykes, Sir Mark 66, 68
Sykes-Picot-Sazanov Agreement 65
Sykes-Picot Agreement 79
Sylhet 119
syphilis 62
Syria 11, 12, 13, 17, 21, 65, 79, 84, 87, 110, 117, 226, 255, 259, 281

T

Tajikistan 296
Tajiks 189
Taliban 9, 45, 61, 151, 152, 153, 154, 155, 168, 171, 174, 179, 181, 182, 183, 184, 185, 186, 187, 189, 190, 221, 227, 244, 292, 294, 312, 313, 314
Talmud 32, 217
Tanzania 153
Tarik Bin Ziyad 26
Tashkand 43
Taslima Nasreen 94
Tel Aviv 91, 100
Tenet, George 111, 174
Texas 59, 138
Thatcher, Margaret 102
Thatcher, Mark 278
The Guardian 6, 7, 103, 136, 137, 154, 167, 179, 182, 227, 260, 297

The Hague 89
The Independent 63, 71, 158, 181, 185, 248, 283
The Mirror 171
The Observer 159
The Washington Post 1, 100, 111, 142, 180
Thomas, William 155, 182
Tiananmen Square 220
Tibet 209
Time 49, 181
Times' of London 109
Tirah Valley 312
Toby Gati 144
Toffler, Alvin 208, 209
Tomahawk 161
Torah 82, 217
Tora Bora 312
Towns, Edolphus 220
Toynbee, Arnold 67
Toys R Us 275
Trent, William 60
Trilateral Commission 208
Trnopolje 136
Tsunami 302
Tudeh Square 74
Tunisia 19, 95, 228, 231
Turcoman-Chai 47, 48
Turkey 39, 47, 66, 67, 80, 84, 116, 130, 139, 147, 228, 261, 312
Turkish Empire 41, 47, 65, 79, 130
Turkmen 42, 43, 44
Turkmenistan 295
Tutsis 266

U

U.N. Development Program 104
U.N Security Council 101
UAL Corp 159
Uganda 76
Ukraine 49
ulema 73

ULFA 246

UN 5, 46, 85, 88, 92, 95, 104, 105, 106, 107, 108, 110, 112, 113, 116, 121, 122, 129, 137, 138, 139, 140, 141, 148, 179, 184, 210, 212, 228, 243, 251, 259, 260, 262, 268, 274, 292, 313

UNESCO 104, 106

UNHCR 138, 148

UNICEF 104, 105, 210, 272

Unilever 200

United Kingdom 212, 247

United Nations 46, 49, 87, 88, 101, 102, 103, 121, 122, 133, 136, 138, 139, 141, 144, 146, 147, 151, 179, 184, 186, 209, 219, 224, 246

United States ix, x, 2, 5, 40, 49, 50, 63, 72, 73, 74, 77, 80, 81, 85, 87, 88, 90, 91, 94, 98, 99, 100, 101, 107, 109, 112, 113, 117, 123, 132, 134, 140, 141, 142, 143, 148, 150, 152, 154, 162, 165, 174, 175, 182, 185, 190, 198, 199, 202, 203, 212, 214, 215, 220, 222, 224, 225, 226, 229, 241, 243, 244, 247, 249, 253, 259, 263, 280, 282, 293, 297, 304

Universal Declaration of Human Rights 134

UNOCAL 153, 154, 190, 292

UNPROFOR 138, 148

UNSCOM 106

uranium 100, 103, 107, 111

Urban Moving 162

Uri Avnery 91

US 1, 5, 59, 62, 63, 68, 70, 77, 82, 85, 87, 90, 91, 92, 95, 96, 99, 100, 101, 102, 103, 105, 106, 108, 109, 110, 111, 112, 113, 115, 116, 122, 124, 136, 139, 140, 141, 145, 152, 153, 154, 155, 157, 158, 162, 166, 167, 168, 171, 172, 173, 174, 175, 176, 177, 178, 180, 181, 182, 183, 186, 189, 190, 191, 196, 197, 198, 200, 201, 202, 203, 204, 205, 207, 208, 209, 210, 212, 222, 224, 225, 226, 227, 228, 229, 235, 242, 243, 244, 246, 248, 250, 252, 253, 260, 262, 263, 264, 269, 270, 272, 273, 274, 275, 278, 279, 281, 284, 291, 292, 293, 294, 296, 298, 299, 301, 302, 305, 310, 311, 314, 315

USA ix, 5, 6, 59, 69, 78, 82, 84, 88, 102, 103, 104, 108, 133,

146, 158, 161, 173, 177, 178, 199, 200, 203, 206, 224, 237, 247, 249, 253, 259, 263, 312
USS Maddox 167
Uzbekistan 296, 297
Uzbeks 189

V

Vajpai 72
Valencia 29
Vasco da Gama 56
Versailles Peace Conference 67
Vietnam 103, 109, 117, 229, 274
Voltaire 39
von Buelow, Andreas 159
von Sponeck, Hans 105, 210

W

Walkom, Thomas 245
Wall Street Journal 68, 210
Wana 312, 313
Wars of Western Civilization 230
Washington 1, 70, 77, 84, 91, 92, 100, 111, 112, 115, 116, 142, 143, 144, 155, 160, 164, 172, 174, 180, 181, 227, 243, 281, 291
Washington, George 83
weapons of mass destruction 100, 108, 109, 111, 113, 207, 214, 219, 231, 269, 276
Weathermen 117
Weinberger, Caspar 201
Weizmann, Chaim 68, 85
Wesley Clark 141
West Bank 77, 86, 87, 93, 270, 291
White, Jerry 183
Whitehall 68, 212
Whitehouse 243
White House 1, 8, 71, 150, 153, 157, 159, 175, 181, 205
Whitney, Mike 302
Wilson, President 85

344

Winfrey, Oprah 253
Wolfowitz, Paul 170, 207, 223
Woodward, Bob 169, 173, 180
World Bank 208
World Food Program 105
World Health Organization 104
World Trade Centre 8, 104, 110, 155, 158, 160, 162, 164, 170,
        179, 181, 189, 227, 241, 250, 262, 274, 304
World Trade Organisation 208
World War I 23, 65, 79, 80, 84, 85, 266
World War II 69, 97, 119, 135, 179, 199, 228, 249, 305
World Zionist Congress 76
WTC 163, 164

Y

Yahya Khan, General 178
Yale 223
Yamud 43
Yeltsin, Boris 8
Yugoslavia 131, 133, 145, 229, 244, 250

Z

Zakat 264
Zakheim 223
Zamorin 56, 57
Zernovodsk 54
Ziad Jarrahi 241
Zinn 214
Zinni, General 207
Zionism 79, 81, 82, 85
Zionist 76, 79, 80, 81, 82, 85
Ziryab 30
Zoroastrians 25
Zulfikar Ali Bhutto 88
Zvornik 136

ABOUT THE AUTHOR

Khan Hussan Zia was born in a family with connections to Afghanistan. He was educated in Pakistan and England and later served in the Pakistan Navy. He is an old student of Islamic and Indian history and contributes to newspapers and magazines mostly on geo-political subjects. His earlier books include The Pathans of Jullunder ----- the social history of a community in India that was uprooted in the partition of the sub-continent and Soft War on Pakistan ------ an analysis of the media campaign against that country.

34546691R00217

Made in the USA
Lexington, KY
09 August 2014